UNDERSTANDING JUVENILE JUSTICE

UNDERSTANDING JUVENILE JUSTICE

ALLISON MORRIS   HENRI GILLER

CROOM HELM
London • New York • Sydney

© 1987 Allison Morris, Henri Giller
Croom Helm Ltd, Provident House, Burrell Row,
Beckenham, Kent, BR3 1AT
Croom Helm Australia, 44-50 Waterloo Road,
North Ryde, 2113, New South Wales

Published in the USA by
Croom Helm
in association with Methuen, Inc.
29 West 35th Street
New York, NY 10001

British Library Cataloguing in Publication Data

Morris, Allison
    Understanding juvenile justice.
    1. Juvenile justice, Administration of —
    England
    I. Title II. Giller, Henri
    344.205'8   KD8471

    ISBN 0-7099-3832-2
    ISBN 0-7099-3890-X Pbk

SB   35367 £10.95. 10.87

Printed and bound in Great Britain
by Billings & Sons Limited, Worcester.

CONTENTS

INTRODUCTION

Our objective in writing this book is to contribute to attempts to understand the philosophy and practice of dealing with juveniles who commit offences.) Information on this is found in a wide range of sources (some unpublished) and is, therefore, not always easily accessible. Moreover, much pre-dates recent legislative changes. Our intention is to pull these diverse sources together in order to provide an over-view of juvenile justice in England and Wales. The majority of the book deals with the philosophy and practice of juvenile justice in the 1980s. However, we also discuss the historical development and context of the system as this aids our understanding of its current shape and of debates about its future. Likewise, where relevant, we have referred to information on other systems of juvenile justice, in particular to Scotland and the United States.

Systems of juvenile justice do not, of course, exist in a social policy vacuum. They co-exist alongside other systems or networks of social control which also seek to regulate the lives of juveniles: for example, child care, health and education. Each is inter-related and frequently, although not invariably, compliments the other. So, for instance, juveniles appearing in the juvenile court for offending may have previously been made the subject of an order of that court on account of their parents´ inability to provide them with proper care and attention; or reports about juveniles´ school behaviour and attendance may be referred to by magistrates in determining their sentence. Also, disruptive juveniles in the child care system may be accommodated in the same secure establishments as juveniles who have committed offences.

The inter-relatedness of these spheres of

1

control does not necessarily mean, however, that trends and developments in one parallel those in others. For example, some programmes of intermediate treatment are comparable with some youth training schemes, thus indicating a similarity in the regulation of juveniles who offend and juveniles who are unemployed. On the other hand, the current form of legal intervention in the lives of juvenile offenders is very different from that proposed for those who are abused or neglected in the government's recent review of child care law. Indeed, that review also recommends that some forms of deviant behaviour (truancy, being in moral danger or being beyond parental control) should no longer form the basis for compulsory state intervention. It would also be wrong to assume that consensus about the appropriate methods to be used exists in any one system. In the sphere of delinquency, this is illustrated by the debate between those who wish to retain custody for offenders and those who seek to provide community-based alternatives. In the educational system, the recent introduction in schools of the Manpower Services Commission's Technical Vocational Education Initiative (TVEI) is seen by some educationalists as undermining liberal educational values and as imposing instead a vocational curriculum.

Recognising these inter-connections does not mean that we cannot discuss the format for dealing with juveniles who offend on its own. It does mean, however, that we must do so with an awareness that debates and policy and practice developments take place within a context which influences other control systems.

Finally our thanks to Nigel Walker, Ray Corrado and Loraine Gelsthorpe who commented on our work and made us clarify our thoughts. Any errors and omissions are, of course, our responsibility. We are also grateful to Pat Cochrane, Freda Mainwaring and Pam Paige who patiently typed the numerous drafts.

Chapter One

THE HISTORICAL FOUNDATIONS OF JUVENILE JUSTICE

Introduction

It is important to place juvenile justice in its
historical context. Rather than present a detailed
descriptive account (for this see Parsloe, 1978;
Sanders, 1970 and Radzinowicz and Hood, 1986), this
chapter explores themes which occurred in a number
of countries at a similar time. The parallels in
ideology are striking (see, for example, Stang
Dahl´s (1974) account of the emergence of the
Norwegian child welfare boards and Platt´s (1969)
account of the early American juvenile courts.) This
chapter will first outline and then critically
examine conventional accounts of the development of
juvenile justice. We detail changes both in the
processes for dealing with delinquents (for example,
the development of juvenile courts) and in the
penalties available to deal with them (for example,
the emergence of the reformatory schools). Frequently, the distinction between these two types of
change is ignored. They have to be viewed as two
inter-related issues which, while not necessarily
changing contemporaneously, reflect the dynamic
development of juvenile justice. Each is influenced
by changes in the understanding of the causes of
crime and by demands to respond to what is seen as
´the crime problem`.

Retribution to Reform

Children have not always been seen as a
distinct social problem. Until this century,
childhood was a brief and unimportant phase of life
(see Aries, 1962). Indeed Aries notes that various
languages did not even have words to describe
childhood: (1)

> In its attempts to talk about little children, the French language of the 17th century was hampered by a lack of words to distinguish them from bigger ones. The same was true of English, where the word ´baby` was also applied to big children (1962, 28-29).

Gillis makes the same point:

> By the standards of today´s biologically exacting vocabulary, the language of age in pre-industrial Europe is hopelessly vague. Even as late as the 18th century, the French and German words ´garçon` and ´knabie` referred to boys as young as six and as old as thirty or forty (1974, 1).

The word ´adolescence` is said to be even more modern and its creation is attributed to G. Stanley Hall who wrote a 2-volume book called <u>Adolescence</u> in 1890.

Until this century both the birth and death rates were high. It is estimated that the odds were two or three to one against a child living until the age of five as late as the 18th century. From a very young age, most children, rich and poor alike, began to work and take part in communal life. According to Gillis:

> Ready for semi-independence, they were dressed as miniature adults and permitted to use the manners and language of adult society (1974, 8).

Child labour was traditional, universal and inescapable, but its intensification occurred between 1780 and 1830. For example, in the first decades of the 19th century, 80 per cent of workers in English cotton mills were children (Gillis, 1974, 56). Children were viewed as economic assets, as a source of cheap labour. For many, this meant exploitation in the mines and factories. These hardships are well documented in such novels as ´Hard Times` and ´Oliver Twist` and in official inquiries (for example, the Report of the Select Committee on Factory Children´s Labour 1831-2).

This early assimilation of children to adults is also visible in the criminal justice and penal systems (see, for example, Hibbert, 1963). The most common punishments in 18th century England were the

4

fine and the whip though wide use was also made of the stocks, the pillory and branding. Hay (1977) describes the system of criminal law then as based on terror. Capital statutes had grown from about 50 to over 200 between the years 1688 and 1820. Almost all were offences against property. Yet there was a paradox: the actual number of executions was low, and remained relatively stable. This is explained by the fact that more of those sentenced to death were pardoned than were hanged and that juries often declined to convict. Indeed, both Romilly (1810) and Beccaria (1764) had argued that convictions would have become more numerous if capital punishment was removed and replaced with a fixed and graduated scale of more lenient but more certain punishments. But Parliament did not act. Why this contradiction? Hay explains it through the power of the pardon. It maintained 'the fabric of obedience, gratitude and deference' (1977, 49). Hay goes on to suggest that 'the law made enough examples to inculcate fear, but not so many as to harden or repel a populace' (1977, 57). Langbein (1983) disputes Hay's conclusion and argues that the criminal law and procedures served to protect the interests of those who suffered as the victims of crime. Further, he argues that it was prosecutors and jurors who exercised most of the discretion, not members of the ruling class and that the discretion was exercised on good faith considerations not arbitrarily. However, Langbein and Hay both agree that deterrence was the explicit rationale for capital punishment.

What is important in all of this is that there was no distinct legal category of 'juvenile delinquent' or 'child offender'. In the 19th century half of those convicted of crimes were under 21 and both adults and juveniles were subject to the same laws and penalties. The age of criminal responsibility was seven in common law. Children between seven and fourteen were presumed incapable of committing crimes (doli incapax) but this presumption was rebuttable and was usually rebutted by the fact of the offence. In some American states, the age of criminal responsibility was ten with a chance of avoiding responsibility up to twelve if the child was lacking in mental or moral maturity. However, the position was the same as in England: adults and juveniles were treated alike. The reasoning was that the law sought not to reform the offender, but to punish him in order to expiate the crime and to deter potential offenders. An

English judge, sentencing a ten year old child to death, said that the child was a 'proper subject for capital punishment and ought to suffer; there would be a very dangerous consequence to have it thought that children may commit such atrocious crimes with impunity.' One day in 1814, five children between eight and twelve were hanged for petty larceny (Pinchbeck and Hewitt, 1973, 352). Deterrence was the main objective. As Hale wrote:

> Experience makes us know, that every day murders, bloodsheds, burglaries, larcencies, burning of houses, rapes, clipping and counterfeiting of money, are committed by youths above fourteen and under twenty-one; and if they should have impunity by the privilege of such their minority, no man's life or estate could be safe (1736, reprinted 1971, 25).

Typical of the treatment meted out to young offenders was that of Thomas Miller described by Pearsall:

> In 1845 he stole some boxes, and was whipped, and sent to prison for a month. He was then eight. In 1846 he robbed a till, and was sentenced to seven years transportation. He was too young, and spent three months in prison instead. Immediately on discharge he committed larcency again, and spent two further years in prison. In May 1848 he was discharged, but in July he was back again for fourteen days. In April 1849 he was whipped and imprisoned for two days. Thomas Miller was then aged twelve. His height was four feet two inches (1975, 164).

Platt (1978) has queried this suggestion that adults and children were dealt with similarly. In relation to capital punishment, he argued that on occasions the prosecution refused to charge, juries refused to convict and pardons were frequently given. Sentences of transportation were sometimes substituted and charitable institutions took responsibility for young people. Still, it does not seem that these events benefitted children more readily than adults. As King (1984, 45) demonstrates in an analysis of the period 1782 to 1787, 'youth was pleaded not as a legal category, but a general mitigating circumstance`

Concern about children was slow to develop and but for the modern construction of `childhood` probably could not have. According to Empey (1978, 66), the invention of `delinquency`, the setting up of the juvenile court, the drafting of child labour laws, legal requirements regulating education, the emergence of the new professions or specialisms of paediatrics, child psychiatry and teaching all reflect the creation of this concept. (2)

These developments would also probably not have been possible but for the considerable attention given at this time to the collection of criminal statistics. Such statistics figured prominently in the first volumes of the Journal of the Statistical Society of London (founded in 1834). The first continuous series of statistics for the whole of England and Wales dates from 1835. From that year to 1856, Criminal Statistics (the number of those tried on indictment in Higher Courts) were published each year. These were enlarged from 1857 into Judicial Statistics which included information about those in the magistrates' courts as well. The introductory comments to these statistics read remarkably like those published today.

Commentators made much of these statistics. In a prize-winning essay, Worsley demonstrated that the 15-20 age group comprised more offenders than any other age group. (3) Though only ten per cent of the total population, they made up almost a quarter of the criminal population. However, it is noteworthy that the age group Worsley was particularly concerned with in Juvenile Depravity is that under 20; those under 15 only made up six and a half per cent of the criminal population. Worsley (1849, 12) painted a picture of progression from `petty delinquencies to greater and more heinous crimes` and argued that, even if this did not occur, the juvenile offender was `scarcely less dangerous`. He was corrupt himself and corrupted others `like an ulcer on the body`.

Discovery of this `new` problem led to concern. For example, gradually the dangers of holding children and adults together in the same institutions were identified. Bennet, writing of Newgate, refers to:

> boys of the tenderest years, and girls of ten, twelve and thirteen [who] were expo-sed to the various contagion, that predom-inated in all parts of the prison (1818,9).

The 1836 report of the Inspectors of Prisons shows that things had not changed much by then:

> Of many children whom we have seen in prison, we hesitate not to affirm, that absolute impunity would have been far less mischievous than the effects of their confinement.
> ... The boy is thrown among veterans in guilt...and his vicious propensities cherished and inflamed.
> ... He enters the prison a child in years, and not infrequently also in crime; but he leaves it with a knowledge in the ways of wickedness (1836, 86).

And later in the century, Mary Carpenter described prisons as the:

> most costly, most inefficacious for any end but to prepare the child for a life of crime...thousands of young children annually committed to it come forth not to diminish but to swell the ranks of vice (1853, 13 and iii).

Though there was gradually some separation of boys from adults, all kinds of boys (convicted and unconvicted, first offenders and recidivists) were kept together. However, as May stresses:

> Any consideration of the problem of protecting juveniles was incidental. The swelling prison population stimulated reform and in the process the problem of the young offender was revealed (1973,10).

The concern generally was to categorise and segregate offenders. It was a period of reform in prisons. This was the era of the Panopticon and the silent and solitary systems. Pentonville was completed in 1842 and it was a model prison with specially selected, mainly first offender, prisoners. Its objective was ´amending the criminal mind` and ´reformation of character` (Evans, 1982, 2). Thus reform was the objective for both adult and juvenile offenders; it was merely the methods which now began to differ.

Early in the 19th century attempts were made to develop separate facilities for juvenile offenders. The Philanthropic Society, for example, opened in

1806 a house of refuge for young people between twelve and nineteen who had been sentenced to imprisonment. On release, they stayed in the refuge for twelve to eighteen months. Thus the early institutions were in reality after-care facilities. There had also been since 1823, a separate hulk (a ship receiving convicts) for juveniles. But it was not until 1838 that a separate prison for juvenile offenders was opened at Parkhurst. (4) Proponents of the Parkhurst principle upheld the importance of the deterrent effect of law and argued that the present system of mixing adults and juveniles was making deterrence ineffectual.

During the same period, industrial and reformatory schools were established. The industrial schools received juveniles begging or receiving alms, found wandering and not having any home or visible means of subsistence, found destitute, either being an orphan, or having a parent undergoing penal servitude, and frequenting the company of reputed thieves. Also included were all juveniles under twelve where charged with an offence punishable by imprisonment, but not convicted of a felony and all juveniles under 14 where parents claimed that they were unable to control them and that they desired them to be sent to an industrial school. The reformatories received juveniles up to the age of 16 who had been convicted of an offence punishable by imprisonment or penal servitude.

Foremost among the advocates of this kind of institution was Mary Carpenter whose work with the urban poor caused her to write extensively on the plight of both the destitute and the delinquent. She founded a school in Bristol in 1846 and wrote a book on the principles of the reformatory system which she put into practice in her own school which she opened in 1852. Proponents of her approach rejected deterrence as a basis for intervention in favour of a more pervasive notion of reform. They sought to establish separate institutions for juvenile offenders which afforded both their removal from society and their reclamation but which were also economical. Reformatories were given central government support in the Reformatory Schools Act 1854. (5)

Similar thinking led to modifications in (or attempts to modify) procedures which influenced the trials of juveniles. A Bill for the Punishment, Correction and Reform of Young Persons introduced in 1821 proposed that, instead of committing juveniles to prison to await trial at Quarter Sessions or Assizes for petty offences, summary powers of conviction might be given to two local justices. This was rejected, as were subsequent similar Bills in 1829 and 1837.

In 1847, however, the Juvenile Offenders Act was passed which allowed larcencies and thefts committed by persons under 14 to be heard by magistrates in Petty Sessions. In 1850, this was amended to those under the age of 16. It was not until the 1879 Summary Jurisdiction Act that there was a further major change. Under this Act, juveniles under 16 could be tried summarily for nearly all indictable offences.

Towards the end of the century, some towns began to operate separate juvenile courts. (6) These courts were established throughout England and Wales after the 1908 Children Act. Indeed, the principal claim to fame of the 1908 Children Act has been described as the creation of the juvenile courts. Watson and Austin say of it:

> The Children´s Act 1908, heralded as the Children´s Charter, was a highly progressive measure; the most important of its provisions was the establishing of separate juvenile courts from which the public were to be excluded (1975, 2).

The Act, however, contained much more. As Bottoms notes:

> The provisions as to juvenile offenders appear only in part five and the section creating the juvenile courts does not appear until section III (1985, 96).

Other sections referred to the prevention of cruelty to children, begging and prostitution of young girls. Nor does it appear from the Parliamentary debates that the government saw the creation of the juvenile court as the most important part of the Act. Nevertheless, create it it did, though as we have noted some local areas had already set up their own juvenile courts and there was already a long history of allowing summary trial of indictable offences committed by juveniles.

The creation of the juvenile courts, according to Bottoms (1985) ´can be seen as part of the process of individualisation of the penal system` which was taking place around that time: the same period saw the statutory creation of probation, borstal and preventive detention. However, to the extent that this is so, it was an individualised criminal court. Though the 1908 Children Act set out for the first time the principle that juvenile offenders should be heard separately from adults in special sittings of the magistrates' court, in essence, the new juvenile courts functioned as criminal courts and the mode of trial was the same as it was for adults. The prevailing idea was that the juvenile was a wrongdoer and the old procedures for dealing with adult offenders were thought to be appropriate in most respects for dealing with juveniles. In addition, though the courts were given a wide and flexible range of dispositions, decisions were governed by such considerations as the seriousness of the offence and the interest of the public. Individualisation took the form of some concern for the welfare of the child. For example, Herbert Samuel, in introducing the Bill, stated that one of its main principles was that the juvenile offender should receive at the hands of the law a treatment differentiated to suit his special needs. (7)

Events in the United States took a similar, though not identical, direction. New York City's House of Refuge was founded in 1826. Here, juveniles were separated from adult offenders and given corrective treatment rather than punishment. The Houses of Refuge also took in vagrants and neglected children. Reformatory and industrial schools followed, as did probation (first in Massachusetts) as an alternative to institutionalization. In addition, efforts were made to separate juveniles from adults during the trial stage. For example, in 1861 the mayor of Chicago appointed a commissioner to hear minor cases against boys between six and seventeen years. The first juvenile court in the United States was opened in Chicago in 1899. Juvenile cases were heard in special, separate courtrooms and juveniles and adults had to be kept separate whenever both were confined in the same institution. The purpose of the legislation was to provide the child with the care, custody and discipline that a parent would normally provide. The juvenile court, however, was not to be a criminal court in the traditional sense. The judge was likened to a helpful but stern parent, and his function was to rescue juveniles rather than to punish them. In the words of Julian Mack, the juvenile:

> should...be made to feel that he is the
> object of its [the court's] care and
> solicitude. The ordinary trappings of the
> courtroom are out of place in such
> hearings. The judge on a bench, looking
> down upon the boy standing at the bar, can
> never evoke a proper sympathetic spirit.
> Seated at a desk, with the child at his
> side, where he can on occasion put his arm
> around his shoulder and draw the lad to
> him, the judge, while losing none of his
> juducial dignity, will gain immensely in
> the effectiveness of his work (1909, 120).

Dispositions were to be based on an examination of the juvenile's special circumstances and needs. The rules of criminal procedure were, therefore, inapplicable. The basis of the new juvenile courts was the concept of <u>parens patriae</u>. This is derived from the Chancery Courts which were primarily concerned with protecting the property rights of juveniles and others believed to be legally incompetent, but came to refer to the responsibility of the juvenile courts and the state to act in the best interests of the child. According to Mack it enabled the juvenile courts:

> to get away from the notion that the child
> is to be dealt with as a criminal; to
> save it from the brand of criminality, the
> brand that sticks to it for life; to take
> it in hand and instead of first stigmatiz-
> ing and then reforming it, to protect it
> from stigma (1909, 109).

This early example was rapidly followed throughout the United States., The principles on which the juvenile courts acted were radically different from those of the criminal courts. Herbert Lou described them as 'the first legal tribunal where law and science, especially the science of medicine and those sciences which deal with human behavior, work side by side' (1927, 9). Others have referred to the essential philosophy of the juvenile court as <u>socialised</u> in contrast to criminal justiice. A major consequence of this was that the acts committed by the juvenile were not considered criminal violations; specific crimes were, in a sense, eliminated from the juvenile court. The juvenile was charged with being a delinquent regardless of the crime committed. These moral evaluations of juveniles remain relevant. This is discussed further in Chapter 6.

Reform Revised

The reform movement is usually said to have its roots in the general humanitarianism and philanthropy of the 19th century. It has been variously described as a move from ´retribution to reform` (Boss, 1967), from ´leg irons to leniency` (Berlins and Wansell, 1974) and from ´cruelty to enlightenment` (Ignatieff, 1978). Such accounts deny the many inconsistencies in the reform movement. In England, for example, there was considerable debate between the proponents of Parkhurst (the prison for juveniles) and the proponents of the reformatories. (8) Also, before children went to the reformatories in England they had to serve a sentence of imprisonment first to expiate their crime. Similar tensions existed in the United States. Fox (1970), for example, contends that the 1899 legislation which set up the first juvenile court in Chicago was actually a <u>failure</u> in reform and that sectarian rather than humanitarian interests dominated. In Platt´s words, we need to look beyond the ´rhetoric of benevolence` (1978, XXIX).

There are also, however, difficulties with critical accounts (Platt, 1978; Foucault, 1977; Ignatieff, 1978). They tend to overschematize and oversimplify a very complex sequence of events. Platt dates the ´story` from 1899 with the establishment of the juvenile court whereas the Houses of Refuge were founded much earlier. Further, these accounts tend to reduce the intentions behind the changes to conspiratorial class strategies; for example, they deny the existence of a ´genuine` humanitarianism and ignore both working-class resistance to (Humphries, 1981) as well as support for the changes (Ignatieff, 1981). Indeed, Hagan and Leon (1977) describe Platt´s version as ´either unconfirmed or unconfirmable, plagued by logical errors and, therefore, quite possibly false` . They argue that data available on the social history of Canadian delinquency legislation do not support Platt´s position. There may, however, be threads of truth running through two quite different versions of history. What we need, and what we hope to provide, is an account which aids our understanding of change, but which does not impute conspiracy, which does not assume humanitarianism to have been the sole motive and which does not reduce change to a series of _ad hoc_ adjustments to crises.

Our understanding of the history of this period is not yet complete. Why did the reformatories and juvenile courts develop at this particular time? Whose economic and political interests were served by the juvenile justice apparatus? What changes in the political, economic and social structures necessitated the creation of new institutions for regulating the children of the urban working class? The rest of this chapter attempts to explore these questions by focusing on two areas: an examination of discourse, that is the stated intentions and acknowledged motives of the reformers (9) and an examination of what was actually done. In rhetoric, we can find indications of dominant conceptions of social behaviour and beliefs about the nature of social order. It can be used as an indicator to illuminate some of the central features of the society at that time. Documents and debates are not merely about the format of the juvenile justice system; they can be read as part of a political programme which takes, for example, delinquency as one of the critical axes of the relationship between social life, the family and the state. Discussions about `youth` also carry more than a surface message; youth is a social category which has the power to carry a deeper message about the state of society, about the social and political changes occurring without actually talking about politics. These various problems can thus be rooted in civil rather than political society.

Juvenile delinquency is, therefore, not just a crime problem; it is an indicator of breaks in the normal agents of socialisation and discipline: school and family. Thus certain themes become linked together. In the 19th century, `the state of the poor`, `the state of public morals` and `increases in crime` were all part of the same debate in seeking for remedies. For example, the growth of mass schooling began in the early 1780s through the Sunday School movement. This was triggered by a moral panic about juveniles; the popular image was of groups of begging, thieving, idle children who threatened the citizen and his property. Later the `school of industry` supplemented the Sunday Schools. As Clara Reeve put it:

> It is Schools of Industry that are wanted, to reform the manners of common people; where they are taught their duties every day, and all day long (1792, 84-5).

14

Later still, the monitorial (day) schools were developed. There the acquisition of skill was of secondary importance. More important was the way it was taught. Key phrases were `restraint`, `habit` and `order`. Juveniles were numbered, labelled and graded; `they were formed in obedience and discipline` (Johnson, 1975, 48). Thus the Prison Inspectors in their first report (1836) turned to moral and religious education in an attempt to stem the crime rate, especially among the children of the urban poor (Parl. Pap. 1836, XXXV, 83). (10)

Early reformers resisted state intervention. They believed that the state should be neither charitable nor benevolent. But from the beginning of the 19th century in both England and the United States the activities of the state increased enormously, in such areas as health, education and industry. Initially, the role of the state was limited to providing financial support for the initiatives of the reformers. However, when that involvement became substantial, the state moved from a position of influence to one of direct control, since it regulated the resources needed to operate the reforms. (11) This evolving role of the state with respect to controlling delinquents was only part of a wider 19th Century movement in the state´s regulation of disciplinary networks (Scull, 1977; Rothman, 1971; Johnson, 1970; Donajgrodzki, 1977) and, importantly, it was also an international movement. Not only were there various international conferences which led to the exchange of information and ideas, but key reformers visited the various institutions and each other. Mary Carpenter, for example, visited the recently established reformatories at Mettray in France and at Rauches Haus in Germany before opening two reformatory schools in England (Kingswood and Red Lodge). Also, in her book on <u>Juvenile Delinquents</u> (1853), she devoted a chapter to the American and another to Continental experience.

There was a sense of crisis in the early 19th century. Among the various social themes emerging were urbanization, industrialization, the growth of working-class militancy (e.g. through Chartism and trades unionism) and concern about rising rates of vagrancy, pauperism and juvenile crime. Referring to Regency London, Low quotes Henry Grey Bennett, Chairman of the 1816 Select Parliamentary Committee on the Police, that there were:

about 6,000 boys and girls living solely

on the town by thieving, or as companions and associates of thieves (1982, 64).

Juveniles (some as young as six) were engaged in pickpocketing and shoplifting, often as the tools of adults. Donajgrodzki argues that it was for these reasons that the early Victorians were obsessively interested in discovering the bases of social order (1977, 51). But the fact of a crisis does not explain the choice of remedies. Why not hang more? Why shift from the belief in deterrence and punishment which was used to control the 18th century population?

Contemporary Theories of Criminality

The dominance of particular theories of crime causation was certainly relevant. Early theories of criminal behaviour were derived from religious ideas: crime and sin were synonymous. At the beginning of the 19th century classical criminology was a dominant force in crime control. (See, for example, Beccaria 1764.) Central tenets were the role of free will and the function of punishment as a manipulator of this will. Men were seen as choosing between the anticipated pleasures of criminal acts and the pains imposed by society upon such behaviour, and it was believed that a fixed schedule of penalties could affect this calculation.

The challenge to classical criminology came with the growing awareness of the underlying causes of crime. Early in the 19th century classifications of criminal types and lists of aetiological factors were produced. The report of the Committee of the Society for Investigating the Alarming Increase (12) in Juvenile Delinquency in the Metropolis, in 1816, provides a good example of this. (13) In this Committee's opinion, the main causes of delinquency were:

1. the improper conduct of parents;
2. the want of education;
3. the want of suitable employment;
4. the violations of the Sabbath and habits of gambling in the streets.

It also identified "other auxiliary causes". These were:

a. the severity of the criminal code;
b. the defective state of the police;
c. the existing state of police discipline.

These themes are apparent in the case histories collected by the Society:

A.B. aged thirteen years. His parents are living; he was but for a short time at school; his father was frequently intoxicated, and on these occasions the son generally left home, and associated with bad characters, who introduced him to houses of ill fame, where they gambled till they had lost or spent all their money. This boy had been five years in the commission of crime, and been imprisoned for three separate offences; sentence of death had been twice passed on him.

E.F. aged eight years. His mother only is living, and she is a very immoral character. This boy has been in the habit of stealing for upwards of two years. In Covent-garden Market there is a party of between thirty and forty boys, who sleep every night under the sheds and baskets. These pitiable objects when they arise in the morning have no other means of procuring subsistence but by the commission of crime; this child was one of the number; and it appears that he has been brought up to the several police offices upon eighteen separate charges. He has been twice confined in the House of Correction, and three times in Bridewell; he is very ignorant, but of a good capacity (quoted by Low, 1982, 70-71).

Thus the responsibility was not necessarily the juvenile's. Crawford argued before a Select Committee of the House of Commons in 1817 that it was:

easy to blame these poor children and to ascribe their misconduct to an innate propensity to vice; but I much question whether any human being, circumstanced as many of them are, can be reasonably

expected to act otherwise (quoted by
Tobias, 1972, 11).

Contemporary religious views fitted in well
with this. They emphasized that the criminal was
not innately depraved, but rather that delinquency
could be traced back to early childhood. It was due
primarily to a breakdown in parental discipline.

In addition to family corruption, however,
commentators and investigators also focused on the
corrupting influence of city life: the combination
of criminal classes and criminal areas. (14) The
criminal areas of Shoreditch, Bethnal Green, White-
chapel and Clerkenwell (15) were all well documented
and mapped out by intrepid city explorers. Tobias
quotes the picture of the pedestrian who:

> traverses narrow dirty streets and courts,
> crowded and filthy - miserable and
> destitute of light, water, almost of air;
> he sees property dilapidated and falling
> to a mass of foul and ugly rubbish;
> children with pale and ghastly faces;
> forms hideous with premature disease,
> arising from the unnatural and unhealthy
> circumstances into which they are help-
> lessly cast. Of late years public
> attention has been drawn to this solid
> mass of misery, of low vice, of filth,
> fever and crime (1972, 30).

Whole thoroughfares were described as being occupied
by receivers of stolen property with their goods
openly spread for sale. Field Lane in Clerkenwell
was variously described as `this hot bed of crime
and demoralisation` and `one of the great dunghills
on which society rears criminals for the gallows`.
Worsley described such areas in terms of
`barbarism`, `heathenism`, `degradation` and `civil-
ization uncivilized` (1849, 120). They were assoc-
iated with the decline of the family and bonds of
kinship and the erosion of traditional methods of
social control. Thus there was a linking of moral
evils with physical conditions. Worsley, for example, wrote:

> The general state of dwelling houses and
> domestic comfort is closely linked with
> moral habits; that discomfort at home is
> both cause and effect of immorality and
> vice (1849, 90).

Consequently it was widely felt that if the <u>physical</u> conditions of the poor were improved, so too would their <u>moral</u> condition. Neale, for example, referring to Manchester, argued that if society:

> improved the habitations and thus promote the physical wellbeing of the poor, an immense saving would speedily be effected to the public - crimes of every kind would be lessened (quoted in Tobias, 1972, 35).

The causes of poverty were believed to have changed. Earlier accounts referred to drink, idleness and irreligion. By the 1880s, it was the pressures of city existence, the degenerating conditions of city life, which were blamed.

These beliefs provided the basis for the reformers´ proposals. The notion of the ´dangerous or criminal classes` and their predisposition to crime formed the bedrock on which the reformatory movement expounded its principles of treatment. The line between these and the labouring class was not viewed as drawn by actual poverty. It was rather, in Carpenter´s words, ´in the utter want of control existing among the children of the lower class, and in the entire absence of effort on the part of the parents to provide proper education for their children` (in her evidence to the Select Committee on Criminal and Destitute Juveniles, 1852). Therefore, to some extent, the conditions of the <u>whole</u> class had to be considered.

The idea of a criminal class was a powerful influence by the early nineteenth century. The threat that the criminal classes, increasingly congregated in urban settings, would join together and produce an uncontrollable ´mob` was an ever present fear (Tobias, 1972; Pearson, 1975). Also feared was the possibility that the respectable working-class might be corrupted by this mass of undeserving poor. The separation of this class from the others and the placation of their most obvious grievances were two recurrent themes in nineteenth century social policy. The reformatory movement provided a ready panacea to this social threat by offering the segregation of potential mob members in an isolated and controlled setting. (16) When coupled with a programme of labour, religion and education which would ensure the return of such individuals as useful members of their social class, the appeal was irresistable (Scull, 1977, 26). In essence, the reformatory movement perpetuated the notion that the remedy of social problems lay primarily in personal rejuvenation rather than in the more politically radical solution of changing fundamental aspects of the social structure.

The importance of personal rejuvenation was reinforced by the emergence of positivist criminology later in the century. Within the framework of positivist criminology, determinism replaced free will; individuals were seen as able to exercise little control over the factors leading to their criminal behaviour. In time, the emphasis in the search for explanations of criminal behaviour shifted from socio-economic and hereditary factors to the psychology of the individual offender. Criminals and the law abiding were viewed as different in certain characteristics, but the characteristics assigned at any one time depended on the theories in fashion. Crime was a disease and, consequently and more importantly, was something that could be cured. The factors which caused crime could be controlled by others. In determining penal measures, the offender´s hereditary, personality and environment were to be taken into account. The maxim was ´punishment should fit the individual, not the offence`. Persons without choice, it was argued, could not be seen as responsible for their behaviour, and so they could not be punished; rather they required treatment. Positivism justified intervention and provided the impetus for change. Further, the new sciences of psychiatry and psychoanalysis highlighted the importance of childhood experiences in the development of the personality. It was simple logic to spend more money on and provide more resources for the juvenile offender. The vital difference in this approach is that class discourse is less apparent. Personal pathology superceded class membership as the key signifier of susceptibility to criminal behaviour.

Also seminal, however, in the choice of remedy was the reformers´ image of childhood, of family and, later in the century, of adolescence. In the middle-class family, children remained children into their mid and late teens. They were protected and dependent. Purity was maintained by ignorance of realities outside the home. The ideal child was submissive, hardworking, obedient, modest and chaste. (See Empey (1978, 53-55) for an outline of child-raising principles commonly held in the 19th century.) Similarly, the ideal adolescent was organized, disciplined and supervised. Not that children or adolescents were naturally so. Dominant beliefs were of the need for parents to mould children. `Spare the rod and spoil the child` was a favourite maxim. In contrast to the ideal, working-class children seemed alarmingly unchildlike to middle-class observers (Worsley, 1849, 92-3). For example, Mary Carpenter wrote:

> We have beheld them prematurely old in vice when scarcely beyond childhood...and have shuddered if we contrasted them with our own young children (1853, 118).

Often working-class children were economically independent and played an active part in street life. They were not even necessarily living within the parental roof but in common lodging houses, themselves viewed as a corrupting influence. Here, according to Neale, juveniles:

> become familiarised with scenes of infamy offensive to every principle of morality, and here it is that they become initiated into every species of criminality by the precept and example of adult and hardened offenders (quoted in Tobias, 1972, 34).

Moreover working-class families (17) were seen as ineffective, unreliable and corrupting. In Worsley's words:

> Juvenile crime must be mainly attributed either to parental neglect or parental example (1849, 218).

The stereotypical image was of a life which centered round gambling, drinking and promiscuity. The finger was frequently pointed by reformers at the dangers of cheap publications, popular entertainments, street fairs and pubs (Worsley, 1849). (18) The same images were held in the United States but there was an added dimension there: immigration. (19) European immigrants were thought to present a serious social problem. A leading penologist of the period, W.D. Morrison, believed that juvenile delinquency was due to the `boundless hospitality` shown by the United States to immigrants. The confinement of immigrant children, therefore, was an assertion that <u>American</u> children were moral and well-balanced. Immigrant children were to be turned into paragons of middle-class protestant virtue (Finnestone, 1976; Fox, 1970).

The Remedies

One response to the assumed deficiencies in working-class life styles was to enforce respectable (middle-class) standards of family obligation. This marked the start of the state's promotion of desired family life and intervention to enforce it. In England, for example, in the 1870s and 1880s, various Acts of Parliament required parents to carry out certain parental duties by the threat of a penalty or even the loss of the child if they failed to. Jones (1982, 26) quotes John Glover saying that soon all 'the children (would be) in the workhouses and the parents in prison.' In 1892, there were 86,149 cases brought against parents under the 1870 Education Act alone.

Another response was to remove working-class children to the reformatories. Pinchbeck and Hewitt quote the Chief Bow Street magistrate in his evidence to the Select Committee on the Police of the Metropolis as saying that:

> To get away those boys before they are completely contaminated...would be a great national object. ...that if they could be taken from their parents when they are found in the streets, and put into some asylum, where they could be trained up to industry, it would be an immense thing, and then the gangs would want recruits, and would fall to decay (1973, 446).

The assumption was 'that proper training can counteract the imposition of poor family life, a corrupt environment and poverty, while at the same time toughening and preparing delinquents for the struggle ahead' (Platt, 1969, 53). The aims were to insulate working-class juveniles from the adult, working-class world by placing them in small, country communities, to teach them how to fulfill appropriate adult roles (by the inculcation of the values of humility, discipline, honesty and industry) and to return these 'youth heathens' (Carpenter, 1853, V) and 'morally diseased children' (Carpenter, 1853, 292) to the 'true position of childhood'. In the words of Mary Carpenter:

> He must be brought to a sense of dependence...(to) yield his own will in ready submission (to be)...gradually subdued and trained (1853, 298).

Davenport Hill echoed this in his description of the delinquent as ´a stunted little man` who must be ´turned into a child again` (quoted in May, 1973, 7). Similarly the Commander of the <u>Akbar</u> (a reformatory ship) is quoted in May as saying:

> The first great change which has to be effected when they are received on board in their vagrant state is to make them ´boys`. They are too old, too knowing, too sharp when they come on board, too much up in the ways of the world (1973, 28-9).

Thus writers tended to regard offenders as creatures of a different species.(20) Tobias quotes an account published in 1832:

> Some of the boys have an approximation to the face of a monkey, so strikingly are they distinguished by this peculiarity. They form a distinct class of men by themselves (1972, 40).

They had to be humanised, re-formed.

The reformatories were modelled on inculcating the norms of the middle-class in a quasi-family structure. (21) The first of the new reformatories was the Colonie Agricole at Mettray, conceived by Auguste Demetz in 1839. Central supervision of the type provided in the new prisons was not followed; it was rather replaced with twelve independent family units, designed to appear as part of a small rural village. The example of ´parents` was substituted for solitude, the ´house` for the cell.

American penologist Enoch Wines talked of the reformatories there in similar terms. There was:

> nothing of the prison about them - no walls, no spies, no guards: family influences are made prominent and predominant (1880, 224).

One of the principles stressed by the Rev. Sydney Turner, in charge of the Royal Philanthropic Reformatory, was that of ´Family Division`. This meant separating the boys into ´distinct households ...making each a family.` He argued: ´if you want success, follow the new plan of family division` (quoted in Hinde, 1951, 107). This is repeated by Carpenter: the delinquent must, in short, be placed in a family. The staff were to assume `the holy duties of a parent` (22) (Carpenter, 1853, 298). In Donzelot´s language, the family appears as though `colonized`:

> There are no longer two authorities facing one another: the family and the apparatus, but a series of concentric circles around the child: the family circle, the circle of technicians and the circle of social guardians (1979, 103).

Or, to quote Evans:

> Authority had been given another structure, equally severe yet more domestic (1982, 393).

But there were also elements in the reformatory movement of the 1850s of the church (Protestantism in the early years of the movement) and of the school. According to Foucault (1977), the religious and educational element masked the repressive function of the reformatories, which would have been apparent in prisons for juveniles, and enabled a continuity of control: what he calls `the carceral network`. The reformers, therefore, wanted fundamental and lasting correction by means of inner change: `domination of the soul` (Foucault, 1977). In Davenport Hill´s words, the means employed operated on `the mind and the heart` (quoted in Tobias, 1972, 172). Carpenter (1853, 169) used similar language. Reform occurred `only when the child´s <u>soul</u> is touched, when he yields from the <u>heart</u>` and this was preferred to discipline through punishment as that was now viewed as ineffective. (23) Thus the issue was one of proposed or assumed effectiveness and not of benevolence. The aims of Parkhurst and the reformatories were similar; only the methods differed. The reformatories allowed greater potential for controlling juveniles. Indeed statistics show a decline in the total number of juvenile offences recorded in the second half of the century. The main reason for this was said to be the removal of potential or actual delinquents from the streets to the reformatories (Jones, 1982).

The reformatories promised increased social control in three ways. First, more juveniles came under their control for longer periods of time. In

England, instead of a norm of three months imprisonment, juveniles spent between two and five years in the reformatories. (24) Further, many juveniles who would not previously have been brought into the penal system were sent to the reformatories. In the United States, Platt (1978) suggests that the child-savers promoted institutionalisation and that, therefore, juveniles were increasingly committed to reformatories. Mary Carpenter also saw the reformatories as widening the possibility of official intervention: ´Convictions would be far more frequent than at present` (in her evidence to the Select Committee on Criminal and Destitute Children, 1853, 98). She felt that there were too many acquittals and too few prosecutions but argued that if the public knew that juveniles would be reformed then they would be more likely to be prosecuted and convicted. This was echoed by Hugh Maxwell in New York. He observed that the opening of the Refuge had removed all objections to convictions. Carpenter further argued that the reformatories could deter more effectively than the prisons:

> ... If boys knew that their school fellow was secluded for two or three years according to his conduct, that he was withdrawn from his liberty, that he was compelled to work without wages...not only would they be far from thinking it a "bonus on crime", but they would dread such a punishment infinitely more than conviction, the effects of which they would very likely escape (in her evidence to the Select Committee on Criminal and Destitute Juveniles, 1852, 98).

Thus, in England, between 1854 and 1873, 26,326 juveniles were sent to reformatory or industrial schools.

Secondly, the reformatories encouraged early intervention unrelated to the nature of the juvenile´s offence. For example, around half of the juveniles sent there went on their first conviction. (25) The report of the Inspector of Reformatory Schools for 1871 stated:

> The facility with which boys have been sent to reformatories for very trifling offences, and after very trifling punishment, has tended in many cases to

increase rather than lessen the number of quasi criminals who are candidates for such treatment (Inspector of Reformatory and Industrial Schools, 1871, 6).

Furthermore, criteria for referral to the reformatory and industrial schools were wide and vague. Intervention became based on the status of juveniles qua juveniles, not on the basis of their conduct. The neglected and pre-delinquent (often referred to as ˊthe perishing classesˋ) became as much the legitimate objects of the stateˊs intervention as the delinquent (part of ˊthe dangerous classesˋ). Mary Carpenter, in her book <u>Reformatory Schools</u>, described the ˊperishing classesˋ as:

> ...those who have not yet fallen into actual crime but who are almost certain, from their destitution and the circumstances in which they are growing up to do so, if a helping hand be not extended to raise them (1851, 2).

The ˊdangerous classesˋ comprised:

> ...of those who have already received the prison brand, or if the mark has not yet visibly set upon them, are notoriously living by plunder who unblushingly acknowledge that they can gain more for the support of themselves and their parents by stealing than by working... (1851, 2).

The reformers, therefore, were concerned with deviant character and life-style, with the immoral and the incorrigible as much as with the delinquent. The determination was to control not just crime but all activities which could contribute to a deviant life style. Thus restrictions were imposed on juvenilesˊ drinking alcohol, gambling, playing games, reading certain materials and attending certain entertainments. Even seemingly legitimate activities such as work were controlled when they were thought inappropriate, for example, street trading (Pearson, 1983). The extension of such controls, of course, exacerbated the risk of juveniles running foul of the law. Gillis (1974) shows that, in some towns, for example Oxford, towards the end of the 19th and early in the 20th century, there were increases in the <u>official</u> rate of juvenile crime despite a general improvement in juveniles´ behaviour. Interestingly, by 1894 in England, there were only 4,800 juveniles in reformatories compared with 17,000 in the industrial schools (which catered for the neglected and pre-delinquent juveniles). In the United States, the original 1899 legislation termed ´delinquent` any juvenile who violated any law of the state or any city or town ordinance. This statute was broadened in 1901 to embrace a list of peculiarly juvenile offences (e.g. frequenting places where a gaming device was operated, ´incorrigibility` and ´growing up in idleness`). Legislation in 1907 extended delinquency to, amongst other things, running away, loitering and using profanities.

Thirdly, a new technique of reform was promised by the reformatory and industrial schools: discipline through work. What was stressed, however, was the inculcation of the work habit rather than the provision of useful training in a trade. (Oakum picking, wood chopping, matchbox making were common.) Carpenter referred to mundane work creating the ´salutary fatigue of the ,body` which removed ´from the minds evil thoughts` (1853, 306). Paterson (quoted in Humphries, 1981, 229) said of the juvenile after reformatory training:

> He will be able to keep any sort of job, however laborious and monotonous it may be... Many were born to be hewers of wood and drawers of water...for them laboring work, arduous and continuous, is the best preparation for the life that ensues.

With respect to the American institutions, Platt stressed that:

> The content or the type of work to be learnt was almost certainly of less relevance to the reformers than that the child could learn the form of work...[and] be normalized to work in general (1978, 69).

In practice, the work was geared more often to the institution´s profitability than to the individual´s reform. For example, Carlebach wrote:

> Since it was considered to be a measure of an institution´s worth to run it as cheaply as possible and since it was

necessary to convince those who subscribed
funds towards the management of institutions that their money was being well
spent, a number of undesirable factors
became deeply entrenched...A number of
institutions eventually confined themselves to industries which were not only
useless in a training sense but which were
often very harmful to the children, in
order to achieve a maximum profit from the
labour force which the children represented (1970, 68).

The Poor Law principle of less eligibility also
influenced the running of the schools. An article
in the Economist (13th October 1860) argued that
both industrial and reformatory schools should be
'marked by some disagreeable conditions which will
effectively prevent them from gradually superseding
the schools where payment is required.' Accordingly,
when the movement for compulsory education was
gaining ground in England, the reformatories
initially resisted the introduction of formal
educational classes into the syllabus and insisted
on continuing to teach only the scriptures. It was
argued that anything else would produce in them a
disrelish for the laborious occupations of life
(Williams, 1965). Later, they were given learning
suitable to their status (Flinn, 1967). In the New
York Refuge, inmates spent four hours in the
classroom compared with eight at work (Schlossman,
1977).
The early reformers in England had a clear
class orientation. Mary Carpenter, for example,
wrote:

We have thus indicated the way in which
young children of the labouring classes
may be prepared for their station in life
(quoted in Morris and McIsaac, 1978, 7).

Moreover, this legacy persisted. For example, the
Chief Inspector of Reformatory and Industrial
Schools stated in his annual report in 1915 that the
aim of the reformatories was:

to train it (sic) in all the little habits
of refinement and self-respect which are
reckoned among the conventions of decent
working-class folk, to teach it to take
pride and pleasure in wearing seemly

clothes and neat boots (Inspector of Reformatory and Industrial Schools, 1915,35).

Schlossman presents a similar picture in the United States. He argues that the managers of the House of Refuge in New York frankly described the Refuge as an instrument for compelling lower-class children to conform to middle-class standards of behaviour. Rather than instil inmates with a success ethos which implied social advancement, they emphasized the traditional expectations for a lower-class citizenry: 'the habitual practice of orderly, meek existence' (Schlossman, 1977, 30).

The regimes generally were harsh. The early industrial schools tended to replicate the brutality and harsh conditions of industrial employment. Ten hour working days were not uncommon. Humphries (1981) documents birching, solitary confinement and dietary restrictions as punishments. Carpenter herself stressed the importance of strict discpline:

> I would not object to really severe measures being resorted to if they were found to be necessary from the conduct of the child...they must feel they are under positive and firm discipline, and I believe that when boys do find themselves under the firm discipline, they will yield to necessity (in her evidence to the Select Committee on Criminal and Destitute Juveniles, 1852, 97 and 109).

Though the New York Refuge was primarily presented to the public as an educational enterprise, the managers also stressed that it was a 'juvenile penitentiary'. Indeed, by the middle of the 19th century, the Houses of Refuge and reform schools were generally under attack. Exposés revealed a wide gap between the public claims of the administrators and actual practices. Schlossman lists the charges:

> Educational achievements were minimal; rehabilitative accomplishments were exaggerated; corruption was rife; political considerations intruded into the appointment process and inflated expenses; active proselytizing of Catholic inmates was pursued against the wishes of their parents; hardened and relatively innocent offenders mingled at will, negating the original

purpose of the institution to prevent "contamination"; sexual segregation developed homosexual tendencies, encouraged sexual exploitation, and exacerbated emotional problems; vocational training programs amounted to no more than busywork or worse still, exploitation of cheap child labor for private profit and finally, incarceration provided a perfect setting for mutual instruction and reinforcement of the norms and techniques of criminal behavior (1977, 35-6).

Scull (1983), therefore, cautions against taking reformers' claims at face value and suggests that there was considerable discrepancy between intentions and consequences, between words and actions.

By the end of the 19th century the desirability of the reformatories and the industrial schools began to be questioned (26) and alternatives introduced. The Summary Jurisdiction Act of 1879, for example, enabled magistrates to admonish a juvenile who had committed a petty offence without entering a formal conviction. Later, the Probation of First Offenders Act, 1887, gave magistrates the power to release, on their own recognisance, any offender convicted of an offence punishable by not more than two years imprisonment. (27) Later, the Howard Association promoted a supervised system of probation. This was achieved in the Youthful Offenders Act of 1901 and the Probation Act of 1907. The era of the reformatories was diminishing just as the juvenile courts emerged.

The creation of the juvenile courts in 1908 can be viewed as simply the logical outcome of increased awareness of the differing needs of juveniles and adults. But these concerns were fuelled by an awareness of declining birth rates (each census after 1881 confirmed a falling birth rate) and of the poor physical state of the working-class population (as revealed in recruits for the Boer War.) (28) It was also a period of economic and social uncertainty. From the 1890s on, there was increased industrial competition from abroad, the expansion of the war power of Germany, the growing strength of organised labour and the Labour Party, and the emergence of the suffragette movement. It was an era of conflict between old and new ideas: property, family, Christianity, class, and the dominance of men were all under attack. Concern for juveniles (delinquent or not) in the 1908 Children Act reflected concern for the future; juveniles' health and well-being was one of the nation's greatest assets. (29)

Conclusion

Our conclusion is that the characterisation of this period as one of benevolence and reform is an ex-post facto rationalisation. The reforms were authoritarian and conservative. Conventional accounts stress the humanitarianism of the reformers, but their motivations were complex. Evangelical groups, industrialists and women were all much involved in and had much to gain from the child-saving movement. With respect to women, Prochaska (1980) goes as far as to suggest that it is difficult to tell who benefited most from their labours, the objects of their sympathy or themselves. Philanthropy was an obvious alternative to the refined idleness of middle-class women. After all, they traditionally cared for the young, the sick, the elderly and the poor. Visiting workhouses, schools, refuges and prisons were viewed as fit and proper concerns for women. A reformatory without a woman, it was said, was 'like a home without a mother - a place of desolation' (Sichels in the Proceedings of the National Conference of Charities and Correction, 1894, quoted in Platt, 1978, 79). Women, therefore, lobbied for protective legislation for juveniles, particularly for statutes creating juvenile courts, and actually served as probation officers or assistants in institutions or participated in the selection of such persons.

Evangelical groups were involved in all the major reforms of the period. Specifically in relation to delinquents, the Reformatory and Refuge Union, which represented a thousand charities, made clear that its chief aim was 'to reclaim and elevate the neglected and criminal classes, by educating them in fear of God and in the knowledge of the Holy Scriptures' (quoted in Prochaska, 1980, 158).

Platt argued that the juvenile court system was part of a general movement 'directed towards developing a specialized labour market and industrial discipline' (1974, 377). Others (e.g. Hagan and Leon, 1977 and Empey, 1978) are more cautious, but it is likely that the reform movement was quite diverse reflecting different social conditions in different areas. At the very least, we can question the belief that humanitarianism was the sole motivation underlying the reforms.

Rather than a radical break from the past, the reformatories reaffirmed traditional ideas about family, parental authority, education and rural life. Their aims were to stablize the emerging industrial order, promote stability at a moment where traditional ideas and practices appeared ineffective and to forestall threats to the <u>status quo</u>. The argument was mainly about the best way of achieving this. Social reforms in one area, however, also created social problems in another. For example, the various Factory Acts early in the 19th century restricted job opportunities for juveniles. This led to an increase in the number of juveniles on the streets, hence their high visibility and consequent concerns about their behaviour.

We are not rejecting benevolence outright; the social construction of childhood did prevent the economic exploitation of juveniles and general indifference to their needs. But most reforms were <u>also</u> implicitly or explicitly coercive. This is not inconsistent, for humanitarianism and coercion are essentially two sides of the same coin: they are mutually supportive.

NOTES

1. Cf. Pollock (1983) accepts that the concept of ´childhood` is new but disputes the view that childhood as a separate sphere is a recent phenomenon.

2. Though much of this was the result of humanitarian motives, there is also what Empey calls ´a darker side` (1978, 68) – for example, the definition of an increasing number of acts as deviant and greater intervention into the lives of children. Jones (1982, 27) quotes John Eardley-Wilmot saying in the 1820s ´many offences for which a lad is now sent to gaol were formerly disregarded or not considered of so serious a character as to demand imprisonment.` He went on to say that ´crowds of young offenders who formerly escaped

detection have been brought to justice.` The net-widening effect of the cautioning of juvenile offenders by the police is a modern equivalent of this process. This is discussed in Chapter 5.

3. Plint (1851) is critical of Worsley's figures. He claims that rather than increases in crime in the period 1842-6, crime had decreased by 20 per cent and that the decreases were even larger in the manufacturing counties, the conditions of which Worsley had blamed for crime. Of course, the accuracy or otherwise of the statistics (see Chapter 2) is largely irrelevant. It is the supposed scientific nature of the inquiry which gives credibility to the exercise of defining the extent of crime and its control. This association remains valid today.

4. At Parkhurst, boys were classified in various ways. There was a general ward for 14 years old and over, a junior ward for the under 14s, a probationary ward where all boys stayed for their first four months, a refractory ward for punishment and an infirmary ward for the sick. It operated as a boys' prison for only twenty-five years until it was closed in 1864 after considerable criticism of its repressive regime and harsh discipline.

5. It has to be kept in mind, however, that there was no immediate transfer of children from prisons to reformatories. Though the number in the former decreased while those in the latter gradually increased, the vast majority of children continued to serve prison sentences. The following figures were printed in the Economist (7 July 1860):

	Reformatories	Prisons
1856	534 boys and girls	13,981 boys and girls
1859	921 boys and girls	8,913 boys and girls

6. For example, magistrates in both Birmingham and Manchester had since the 1880s dealt with juvenile offenders in a separate court.

7. Juvenile courts in France seem to have been similar. Donzelot refers to them as being the same arrangements as for adults, but `miniaturized`: `in short, a theatrical deployment that does not differ a great deal from that used for adults` (1979, 100). There was a difference, however, in the way they functioned. Donzelot argues that there were a series of fundamental shifts in judicial practice: a shift in the content of the thing judged and a shift in the mode of trial. To this extent then `the child` was recognized as different.

8. Carpenter, for example, was highly critical of the harsh punishments imposed at Parkhurst. `It

attempted to fashion children into machines through iron discipline, instead of self acting beings` (1851, 321).

9. Prominent amongst these, in England, was Mary Carpenter but Matthew Davenport Hill, Walter Crofton and Alexander Maconochie were also active. In the United States the main campaigners were Enoch Wines, Lucy Flowers, Sara Cooper and Sophia Minton.

10. Wyse wrote of the impact of education on the working class in similar terms:

> He will not be found, each Saturday night, in these dens of iniquity, with pale and haggard cheeks, applauding the licentious or infidel jest, plotting the next strike, devising some new means of intimidation or aggression against the resisting or industrious...returning on Monday to his work...the seeds planted of crimes which perhaps, ere long, may consign him to the transport vessel, or the scaffold (1836, 310).

11. For example, full state control of the reformatories became complete with the establishment in 1898 of the Children´s Department within the Home Office although it had contributed financially to them since 1854.

12. The Committee, in fact, provided no statistics on juvenile crime, but was convinced that it was rising.

13. Later reports echo these themes. See, for example, the Select Committee on Criminal Commitments and Convictions (1827) and the Select Committee on the Police of the Metropolis (1828).

14. At this point it was believed that it was the working class family and area which corrupted. When the Puritans left England for the New World, it is interesting that they did so because of the corruption of the Old World generally.

15. They were also found in other cities (Jones, 1982) but what was happening in London dominated policy discussions and practice. London was regarded as the Mecca of the dissolute, the lazy, the mendicant, ´the rough` and the spendthrift (Stedman Jones, 1984, 12). It was also by far the largest city in the world: 2 million in 1850, 5 million by the end of the century.

16. Segregation was viewed as the panacea to most 19th century ills, but this could not be undertaken on an individual basis. Hence the development of institutions like prisons, asylums and work-houses as the medium for the panacea

(Melossi and Pavarini, 1981).

17. As in modern literature, in reality it is often the <u>mother</u> who is blamed. Worsley (1849, 79) referred to working women: 'The result is a house in the grossest disorder, and a home without comfort'. He also explained increases in juvenile crime by reference to increases in women's crime (1849, 118).

18. Such 'vices' and their modern equivalents are still viewed as stimulants to criminal behaviour (for example, video 'nasties' and football matches). See Pearson, 1983.

19. This was relevant to a more limited extent in certain English cities with respect to Irish immigration (Pearson, 1983, 236-7).

20. Of course, 'scientific' credibility was subsequently given to this by the work of Lombroso (1911). Although his work was not translated into English until 1911, his findings were known by the early 1890s.

21. According to Donzelot the same ideology underlined the first juvenile courts in France. He refers to them as: the 'family law court' providing 'family justice' (1979, 100) and later to the juvenile court as a visible form of the state-as-family (1979, 104).

22. This kind of language is also apparent in debates on education. The idea was that the school and the teacher would take over many of the responsibilities of the parent. This was at its clearest with respect to pauper children, but attempts were also made to import similar ideas into the education of other children too. The teacher, therefore, had to become a 'substitute' parent, occupy 'the father's place' (Kay, 1841, quoted in Johnson, 1970, 112), because the parents were seen as not fulfilling that role, or, at least, not fulfilling it in the ways expected of them by the educationalists.

23. Reconviction figures were frequently referred to in promoting reformatories.

24. Until 1899, they also had to first serve a sentence of imprisonment to expiate the crime. Reformatory training, therefore, was <u>after</u> and <u>in addition</u> to imprisonment.

25. This practice was paralleled in the use of care orders for offences in England and Wales during the 1970s. See Chapter 4 for an elaboration.

26. The Howard Association, for example, blamed them for increases in juvenile crime. In their annual report of 1896 it stated:

> Reformatories do reform. But a certain residuum of their boys are very bad. These institutions need more attention. They are often carried on too much for mere pecuniary profit; the boys´ moral interest being made secondary (1896, 6).

The report of the Departmental Committee on Reformatory and Industrial Schools in 1896 was also critical of the schools and recommended limiting their use to situations in which removal from home was necessary for the protection of the community.

27. This was not, however, like the system of probation operating now or even at that time in certain American states which involved supervision by a designated officer. There was then in England no element of supervision and so magistrates were reluctant to use the Act.

28. The Royal Commission on Physical Training 1905 (Scotland), the Interdepartmental Committee on Physical Deterioration 1904, and the Royal Commission on the Care and Control of the Feeble-Minded, 1904-8, all provided details on the physical and mental state of the nation.

29. This period also saw the development of the youth club movement: scouts, boys brigade, etc. Nationalism and imperialism were key issues. See Blanch, 1979, for an elaboration of this.

Chapter 2

YOUTH AND CRIME

The (Labour) Government fully recognise
and share the widespread anxiety that is
felt...about the continuing problem of how
to cope with a small minority, among
children, of serious and persistent
offenders (Home Office et al., 1976, para.
3).

The (Conservative) Government shares the
general public concern about the level of
juvenile offending (Home Office et al.,
1980, para. 34).

Juvenile delinquency has of late years
increased to an unprecedented extent, and
is still rapidly and progressively
increasing (Society for the Improvement of
Prison Discipline and for the Reformation
of Juvenile Offenders, 1818, 11).

Introduction

Concern over juvenile crime (1) is not new (see, for
example, Pearson, 1983; Dixon and Fishwick, 1984)
though there is a tendency to see increases as
exceptional. However, the history of crime is in
many ways a history of crime waves. Those living in
the 18th and 19th centuries felt just as much as we
do today that they were living in the grip of
immense crime waves; they experienced and we are
experiencing recurrent social panics about increases
in crime, especially in relation to juvenile crime.
Comparisons with earlier times are always problematic, but it is quite likely that London streets
are far safer now than in Dickens' time and that few
American cities match now the lawlessness of the

Wild West in the 1830s. This is not, of course, the public's view.

Taylor (1981, 2) refers to a 'widespread belief in British cities that crime in general is on the increase and that it is becoming more violent and predatory'. This belief is particularly strong in relation to juvenile crime. Between 1965 and 1979 national opinion polls showed that juvenile crime was considered to be one of the most serious social problems in Britain (2) (New Society, 1980, 220).

Pearson (1983) has shown that moral panics about young working-class males repeatedly appear in Britain. He traces a history of what he calls 'respectable fears' which consistently and unfavourably compare present generations with previous 'golden ages', and identifies the 'twenty year rule': the fact that things now are perceived to be worse than some twenty years ago. Through a series of case histories, Pearson shows that this image of a harmonious past fails to stand up to scrutiny; he points to the gangs of street urchins in the 1840s, the garrotters of the 1860s, the football violence of the 1920s, the teddy boys of the 1950s and the football hooligans of the 1980s.

These fears or concerns represent a means by which much wider social anxieties are articulated and expressed. The use made of 'law and order' issues by the Conservative Party in its election campaigns is well documented (Taylor, 1981; Downes, 1983) and it seems that a significant number of voters supported the Tories in the 1979 general election because they believed that they could be relied on to maintain law and order. Yet if one examines the criminal statistics, this belief has little empirical support. Downes (1983, 2) clearly demonstrated that there was no association between the party in government and crime rates. Of course, because of their limitations, criminal statistics cannot not be conclusive in such exercises, but the point is: they are taken to be.

These social anxieties run deeper than party politics, however; they signify uncertainties about the stability of the 'British way of life'. (3) The precise nature of these uncertainties varies with time. In the 1850s, they focused on working-class families and their child-rearing practices (see pages 16-21). In the more recent past, Pearson has drawn attention to:

> The decline of family life, the lowering
> of standards in the schools, the

´permissive` worm within, the irresponsi-
bility of working mothers and their delinquent ´latch-key` children, the excessive
leniency of the law, and the unwarranted
interference of the ´softly-softly, namby-
pamby pussyfooting` of the so-called
experts - these were all well trodden
avenues of complaint by ´law and order`
enthusiasts and ´anti-permissive` moral-
ists, warning of a vast historical degen-
eration among the British people (1983,
4).

Present ´law and order` attitudes in Britain and
discussions about ´juvenile crime` must, therefore,
be understood and situated within a framework of
these deeper preoccupations. (4)
    Much of our information about juveniles comes
from newspapers. Porteous and Colston (1980) found
that British press coverage of events involving
adolescents showed a strong emphasis on violence and
crime, both perpetrated on and committed by them. A
total of 913 articles were analysed. Eleven per
cent were sporting stories (Wimbledon was taking
place during the period of the research), seven per
cent were about education, but 35 per cent were
about crime (about half of these were about
juveniles as offenders, the remainder as victims).
Porteous and Colston conclude:

    According to our daily press a typical
    adolescent is a sporting youngster
    criminally inclined, likely to be murdered
    or injured in an accident (1980, 202).

Only two per cent of the articles discussed youth
employment though, in 1979, 20 per cent of under 18s
were without a job. (5) The researchers also evaluated the stories: 52 per cent were evaluated
neutrally, 24 per cent positively and 24 per cent
negatively. However, much of the positive coverage
was due to a small number of media ´stars`.
Adolescents from other sectors of society tended to
be presented as ´frequent victims of accidents or
crime, or as subversive or criminal themselves`
(1980, 206). Porteous and Colston continue:

    The newspapers present, to some extent, an
    unimaginative view of adolescents, feeding
    their readers with a diet of glitter,
    shock and horror, and self-righteous

indignation. Such a menu is generally unedifying, factually incorrect and socially divisive (1980, 206).

In short, the newspapers reported the unusual or sensational behaviour of a small minority of juveniles.

Society also gets much of its information about crime from the media which provide impressions, definitions, explanations and make events meaningful. They tell us what is taking place and how to interpret and understand it. So how do events become newsworthy? According to Young (1973, 316) people read avidly news which 'titillates their sensibilities and confirms their prejudices', that is newspapers give the public what it wants. This means, of course, that coverage of crime is selective. Young, however, also suggests that images of the deviant perform certain functions: the reinforcement of the consensual part of public consciousness and the denigration of any subversive notions. With respect to the presentation of deviant behaviour, Cohen (1973) suggests from his research on mods and rockers that there is much exaggeration and distortion. He identified ten elements in the media description of events and analysed them for their truthfulness. Basically, they were not. For example, the mods and rockers were described as affluent. Though it was impossible to get precise information on this, Cohen quotes the evidence available from those charged in the courts. The average take-home pay in Barker and Little's (1964) Margate sample was £11 per week and his own sample (in Clacton) had on them an average of 75p for the whole Bank holiday weekend.

What do the criminal statistics themselves say? We do not know how much crime is actually committed; all that we can talk about is 'crimes known to and recorded by the police'. From self-report studies (involving offenders or victims), we know that recorded crime can be a small proportion of all crimes committed and that the nature of crimes committed might be quite different from that recorded. We must keep in mind two crucial variables in attempting to make sense of criminal statistics:
   1. decisions by the public (whether or not to report a crime); and
   2. decisions by the police (whether or not to record a crime).
'Youth' is a factor in this discretionary process:

the public may or may not report offences because of the youthfulness of the defendant; the police may or may not prosecute offenders because of their youthfulness. However, imperfect though the official picture is, it tells us where society´s and the police´s interests lie and so we will start there.

Crimes Known to the Police in England and Wales

The number of offences (6) recorded by the police in England and Wales increased from 81,000 in 1901 to over 3.6 million in 1985: this 1985 figure represents 3 per cent more offences than in 1984. The largest increases were in the number of recorded offences of violence, robbery and criminal damage – each around 10 to 17 per cent. The increase for recorded sexual offences was smaller (6 per cent) and the recorded number of burglary offences fell by 3 per cent.

Since the beginning of the century, the population has increased from 32.5 million to about 55 million. Consequently, a more accurate represent-ation of the growth of crime is provided by looking at the incidence of crime per 100,000 of population:

    249 per 100,000 in 1901
  1,299 per 100,000 in 1951
  5,971 per 100,000 in 1981
  7,258 per 100,000 in 1985

The crime rate varies, of course, according to the nature of the offence. In 1985, it ranged from just over 3,786 per 100,000 population for offences of theft and handling stolen goods to 55 per 100,000 for offences of robbery. There are also consider-able variations among police force areas. In general, the highest rates of recorded crime per head of population are in the police force areas which include the large cities and the lowest rates are in the most rural police force areas. In the Metropolitan Police District (London), for example, 211 offences of robbery were recorded per 100,000 population in 1985 compared with only ten per 100,000 in Wales. In 1985, the highest rates for violence against the person were in Nottinghamshire, Humberside and Staffordshire. For offences of burglary, the highest rates were in Merseyside and Northumbria. These kinds of differences are likely to be due to a number of inter-related factors: for example, the number of potential victims and offenders in each police area, and variations in reporting and recording practices (Farrington and Dowds, 1984).

The majority of recorded serious offences are offences against property: in 1985, they made up about 80 per cent of all offences recorded. Robbery and sex offences each amounted to less than 1 per cent of crimes recorded, criminal damage to 15 per cent, fraud and forgery to 4 per cent and crimes of violence to 3 per cent.

Comparisons of recorded crime over time are beset by problems, (7) but, generally, the picture has remained constant. The theft offence with the greatest increase in the number recorded over the ten years 1975-85 was theft from a vehicle which doubled, an average annual increase of 7 per cent. This rate of increase was more than twice that for theft or unauthorised taking of a motor vehicle, but, taken together, these offences account for about 45 per cent of all theft offences recorded. In numerical terms, the number of violent offences has risen consistently throughout the post-war period: 4,746 in 1945 to 122,000 in 1985. This probably reflects changes in society's tolerance level rather than real increases, however, (McClintock, 1963; Sparks et al., 1977) as the majority of these offences are minor in nature. The number of the more serious violent offences, which accounted for only 7 per cent of the offences of violence recorded in 1985, increased at a much lower rate in the period 1975-85 than did the less serious offences: less than 3 per cent per year on average compared with 6 per cent.

Clearly not all offences known to the police are detected: the overall clear-up rate in England and Wales in 1985 was 35 per cent, (8) but there were wide disparities according to the nature of the offence. Amongst the theft offences, the clear-up rate in 1985 ranged from 13 per cent for theft from the person to 87 per cent for theft from shops and to almost 100 per cent for handling stolen goods. In violence against the person, the clear-up rate was 73 per cent; for robbery it was 22 per cent. Detection rates do not necessarily reflect police efficiency. Shoplifters, for example, are not reported to the police unless already detected.

In 1985, 587,000 offenders were found guilty of, or cautioned for, indictable offences, about 1,500 more than in 1984 and about one-fifth more than ten years earlier. The largest offence group, as expected, was theft and handling stolen goods, which accounted for 55 per cent of offenders. Burglary accounted for 14 per cent, violence against the person 10 per cent, fraud and forgery 5 per cent, indictable motoring offences 5 per cent, criminal damage 2 per cent, sexual offences and robbery each about 1 per cent.

Information on these offenders shows that they were predominantly male: about 83 per cent of the total. For both sexes about a third of the total (29 per cent for men and 36 per cent for women) were juveniles. Among known offenders in 1985, the proportionate involvement of juveniles was highest for offences of burglary, theft and handling stolen goods and indictable offences of criminal damage (each just over one-third).

For both boys and girls, theft and handling was the most common offence for which they were found guilty or cautioned, as Table 2.1 shows.

Table 2.1   Percentage of Juvenile Offenders Found Guilty at all Courts or Cautioned by Type of Offence, Sex and Age

	Males		Females	
	Aged 10 & under 14	Aged 14 & under 17	Aged 10 & under 14	Aged 14 & under 17
Violence against the person	3	8	3	8
Sexual offences	1	1	–	–
Burglary	20	22	4	4
Robbery	1	1	–	–
Theft and handling stolen goods	69	60	91	84
Fraud and forgery	1	1	1	2
Criminal damage	4	3	1	1
Other	–	3	–	1
Total	100*	100	100	100

Sources: Home Office, 1986d
* Less than 100 per cent due to rounding

The rate of recorded crime among juveniles is much higher than for any other age group. In 1985, the number found guilty or cautioned was 8,128 per 100,000 for boys aged fourteen to seventeen and

2,018 per 100,000 girls in this age group. In comparison, the figures for those aged 21 and over were 1,328 for males and 254 for females. The peak age for those found guilty or cautioned is fifteen for boys (8,796 per 100,000) and fourteen for girls (2,346 per 100,000), the same as in nearly every year for the period 1975-85. This has often been linked to the final year of compulsory education, but it does not seem to explain the different peak ages for boys and girls.

A sharp rise has occurred over the years in the rate of crime attributed to juveniles: (9) it increased threefold in the last twenty years and throughout the ten year period 1975-85 the highest rate of known offending per 100,000 was amongst males aged fourteen and under seventeen. The average annual rate of increase in the rate of known juvenile offending per 100,000 population was between 2 and 3 per cent a year. For women, although the rates were much lower than for men, the average annual pecentage increases in the rate of known offending per 100,000 population were greater: around 4 per cent per annum for the under twenty-ones. But, as we have seen, crime in general has increased and the relationship between adult and juvenile crime rates has remained relatively constant. Further, within the criminal statistics, there are considerable variations from year to year. In 1975 and 1976, for example, the rate of crimes committed by boys fell for both the 10-14s and the 14-17s. Although it rose in 1977, it fell again in 1978. Appendices I and II provide information on these changes.

A recent government survey (D.H.S.S., 1981a) examined trends in juvenile crime in an attempt to understand the reasons underlying these changes. It showed that the overall rise in the number of known juvenile offenders could be understood in terms of changes in five factors: the number of juveniles in the population, police cautioning practices, different patterns of offending for boys and girls and for older and younger children, the commission (or detection) of different types of offences, and social factors. It concluded that about a quarter of the increase in offending could be attributed to changes in the number of juveniles in the population. Over two-fifths was attributable to the higher offending rates for 14-17 year old boys and almost a quarter of the total increase to higher offending rates for girls. Almost all the increase in known offenders, however, was due to increases in

the number cautioned - by definition, the more
trivial offences - rather than to increases in the
number sentenced. This indicates that changes in
police practices were in part responsible for these
increases in juvenile crime.

In some senses, the police create or ´make up`
statistics: they are a ´rate producing` agency.
Simple changes like the reallocation of resources or
the creation of specialist bureaus can influence
crime rates. In the 1970s, there was a tremendous
increase in the number of juveniles cautioned by the
police. This could well have influenced the
juvenile crime rate by reducing the number of
informal cautions given and by encouraging the
reporting of juveniles to the police by other
agencies, for example, by schools or shopkeepers.
Research (Ditchfield, 1976; Farrington and Bennett,
1981) supports this suggestion and is explored
further in Chapter 5.

Talk of increases in juvenile crime is at odds
with evidence that the pool of potential juvenile
delinquents is contracting. In 1977, the number of
juveniles cautioned or found guilty of indictable
offences was 184,100. In 1985, it was 175,700, a
decline of 5 per cent. Changes in cautioning procedures between 1977 and 1985 may have led to some
decline, but as we have just noted, there are
other factors which could equally have led to
possible increases: the ´net widening` effect of
police cautioning and increases in police manpower
(Clarke and Hough, 1984). Pratt (1985a) accounts
for the decline by reference to demographic changes
in recent years: especially the decline in the
10-17 age group. (10) However, if we turn to the
number of juveniles found guilty or cautioned per
100,000 population, a different picture emerges:
there is an <u>increase</u> in the involvement of young
persons with the criminal justice system and a
decrease for children. Overall, juveniles are
generally more, not less, likely to be <u>processed</u> as
delinquents, a further indication of the impact of
policing policies. Table 2.2 demonstrates this.

According to Radzinowicz and King (1977,30)
the young contribute the highest share of violent
offences: ´daring, lack of foresight, uncritical
enthusiasm, sheer physical strength and endurance,
all play their part`. They go on to say: ´the young
may be, as they almost certainly are, indulging in
more damage, shoplifting and stealing, violence...`
(1977, 31). In similar terms, Hoghughi (1983, 97)
refers to the ´horrific reality of juvenile crime,

Table 2.2   Persons   Found Guilty of   or Cautioned for
            Indictable Offences per   100,000   Popula-
            tion in the Age Group by Age and Sex

	1977	1985
Males aged 10 and under 14	3517	3231
Males aged 14 and under 17	7519	8128
Females aged 10 and under 14	1041	1048
Females aged 14 and under 17	1570	2018

Source: Home Office, 1986d

both in its extent and   impact`.   In   fact,   serious
offences are very rarely committed by juveniles. For
example, of   around   25,000   offences   committed   by
juveniles in the Metropolitan area in 1985,   only   5
per cent involved violence against the   person.   But
more importantly, we   have   to   bear   in   mind   that
criminal   statistics   represent   a   partial   and
imperfect representation   of   the   world   of   crime.
These are not `true` figures.   At   the   very   least,
clear-up rates are   low   and   there   are   many   good
reasons why young   people   are   more   likely   to   be
detected than adults. Their crimes,   for example,   are
often unplanned and impulsive. Acts of vandalism, an
activity commonly   associated   with   juveniles,   are
often viewed, at least by the   juveniles   concerned,
as   spontaneous   acts,   associated   with   play
(Gladstone, 1978; Wilson, 1978). Juveniles are   also
a highly visible group which makes them particularly
susceptible to contact with the   police   (Riley   and
Shaw,   1985;   Ekblom,   1979).   These   factors   which
relate to the social situation of juveniles need   to
be   considered   in   trying   to   understand   their
contribution to the official   statistics   on   crime.
Recorded offences of shoplifting illustrate some   of
these issues.
     In 1985 there were 281,557 shoplifting offences
known to the police.   The   average   value   of   goods
stolen was £44.   The total   value   of   the   property
stolen was   £11,648.   76   per   cent   of   shoplifting
offences involved goods worth less than   £25.   There
were 147,338 offenders found guilty at all courts or
cautioned for thefts from shops. Juveniles accounted
for about half of these, and this is, in   fact,   the

most common juvenile crime. The bulk of juvenile shoplifters, however, are cautioned: especially girls and those under fourteen years old. The age and sex distribution of people dealt with for shoplifting in 1984 is presented in Table 2.3.

TABLE 2.3 Number of Offenders Found Guilty at Magistrates' Court or Cautioned for Thefts from Shops by Age and Sex

	Age	Male	% cautioned	Female	% cautioned
Number	10 to 14	16,882	88	8,834	95
cautioned	14 to 17	19,355	70	11,715	81
and found	17 to 20	8,989	8	6,234	11
guilty at	21 or more	31,324	13	23,020	22
magistrates'					
court*					

* 35 juveniles were dealt with in the Crown Court for shoplifting

Source: Home Office, 1985a

This high cautioning rate probably reflects the low value of the goods stolen by juveniles. Other factors relevant in the decision to prosecute are the policy of the store, the age, attitude and record of the individual, the circumstances of the offence (e.g. whether it seems planned or professional) and the prevalence of shoplifting in the area.

Shoplifting, of course, has a very high dark figure. Shopkeepers for example, may not realise that an offence has taken place. Stock shortages may be due to many factors: theft by employees or shortages in delivery. Many researchers (Walsh, 1978) believe that theft by employees, by definition adult or young adults, accounts for the largest losses. A second factor is that the shopkeeper or store detective may decide not to report the offender to the police but rather deal with it informally (by, for example, a warning to the offender and the return of the goods to the store). Shops may be particularly unwilling to involve the police where the offender is very young or very old, or clearly disturbed. Conversely certain types of individuals are more likely to be both observed and referred to the police (May, 1977; Steffensmeier and Terry, 1977). This could mean that juveniles become over-represented in the detected population. Juveniles, because of their relative lack of sophistication, may also be easier to detect than adults.

All of this raises the question of how far we can rely on the criminal statistics. Rutter and Giller (1983) recently reviewed the criminal statistics over the last thirty years or so and concluded that it was virtually certain that some of the apparent rate of increase in the number of offenders was illusory (due, for example, to changes in the classification of offences and to alterations in police recording practices), but that some of the increase was nevertheless real. The evidence was stronger for some crimes than others. In the case of serious personal violence, for example, they suggested that it was more likely that both victim and police would respond than in minor property offences. However, Rutter and Giller (1983) stress that the evidence for a real increase in crime is greater for the 1950s and 1960s than for the 1970s.

Other Sources of Information

Criminal statistics may not be an adequate measure of crime. Law enforcement practices may vary from one area to another, and from one year to another; there may be wide variations in the reporting of different offences by victims; and the social and personal characteristics of offenders may influence whether or not an arrest is recorded. For these reasons, criminologists have turned to other sources of information about crime.

The problem of knowing the precise nature and extent of crimes committed is the ´dark figure`, that is crimes which have not been reported to the police or which have not been recorded by the police. We do not know the relationship between the actual amount of crime committed and crimes known to the police and recorded by them and so it is not posible to say with certainty that crimes committed have increased by so much over a given period, or that juveniles commit a certain percentage of all crimes. It may be that actual crime has been increasing at the same rate as recorded crime, that is that the proportion of unrecorded crime has remained constant; but, equally, this proportion may have varied.

A number of factors suggest that the dark figure is not a constant. Offences vary in their likelihood of being reported to the police. The dark figure in sexual offences may be as high as 90 per cent (because of such factors as embarrassment or self-blame). On the other hand, the probability of reporting the theft of a motor vehicle is high (because of insurance requirements). The percentage of crimes reported to the police by a representative American sample of households and businesses (Criminal Justice Sourcebook, 1981) varied between 86 per cent (for vehicle theft) and 13 per cent (for larceny under $50). These percentages changed hardly at all between 1973 and 1979 although the estimated number of offences did.

Sparks et al., (1977), in an English survey, contrasted their respondents' estimates of the nature and extent of crime with police figures. In Brixton, for example, the respondents reported 30 per cent of alleged assaults to the police and the police recorded 17 per cent of these. Overall, Sparks et al., estimated that 11 per cent of the crime in Brixton was reported to and recorded by the police. In Hackney, the equivalent figure was 8 per cent and in Kensington it was 17 per cent.

These findings were broadly confirmed in the reports of the British Crime Survey (Hough and Mayhew, 1983 and 1985) which collected information on offences which had been committed in 1981 and 1983 against a representative sample of 11,000 households in England and Wales. A considerably greater number of offences were revealed than were recorded by the police. The survey indicated around twice as many domestic burglaries, three to four times as many thefts from vehicles, twelve times more thefts from the person and about four times as many woundings as in the official statistics. For only one offence - theft of motor vehicles - were the figures similar, which reflects the relevance of insurance requirements. The researchers suggested, however, that this 'hidden crime' was generally less serious than that which appeared in the criminal statistics, though some relatively serious offences were not recorded and many fairly trivial ones were. (11)

The variable of whether or not a victim reports the offence to the police reflects the importance of the attitude of the victim. Embarrassment may prevent him or her reporting some types of crime to the police whereas the requirements of insurance companies ensure that other types of crimes are reported. Alternatively, the victim may not perceive the act as a crime, or he or she may be antagonistic towards the police because of prior experiences with them. Hough and Mayhew (1983) found that the most common reason for not reporting offences to the police was the triviality of the offence. The next most frequently cited response was that the police could do nothing. Similar reasons have been given in American surveys (for example, Ennis, 1967).

Surveys have also identified those most at risk from crime. In England, contrary to impressions created by the media, the elderly were found to be the group least likely to be the victims of violent crimes though 60 per cent of elderly women living in inner cities said that they felt ´very unsafe` when out on foot after dark (Hough and Mayhew, 1983 and 1985). Those most at risk were young men who spent several evenings out each week and drank heavily. The researchers estimated that the average household could expect to be burgled once every forty years (though for houses in the inner city this falls to, on average, once every thirteen years). (12)

Victim surveys are, however, problematic - victims may be unwilling to report crimes to researchers for many of the same reasons that they are unwilling to report them to the police, or victims may simply forget minor victimizations (Home Office, 1985a, 21-5). But they indicate clearly the dangers of relying on official statistics: trends in the number of offences recorded may differ from trends in the number of offences committed. One of the major justifications for victim surveys has been that they might provide better indications of crime trends. For example, the data collected by the Bureau of Justice Statistics in the United States shows that the percentage of households touched by crime in 1982 was slightly lower than it was in 1981 and 3 per cent lower than the 1975 estimate, despite increases recorded in the official statistics.

Until recently, the only British victimization data providing evidence on crime trends were those derived from the General Household Surveys in 1972, 1973, 1979 and 1980. In each of these years, house-holders were asked the same question: ´During the last twelve months, has anyone got into your house/ flat without your permission and stolen or attempted to steal anything?` The results suggested that about half a million offences of burglary and theft in a dwelling were committed in each of the years covered by the survey (Home Office, 1983). This is about twice as many as the number recorded by the police. However, the findings also suggested that the number of domestic burglaries and thefts committed per 100 households had not changed much over the eight years between 1972 and 1980. The estimated annual increase in the number of such offences averaged 1 per cent per year over the period, much smaller than the increase of about 4 per cent per year in the number recorded by the police. Thus, although the General Household Surveys rates were higher than those based on offences recorded by the police, the rate of increase was lower. The disparity between the two sources indicates that apparent increases in crime may reflect an increase in the proportion of crime reported to the police rather than an actual increase in crimes.

The second British Crime Survey (Hough and Mayhew, 1985) further investigated changes in crime over time. This report contrasts the 1981 estimates of offences with estimates based on interviews with 11,000 people in 1983. Table 2.4 presents these figures:

Table 2.4   British Crime Survey Estimates of Offences in England and Wales

	1981 ,000	1983 ,000	% change
Vandalism	2,714	2,953	+9
Theft from motor vehicle	1,272	1,364	+7
Burglary in a dwelling	745	904	+21
Theft of a motor vehicle	283	283	–
Bicycle theft	214	287	+34
Theft in a dwelling	124	126	+2
Other household theft	1,535	1,671	+9
Assault	1,909	1,852	-3
Theft from person/robbery	596	650	+9
Sexual offences	33	71	+115
Other personal thefts	1,559	1,770	+14
All household offences	6,887	7,588	+10
All personal offences	4,097	4,343	+6

Source: Hough and Mayhew, 1985, 14

Overall, offences against households had increased in this two year period by 10 per cent, offences against the person by 6 per cent.

The changes in these estimates can be contrasted with police figures. Table 2.5 presents this data. Thus the proportionate changes in police recorded offences are not necessarily the same as those reported by victims. Taken together, these tables indicate that although the number of offences reported by victims was much higher than those known to the police, the rate of increase was slightly lower: 10 per cent as against 12 per cent.

Table 2.5 Rising Crime 1981-3: How British Crime Survey Estimates and Offences Recorded by the Police Compare

	% change	% change
	BCS estimates	Recorded offences
Vandalism	+9	+15
Theft from motor vehicle	+7	+12
Burglary in a dwelling	+21	+24
Theft of motor vehicle	–	–2
Bicycle theft	+34	+13
Theft in dwelling	+2	+3
Theft from person/robbery	+9	–1
TOTAL	+10	+12

Source: Hough and Mayhew, 1985, 15

It is clear from studies based on self-reports by victims of criminal behaviour that the dark figure, especially for minor offences, is very large. Studies based on self-admissions of criminal behaviour support this conclusion. In a self-report study of theft, Belson (1975) found that 98 per cent of a sample of 1400 London schoolboys admitted having at some time kept something that they had found, 88 per cent admitted stealing from school and 70 per cent from a shop. Only 13 per cent had been caught by the police (and only half of these had subsequently appeared in court). This confirms many

earlier studies. For example, 43 per cent of Mays'
(1954) sample of eighty boys from a dockside area
of Liverpool had been convicted of some offence, but
a further 28 per cent admitted offences which had
remained undetected. Willmott's (1966) study of
adolescent boys in Bethnal Green in London indicated
that, for them, stealing was part of their normal
behaviour. (See also Downes, 1966 and West and
Farrington, 1973 in London and Parker, 1974 in
Liverpool.)

More serious acts were, however, less frequently admitted to. Only 17 per cent of Belson's
sample admitted having 'got into a place and
stolen', and West and Farrington (1977) found that
only 11 per cent of their sample admitted to
breaking and entering within the previous three
years.

Minor vandalism is also commonly admitted to in
self-report studies. Clarke (1978) found that few
boys in his Manchester study denied such involvement: 85 per cent admitted to scratching desks at
schools, 68 per cent to breaking windows in empty
houses and 65 per cent to writing graffiti on walls.
However, the more serious the acts, the less likely
the boys were to admit to them. For example, only
20 per cent admitted to damaging telephone kiosks
and only 12 per cent to slashing train seats.

Self-report studies, therefore, show that delinquency is a common activity among adolescents, (13) but they go further than this: they
indicate that certain groups are more frequently
involved in criminal behaviour than appears from the
official statistics. Clearly the way in which the
police record criminal activity affects the validity
of statistics and the discretion whether or not to
record is both wide, and, to a large extent,
difficult to regulate. Many factors influence this
decision: the policies and practices of the local
police department, community expectations or
available alternatives to police action. But
research has found (see, Piliavin and Briar, 1964;
Black and Reiss, 1970; Cicourel, 1968) that the
police also rely heavily on the demeanour, attitude
and appearance of juveniles (and also of their
families). This has led, according to some
researchers, to an over-representation of certain
groups - for example, men, working-class people and
blacks.

Crime appears a predominantly male activity.
In England and Wales, women make up 17 per cent of
those found guilty or cautioned: a ratio of about

53

5:1. This ratio varies from offence to offence. For robbery in 1985, it was about 15:1, for burglary 26:1, and for theft and handling 4:1. The ratio of men to women is closest in shoplifting: about 1.5:1. These ratios also vary by age. For under fourteens, it is almost 4:1, for 17-21 it is just over 7:1. Statistics, however, may be constructed in a way which conceals or misrepresents women's crime. For this reason, researchers have turned to self-report studies as an alternative source of data.

American self-report studies suggest that, consistent with the official statistics, boys commit offences more frequently than girls but that the gap is not as wide as the statistics indicate. The patterns of delinquency were also virtually identical for boys and girls, except on assaults (see, for example, Hindelang, 1971: Cernkovich and Giordano, 1979; Jensen and Eve, 1976) and more serious offences (Sarri, 1983a). English studies have produced similar results. Mawby (1980), for example, found that a higher proportion of boys than girls admitted to committing offences of theft, burglary, vandalism and violence. In only three items were there no apparent sex differences: theft from other people's houses, theft from schools, and graffiti writing (see also Campbell, 1981). But again, the sex ratio was narrower than commonly supposed. Riley and Shaw's (1985) study of fourteen and fifteen year olds and their parents showed that while delinquency was more prevalent among boys (49 per cent of the boys admitted an offence in the past year as opposed to 39 per cent of the girls), the difference between the two groups was not constant over the whole range of self-reported offences. Where the opportunities to offend were equal (such as fare evasion, school vandalism, thefts from home, false emergency service calls and graffiti) prevalence was as high among the girls as the boys. Where the offence took place in unstructured groups, however, (e.g. smashing bottles in the street, carrying weapons, breaking windows in empty houses) the male to female prevalence rate was about 3:1. Table 2.6 shows this.

Some projects have compared self-report information with the official statistics over a period of time in an attempt to measure whether apparent increases in women's crime, particularly among the younger age groups, are real. Gold and Reimer (1975), for example, gave self-report questionnaires to a sample of American boys and girls in 1967 and

Table 2.6 Sex Differences in Self-reported Offending (Male:Female Ratios Based on Numbers Admitted Having Committed the Offence at least once in the Past Twelve Months)

	Male:Female Ratio
Damaged seats on buses or trains	0.4:1
Written or sprayed paint on buildings	0.6:1
Stolen something from family or relations	0.9:1
Made hoax 999 calls	1.0:1
Travelled on bus or train without paying correct fare	1.1:1
Shoplifted something worth less than £1	2.1:1
Smashed bottles in the street	2.6:1
Carried a weapon	2.8:1
Bought stolen goods	3.3:1
Broke windows in an empty house	3.6:1

Source: Riley, 1986b, 34.

1972. Apart from an increase in drug use, the delinquent behaviour of girls had not increased (though it had, according to the official statistics). (14)

Studies of self-admissions of criminal behaviour also have their dangers: respondents may exaggerate, conceal, lie and so on. More importantly in this context, these variables may themselves be linked to sex. For example, boys may be more likely than girls to exaggerate; girls may be more likely than boys to conceal (Morris, 1965). Nevertheless we can generally conclude that girls do commit more crime than it appears from the official statistics and that they commit a wide range of delinquent acts.

Researchers have also used self-report studies to investigate social class and delinquency. Official statistics do not refer to social class, but there has long been a widespread assumption that juvenile delinquency is much more frequent amongst those of low socio-economic status than other social classes. Research in England by Wadsworth (1979), May (1975), Rutter (1979) and West and Farrington

(1973) all showed some relationship between social class and delinquency. Self-report studies (for example, Belson, 1968 and McDonald, 1969) have also shown a relationship between these two variables, though the association is less strong than where data on convictions are used. Box (1971) reviewed a large number of self-report studies and concluded that 'a very crude interpretaton` was that 16 studies reported that lower-class adolescents were more delinquent than their middle-class peers and that no such relationship was found in the remaining 24 studies. He stressed, however, that most of the studies were fraught with methodological difficulties (for example, small and unrepresentative samples). After rejecting those he found methodologically weak, he concluded that research did not support the view that lower-class children were more involved in delinquency than middle-class children.

A recent study in the United States by Elliott and Ageton (1980), however, questions this conclusion. Using a national sample of 1,726 youths aged 11 to 17 and a relatively sophisticated self-report instrument, they found lower-class children to be much more likely than middle-class youths to engage in serious delinquent acts like burglary, assault and robbery and to have committed numerous serious personal and property crimes. From this, they conclude that self-report data about class and delinquency confirm the official data. They suggest that those studies showing middle- and lower-class youths to be equally delinquent have relied on measures which are weighted toward minor and status offences. Rutter and Giller´s (1983) review of the literature supports these conclusions.

There has been some concern recently in England and Wales about the contribution of young blacks to crime. For example, mugging is often portrayed in the media as a crime committed by blacks (Hall et al., 1978). Research questions this. Smith (1982), for example, examined the way in which the Metropolitan police presented its summary of criminal statistics in March 1983 and how the media interpreted those statistics. She concluded:

> There is no hard evidence to support the widely held view that the majority of violent street crimes in the inner city (less than 4 per cent of all recorded offences) are committed by coloured offenders against white victims (1982,3).

Ramsay (1982), also found in his survey of Liverpool and Manchester that white people were responsible for a greater proportion of muggings than were blacks. Only in Birmingham did blacks predominate. Ramsay cautions that it is a mistake to see mugging as necessarily a crime committed mainly by a particular racial rather than a particular age group. In several of the disadvantaged areas where the attacks took place, blacks represented almost a majority among the younger people in the local population; and it was younger people (under 20s) who committed over half the attacks.

In contrast, research in the United States suggests that blacks are over-represented in the official statistics because they actually commit more crimes not because official statistics (or, at least, their human collectors) are biased (Hindelang 1978). Elliott and Ageton (1980), in their national sample of young people, found that blacks committed crimes more frequently than whites and committed more serious crimes. (15)

The most systematic study of race and crime in England is one by Stevens and Willis (1979) who examined arrest figures in London for 1975. Their results indicated that the Asian arrest rate was substantially lower than the rate for whites; the arrest rate for blacks (mainly West Indian but including Africans), on the other hand, was much higher than for the white population. The greatest discrepancy was in robbery: a rate of 160 per 100,000 for blacks compared with an expected rate of 22. For most serious offences, the black arrest rate was twice that of the white. Stevens and Willis note a number of possible explanations, including social disadvantage and racial discrimination in the processing of cases by the police.

This was further investigated in a recent study by the Policy Studies Institute. Smith et al., (1983, 100 and 122) found that among male respondents aged 15-24, 63 per cent of the West Indians, 44 per cent of the whites and 18 per cent of the Asians had been stopped by the Metropolitan Police in a twelve month period. The proportion of stops that led to the detection of an offence was said to be one in twelve. This survey also found that a higher proportion of young West Indians than whites said that they had been arrested: 17 per cent of those aged 15-24 compared with 11 per cent of whites in this age group. West Indians account for about 6 per cent of the population of London. Smith's conclusions are more direct than those of Stevens and Willis. He concluded that the level of racial prejudice in the Metropolitan Police Force was a cause for serious concern. This was also commented on by Lord Scarman in his report on the Brixton riots:

> There were instances of harassment and racial prejudice among junior officers on the streets of Brixton (1981, 73).

We cannot be certain how valid self-report studies are (though researchers have attempted to validate their findings by a variety of techniques). As we mentioned earlier, juveniles may exaggerate or conceal their delinquent acts, and these tendencies may be linked to the factors we are attempting to investigate: the class, race and sex of offenders. What we can be certain of is that there are dangers in relying on official estimates of crime and official descriptions of offenders. Some criminologists (e.g. Jensen and Rojek, 1980) argue that, despite the disproportionate share of juveniles in the official statistics, adult-dominated crime is of greater economic and social cost than all juvenile offences combined. White-collar crime, for example, is estimated to cost over ten times the loss attributable to robbery, burglary, larceny and car theft. Organised crime is also an adult-dominated area.

The age-crime curve peaks in the teenage years and then decreases. Most delinquency is transient; it is a phase which many juveniles both go and grow through. Wolfgang et al., (1972) traced the development of 10,000 boys in Philadelphia. A third of them came to police attention (for offences more serious than breaches of traffic regulations), but nearly half of these subsequently kept out of trouble. Only 6 per cent were persistent offenders, in fact, committing five or more offences before they were eighteen. This small group was responsible for over half of the recorded crimes and two-thirds of the violence committed by the total sample. However, the majority of the juvenile offenders became apparently law-abiding citizens.

Overall, the findings of West and Farrington (1973 and 1977) from a sample of London boys are similar. Indeed they argue that persistence can be predicted from such factors as troublesomeness at school and living in a family, one or more of whose members (especially the parents) have a criminal record. Particularly with respect to persistent offending, Osborn and West (1980) raise the question 'do young delinquents really reform?' Drawing from data derived from the Cambridge Study in Delinquent Development (West and Farrington, 1973, 1977 and West 1982), they investigated the extent to which recidivists who were delinquents in their youth but who were not subsequently reconvicted after the age of 24 retained the deviant social habits which they had displayed in their earlier years. Three groups were contrasted: non-delinquents, recidivist delinquents who continued to offend after the age of 24 and recidivist delinquents who ceased to offend after the age of 24. In most respects, the last group was closer to the non-delinquents than to the persisting recidivists. The majority had stable employment, their children were relatively well cared for and their living circumstances were more comfortable and orderly. Osborn and West concluded that many former delinquents, by their mid-twenties, had not only given up criminal offences, but had conformed in most respects to dominant social norms. The recidivists who persisted in criminality differed in that they had acquired convictions at an early age and had more previous convictions. Further, they were more likely to come from large, poor families and to have parents or other family members with criminal convictions. The point is, however, that this group was a small minority.

There is a further research finding which must be taken into account here. Repeated offending is not predominantly a teenage phenomenon. In an exhaustive analysis of the interaction of crime with age, Farrington (1986) concluded that the average age of offenders is 25-30, and that only about a quarter are aged up to and including the peak age in the teenage years. The commonly quoted age-crime curve reflects variations in the prevalence of offending (the proportion of persons who are offending) rather than in its incidence (the rate of offending by offenders).

Conclusion

How situations are perceived are often more important than attempts to assess what they actually are. Juvenile offences and offenders are viewed with considerable public and governmental concern. Indeed, it was this concern which led to the development of special measures for dealing with juvenile offenders and the establishment of the first juvenile courts. It has also provided the impetus for the various changes which have occurred since then. For example, the Ingleby Committee referred explicitly to juvenile crime figures and then related them to the case for change:

> In the fourteen to seventeen age group, the figure (2,274 per 100,000) was just over double what it had been in 1938 and forty seven per cent higher than it was in 1954...It is not possible any longer to feel sure that...our methods of dealing with the problems of children in trouble...are generally sound and sufficient and are necessarily developing along the right lines. We have therefore felt it necessary to reconsider our approach to the whole question (1960, 4).

Similarly, it is widely believed that the 1969 Children and Young Persons Act led to increases in juvenile crime (see, for example, House of Commons Expenditure Committee, 1975, vol. 1, para 13). Evidence from the official statistics does not support such simple connections. A report of a joint working party of the Magistrates´ Association, the Association of Metropolitan Authorities and the Association of County Councils summarised the position as follows:

> There is no statistical evidence that the introduction of the 1969 Act and its implementation in 1971 affected juvenile offending. Firstly the ratio of juvenile offenders to all offenders has remained reasonably constant over the past 10 years, i.e. juvenile offenders generally comprise about 30 per cent of all offenders in England and Wales. Secondly, the rate of increase in offending before and after 1969 is about the same for 14-17 year old boys and for men over 21. There is a slight decrease in the post-1969 rate of offending for 10-14 year old boys and very considerable increase in the rate of young men between 17 and 21. Although the rate of increase in offending by girls has more than doubled in each age group since 1969, the increase is the same for over 17s as for the under 17s and it is therefore extremely doubtful whether the introduction of the 1969 Act can be considered

a relevant factor (1978, 3).

Nevertheless beliefs in supposed changes in the nature and extent of juvenile delinquency were instrumental in the passing of the Criminal Justice Act 1982. The use and abuse of criminal statistics can play a key role in policy developments.

APPENDIX I

Number of Male Offenders Found Guilty or Cautioned
for Indictable Offences per 100,000 Population

	Aged 10 & under 14	Aged 14 & under 17	Aged 17 & under 21	Aged 21 & and over
1964	2,763	4,249	3,366	636
1965	2,741	4,481	3,594	681
1966	2,717	4,611	3,859	742
1967	2,715	4,602	3,898	775
1968	2,809	5,060	4,503	820
1969	3,013	5,709	5,245	907
1970	3,123	6,233	5,673	972
1971	3,235	6,561	5,854	984
1972	3,366	6,871	5,795	979
1973	3,411	7,072	5,810	944
1974	3,809	8,191	6,215	1,011
1975	3,522	7,861	6,689	1,101
1976	3,303	7,567	6,567	1,149
1977	3,792	7,995	6,654	1,164
1978	3,442	7,858	6,685	1,122

Number of Male Persons Found Guilty or Cautioned per
100,000 Population

*
1977	3,517	7,519	6,284	1,222
1978	3,187	7,382	6,245	1,157
1979	2,923	6,810	6,234	1,161
1980	3,075	7,585	6,859	1,269
1981	2,993	7,475	7,049	1,297
1982	2,919	7,659	7,274	1,348
1983	2,926	7,532	6,944	1,349
1984	3,090	7,977	7,008	1,310
1985	3,231	8,128	7,241	1,328

* Indictable offences were redefined in the Criminal Law Act 1977 and new counting procedures were introduced.

Source: Home Office, 1986d

APPENDIX II

Number of Female Offenders Found Guilty or Cautioned for Indictable Offences per 100,000 Population

	Aged 10 & under 14	Aged 14 & under 17	Aged 17 & under 21	Aged 21 & over
1964	367	571	315	117
1965	397	683	333	125
1966	393	743	361	126
1967	396	665	387	138
1968	410	720	428	144
1969	471	824	516	166
1970	533	932	593	178
1971	605	1,125	670	192
1972	736	1,189	692	201
1973	775	1,209	687	189
1974	922	1,490	796	218
1975	894	1,514	889	248
1976	819	1,468	887	275
1977	1,058	1,610	942	282
1978	987	1,617	925	267

Number of Female Persons Found Guilty or Cautioned per 100,000 Population

*				
1977	1,041	1,570	940	283
1978	952	1,572	915	267
1979	913	1,457	925	253
1980	881	1,539	1,009	269
1981	887	1,566	970	258
1982	985	1,721	994	264
1983	941	1,659	962	255
1984	847	1,666	984	249
1985	1,048	2,018	1,055	254

* Indictable offences were redefined in the Criminal Law Act 1977 and new counting procedures were introduced.

Source: Home Office, 1986d

NOTES

1.   A wide variety of anti-social behaviour brings juveniles to the attention of the juvenile justice system - running away from home, truancy from school and the like. We are only discussing offences against the criminal law. The criminal jurisdiction of the juvenile court begins on the 10th birthday and ends at the 17th. Those aged 10 and up to 14 are technically children, and those aged 14 up to 17 are technically young persons. On occasions, we distinguish the two age-groups. In the main, we refer to ´juveniles` to include both.

2.   In an American survey (Hauger et al., 1983) 37 per cent of respondents agreed and 63 per cent strongly agreed that there had been a steady and alarming increase in the rate of juvenile crime.

3.   See also Hall et al., (1978) who link concern about mugging with immigration and decline in the ´British way of life`.

4.   Ambivalence also characterises our attitude to juveniles generally; our interest is coupled with distrust and misunderstanding. Friedenberg (1966) sums this up as follows: the terms ´teenager` and ´juvenile delinquent` are used as if synonymous. The result is that adolescence itself is often seen as a social problem, something that we must do something about.

5. Unemployment disproportionately affects the young. In downturns in the economy, employers tend to stop recruiting, young people are fired on the ´last in, first out` principle and employers cut back on expenditure on training. In 1981/2 there were 304,000 unemployed school leavers (Social Trends, 1983, 190). Since then the method of recording unemployment figures has changed a number of times and comparable figures are not published in Social Trends. It is estimated, however, that in September 1985, 63 per cent of school leavers had no jobs, that is around 328,000 (Pratt, personal communication). In certain cities (especially in the North of England) and for certain groups (for example, blacks), the figure is much higher.

6.   These are referred to as notifiable offences in the annual criminal statistics and are broadly the same as those entitled ´indictable offences` in earlier years. Generally these are the more serious offences but many offences of a trivial nature are notifiable because of the classification in which they fall. For example, the classification ´robbery` can include anything from armed robbery

from a bank to a child forcibly taking something from another child. Notifiable offences are also broadly similar to Crime Index offences in the United States.
    7.   In addition to changes in the public's reporting and the police's recording practices (these are discussed further later in this chapter), there can be numerous technical changes in the coverage of offences recorded. For example, in order to compare the figures for recent years with before 1977, it is necessary to exclude offences of criminal damage where the value of the damage was £20 or less, because such offences were not recorded in the earlier years. A further difficulty is that inflation raises more offences above the £20 limit each year.
    8.   In certain areas it is considerably lower. For example, in 1984 in the Metropolitan Police District it was 17 per cent.
    9.   International statistical comparisons are dangerous to make: definitions of offences may vary, ages of criminal responsibility may differ and the law and practice of alternatives to prosecution may differ. However, it seems that, generally, recorded juvenile crime increased in other countries in the 1960s and 1970s in much the same way as in England and Wales. Council of Europe figures indicate that juvenile delinquency increased in this period in France, Germany, Sweden, Switzerland and the Netherlands. In the United States, however, the picture is somewhat different. Galvin and Polk (1983), referring to FBI arrest statistics from 1973-82, argue that the overall delinquency rate (including status offences) declined there over that period and that serious violent youth crime remained constant. (For a full discussion of international trends see Rutter and Giller, 1983, 95-8.)
    10.   On the basis of estimated and projected figures, a 27 per cent decline will have taken place between 1977 and 1991 in the 10-17 age groups. See Pratt, 1985a and Riley, 1986a for a fuller discussion of trends.
    11.   A recent paper by Mayhew and Smith (1985) further questions the reliability of conclusions drawn from official statistics. It appears from the official statistics that there is more crime in Scotland than in England and Wales. Evidence from the victimization survey throws doubt on this.
    12.   American research has produced similar results. The United States Department of Justice collects each year (through the Bureau of Justice

Statistics) information from victims of crimes. In 1982, 29 per cent of American households were touched by a crime of violence or theft (24.8 million). This ranged from less than 1 per cent for rape to 21 per cent for larceny. Households with high incomes, those in central city areas and those headed by blacks were the most vulnerable to crime.

13. Surveys of adult respondents are rare but see Wallerstein and Wyle, 1947.

14. There are, however, problems with this survey. First, there was a high non-response rate: only 71 per cent of the subjects were interviewed and, secondly, as is common in self-report studies, the measures used were heavily weighted towards minor delinquencies.

15. There is now some support for this conclusion in England too. Pitts (1986) suggests that the statistical over-representation of young black people in street crime and criminal attempts may represent an actual over-representation although not as great as the statistics imply.

Chapter 3

JUVENILE JUSTICE: EVOLUTION AND REVOLUTION

The First Juvenile Courts

The juvenile courts emerged in a variety of jurisdictions at about the same time. Their form, however, differed in some major ways. For example, the
American juvenile courts and the Scandinavian
welfare boards, from their inception, stressed the
welfare of the child and ignored procedural
requirements (Platt, 1978; Stang Dahl, 1974); the
English juvenile courts, on the other hand, viewed
the juvenile offender as a miniature adult who had
to be protected by the due process of law and its
accompanying procedures and safeguards. They were
part of the general system of criminal justice.

The 1908 Children Act established, as we have
already noted, juvenile courts which were special
sittings of magistrates' courts. With the exception
of murder, they dealt with all offences committed by
juveniles from the age of seven to seventeen, unless
they were committed jointly with an adult. The
courts were also given jurisdiction over juveniles
who were thought to be in need of care. The public
were excluded from the juvenile courts and they were
required to sit at a different time or in a
different place from ordinary sittings of the
magistrates' court. Juveniles were also segregated
from adults before trial unless they were considered
so unruly that they could not be detained in a place
other than a prison.

The main dispositions available to the juvenile
courts were: discharge on a recognisance, discharge
to the supervision of a probation officer, committal
to the care of a relative or other fit person,
committal to a reformatory or industrial school,
whipping, payment of a fine and imprisonment if the
juvenile was over fourteen and could not be held

elsewhere. The Act maintained some difference in the treatment of offenders and non-offenders by keeping the more punitive dispositions - whipping, fining, committal to reformatory schools and imprisonment - for offenders only.

Towards Social Welfare

Many English commentators and practitioners looked with favour on the social welfare orientation of the American juvenile courts. Sir William Clarke Hall, former chairman of a juvenile court, for example, wrote:

> The real truth, however, is that no simplification of procedure, no regulations for the 'trial' of children, however perfect in themselves, reach down to the root of the matter. As long as we continue to conceive of the child as a 'criminal' and merely to allow such modification of his criminality as due to youth so long shall we fail to provide the most fitting cure for his misdeeds. What is needed is not the dramatic staging of a trial for a crime, but the provision of the best means for ascertaining and remedying evil tendencies (1926, 64).

The first review of the English juvenile courts was carried out in 1927 by a Departmental Committee on the Treatment of Young Offenders (the Molony Committee). (1) It examined the validity of applying criminal procedures to juvenile offenders. A number of witnesses felt that they should not be dealt with within a criminal jurisdiction and again referred favourably to the juvenile courts in America. But the Committee argued for the retention of the juvenile court. The arguments in favour of this were that there was:

> some danger in adopting any principle which might lead to ignoring the offence on which the action of the juvenile court in dealing with delinquents must be based. It is true that in many instances the offence may be trivial and the circumstances point to neglect rather than delinquency...but there remain cases where serious offences are committed and neither in the public interest nor for the welfare

of the young offender is it right it
should be minimized. Two considerations
presented themselves strongly to our
minds. In the first place it is very
important that a young person should have
the fullest opportunity of meeting a
charge made against him, and it would be
difficult for us to suggest a better
method than a trial based on the well-
tried principles of English law. The
young have a strong sense of justice and
much harm might be done by any disregard
of it...Secondly, when the offence is
really serious and has been proved it is
right that its gravity should be brought
home to the offender. We feel considerable doubt whether a change of procedure
...might not weaken the feelings of
respect for the law which it is important
to awaken in the minds of the young if
they are to realise their duties and
responsibilities when they grow older
(1927, 19).

The Committee viewed delinquents as responsible
for their own fate; their lawbreaking was conscious
and deliberate and, as such, the wickedness of their
action had to be brought home to them by the
formality of court-room procedures. It was also,
however, influenced by a further image: that of
victims of social or psychological conditions beyond
their control. This led to a compromise: the
retention of the juvenile court with the addition to
it of some of the advantages which were claimed for
the American juvenile courts.

The Committee recommended a juvenile court
especially adapted for its purpose (1927, 4). A
major criticism of the early juvenile courts had
centred on their personnel. The selection of
magistrates for the juvenile courts had been
'largely haphazard' with the exception of London
where there was a special procedure. The Committee
accordingly recommended that the juvenile courts
should be staffed with people chosen on account of
their special qualifications - those with a 'love of
young people, sympathy with their interests, and an
imaginative insight into their difficulties' (1927,
25).

The Committee agreed that the main function of
the juvenile court should be to consider the welfare
of the juveniles who came before it and to prescribe

appropriate treatment for them. To this end, the
Committee suggested that the juvenile court
magistrates should have the fullest possible
information about the juveniles appearing before
them: their home surroundings and circumstances,
their career at school and their medical report.
They also recommended that the police and schools
should collaborate more closely. The Molony Committee outlined the basis for these recommendations:

> Once the principle is admitted that the
> duty of a court is not so much to punish
> for the offence as to readjust the
> offender to the community, the need for
> accurate diagnosis of the circumstances
> and motives which influence the offence
> becomes apparent...(there must be) the
> fullest enquiries as to the antecedents
> and surroundings of the offence...for
> estimating the personal factors, including
> especially mental and physical health
> (1927, 43).

The Committee was aware that such principles
might lead to greater intervention in the lives of
juveniles and to longer periods of detention. It
wrote:

> The idea of the tariff for the offence or
> of making the punishment for the crime
> dies hard; but it must be uprooted if re-
> formation rather than punishment is to be
> ...the guiding principle (1927, 48).

An important premise in leading to this conclusion
was the Committee's belief that there was little
difference ´in character or need` between the
neglected and the delinquent:

> It is often a mere accident whether he is
> brought before the court because he is
> wandering or beyond control, or because
> he has committed some offence. Neglect
> leads to delinquency and delinquency
> is often the direct outcome of neglect
> (1927, 71-2).

What is interesting about the Report is that
these dual images of the delinquent were placed not
side by side but in sequence. In the first instance
(the adjudicative stage), the offence was viewed as

70

a conscious act of wickedness. Once the act was proved or admitted, however, it was viewed as a product of personal or external forces and dispositions were to be reached with these in mind.

The Committee's recommendations were subsequently accepted and given statutory force in the Children and Young Persons Act 1932, later consolidated in the Children and Young Persons Act 1933. The new legislation imposed a duty on magistrates to have regard to the welfare of the child in making the appropriate disposition - a major change in the direction of a social welfare approach. But the legislation did not make this the main function of the juvenile court (as recommended by the Committee). Other interests were also recognised. The Act further required juvenile court magistrates to have special qualifications for their work in the juvenile court. But the courts remained, in practice, criminal courts - juvenile court magistrates continued to act also in the magistrates' courts.

One of the concerns which emerged from the War years was the apparent increase in the number of children from broken families and illegitimate children. Consequently the newly elected Labour government initiated in 1945 an inquiry into the child care services to review means of providing substitute families for such children (the Curtis Committee, 1946). The Children Act of 1948 which followed the recommendations of this Committee enabled local authorities to take children considered to be 'in need of care or protection' into their care and to assume the powers and duties of their parents. The distinction between the 'deprived' and the 'delinquent' had already been drawn (see, for example, Molony Committee, 1927, 6 and 71-2), but the establishment of children's departments in each local authority and these new powers provided, in Clarke's words (1980, 73), 'one of the institutional and organisational forms for blurring this distinction further'.

In the same year, however, the Criminal Justice Act increased the range of penalties available for dealing with delinquents. This Act abolished corporal punishment as a sentence and also imprisonment for those under seventeen coming before the lower courts and for those under fifteen dealt with by higher courts. It introduced instead two new dispositions: detention centres (for juveniles between fourteen and seventeen) and attendance centres for juveniles between eight and seventeen). (2) Detention centres were viewed as an alternative to both corporal punishment and imprisonment. They were intended for those who did not require long term training (either in an approved school or borstal) but for whom non-custodial measures were also thought to be inappropriate. Although there was general support for restrictions on the imprisonment of the young, there was less support for the abolition of corporal punishment. (3) At about the same time, there was also widespread concern about increases in juvenile crime. (4) Detention centres, therefore, had to be presented as tough, punitive institutions. They reflected the belief that many juvenile offenders would respond best to strict discipline and that such regimes enhanced the deterrent impact of a juvenile court appearance. According to Land (1975), however, there was also pressure to include elements of training and education. Thus, in their origins, detention centres reflect an ambivalence about the appropriate response to juvenile offenders. In Land's words (1975, 313), they reflected 'both the view that toughness deters and that education reforms'. They appealed, therefore, to those who saw the positive value of a short period of disciplinary training and to those who demanded a penal deterrent. The first junior detention centre was opened in 1952.

Attendance centres, in origin, were intended to punish by the deprivation of leisure time. It was, in fact, with respect to attendance centres that the phrase 'short and sharp punishment' was coined (by Lord Templewood during the debates on the Bill (Parliamentary Debates, H.L. Deb. (1948) vol. 157 col. 39)). Later in the debates he expanded on this:

> Our objective was to deprive young offenders of a half holiday, to prevent their going to a football match or a cinema and, perhaps not less important, to make them ridiculous to their friends and relatives (Parliamentary Debates, H.L. Deb. (1948) vol. 158 col. 297).

At the same time he suggested that attendance centres should be used for 'the young offender who has not yet become anything in the nature of an habitual criminal'. Indeed, the centres were likened to being kept in after school for behaviour which 'went not much beyond a schoolboy's disobedience` (McClintock, 1961, 6) and Section 19 of the 1948 Act expressly excluded boys who had previously been in a borstal, a detention centre or an approved school.

Both the new measures and the two Acts in 1948 reflect ambivalence towards juveniles in trouble. The need to care for those seen as victims of society was countered by the need to discipline those seen as bad. In addition, these changes in legislation reflect the legacy documented in Chapter 1. Reforms in the processing and treatment of juvenile offenders, while inter-related in daily practice, are distinct (and potentially contradictory) policy arenas.

Throughout the 1950s, juvenile crime continued to increase and it was widely believed that there were categories of juveniles with whom the juvenile justice system, particularly the approved schools,(5) could not cope. For example, the Franklin Committee in 1951 had suggested the need to provide closed facilities for persistent absconders from approved schools. Generally, it was believed they would protect the community and remove `trouble-makers` from the open approved schools thereby facilitating the training of the remainder.

Matters reached a head in the summer of 1959 when a disturbance took place at Carlton approved school. Eighty-seven out of the 95 boys there absconded (albeit briefly) and some went on to the roof of the buildings. This led to the appointment of a committee of inquiry (the Durand Committee) which reported in 1960. It identified a further population of boys in the approved school system with whom the schools could not cope: older boys who were `unruly or subversive`. This report influenced the thinking of a Working Party organised in 1960 by the Approved Schools Central Advisory Committee to consider the need for closed and other special facilities. Subsequently, detention rooms were developed as part of the approved school system to deal particularly with persistent absconders and unruly and unco-operative juveniles (Millham et al., 1978: Cawson and Martell, 1979).

These concerns about appropriate responses to juvenile offenders reflected concerns about the juvenile justice process itself. Thus in 1956, the Home Office set up a Committee, chaired by Viscount Ingleby, to inquire into the operation of the juvenile court and to make recommendations for its improvement. The Committee were also invited to consider whether local authorities should be given new powers and duties to prevent or forestall the suffering of children through neglect in their own homes. Perhaps not surprisingly, therefore, the Committee emphasised what had been hinted at in previous reports: the lack of difference in the character and needs of the neglected and the delinquent.

The Committee singled out the lack of a satisfactory home as a major cause of juvenile crime as well as of child neglect and, as a result, supported the provision of housing, health, education and other welfare services to families at risk. But the Committee, though given this opportunity of examining the social services, felt that recommendations involving their radical reorganisation went well beyond its terms of reference. This may have been a consequence of the Committee's composition: it was made up primarily of lay justices, lawyers and administrators. There were no social work representatives.

With respect to the juvenile court, the Committee recognised the conflict mentioned earlier between the court's judicial and welfare functions. It stated:

> The court remains a criminal court in the sense that it is a magistrates' court, that it is principally concerned with trying offences, that its procedure is a modified form of ordinary criminal procedure and that, with a few special provisions, it is governed by the law of evidence in criminal cases. Yet the requirements to have regard to the welfare of the child, and the various ways in which the court may deal with an offender, suggests a jurisdiction that is not criminal. It is not easy to see how the two principles can be reconciled: criminal responsibility is focused on an allegation about some particular act isolated from the character and the needs of the defendant, whereas welfare depends on a complex of personal, family and social considerations (1960, para. 60).

The Committee suggested that a weakness of the current system was that it appeared to be trying a case on one particular ground and then to be dealing with the juvenile on some quite different ground. This conflict resulted, in the words of the

Committee;

> in a child being charged with a petty
> theft or other wrongful act for which most
> people would say that no great penalty
> should be imposed, and the case apparently
> ending in a disproportionate sentence.
> For when the court causes inquiries to be
> made...the court may determine that the
> welfare of the child requires some very
> substantial interference which may amount
> to taking the child away from his home for
> a prolonged period (1960, para. 66).

Although the Committee saw this conflict ´as basic
to its deliberations`, it still argued in favour of
the retention of the juvenile court. It agreed with
those witnesses who felt that, for the proper
protection of those who were the subject of the
proceedings, the tribunal should be a court of law
and that the power to interfere with personal
liberty should be entrusted only to a court.

> It is not the conception of the judicial
> decision that is at fault...What is desir-
> able is that the juvenile court...should
> move further away from its origin as a
> criminal court, along lines which would
> enable it to deal...more readily and
> effectively with (juvenile offenders)
> (1960, para. 76).

The Committee developed a novel procedure for
getting away from the juvenile court´s ´origin as a
criminal court`.

It suggested that the age of criminal responsibility should be raised from eight to twelve, ´with
the possibility of it becoming 13 or 14`, but that a
child below that age should be deemed to be in need
of care if he acted ´in a manner which would render
a person over that age liable to be found guilty of
an offence´. Care and protection proceedings were to
replace criminal proceedings. (6) The thinking
behind the proposal was that by removing the child
offender from a jurisdiction based on criminal
procedures one would also remove the expectations
that the disposition would be based on tariff
principles. This, the Committee believed, would then
lead to more juveniles being referred to the
juvenile court. With respect to older juvenile
offenders the Committee felt that they should stand

on their own two feet and accept greater responsibility for their actions. Criminal proceedings were,
accordingly, to be retained for them and welfare
considerations were to be minimised. The Committee
held a dual image of the delinquent, an image
determined this time by the age of the offender.
Juveniles, it felt, came before the juvenile court
because those responsible for their upbringing
(parents and the school primarily) had failed to
teach them how to behave in an acceptable manner.
During childhood, therefore, the responsibility for
juveniles' actions was to be shared between them and
their parents. The Committee did not go to the
extreme of denying juveniles all personal responsibility for their actions; it was enough that <u>some</u>
of the responsibility was placed on the parents. As
they grew older, the Committee took the view that
their own responsibility increased and that of
others grew less.

At the disposition stage in the proceedings,
the Committee recommended that the juvenile court
should receive reports from the local authority
children's department and the probation department,
that these reports should include any information
which seemed relevant to the treatment of the
juveniles and that they should be given the
treatment they required. The Committee, therefore,
at least to some extent, supported a social welfare
approach towards both categories of juveniles. But
it came out strongly in favour of judicial rather
than administrative discretion in the determination
of dispositions. It argued that:

> Residence in an approved school involved
> considerations affecting the liberty of
> the subject, and we think it important
> that a decision to commit a child to an
> approved school should be taken by a
> judicial body which could not be said to
> have been influenced by administrative
> considerations (1960, para. 341).

Thus its endorsement of a social welfare approach
was modified and the dilemmas, so well portrayed in
the report, were left unresolved. The reforms
suggested by the Committee affected the form and
approach, but not substantially the effect, of
proceedings involving younger juveniles. They were
essentially changes in procedure.

The Committee's major recommendations - 'care

and protection` proceedings for juveniles under twelve - did not become law. The Children and Young Persons Act 1963 raised the age of criminal responsibility from eight to ten (7) and Section 1 placed a duty on local authorities to give such advice, guidance and assistance as was necessary to keep the juvenile offender out of court. No changes were made to the juvenile court´s structure.

The Labour Party had been critical of the Ingleby Committee´s proposals. Indeed, the evidence of the Fabian Society to the Committee (Donnison and Stewart, 1958) and its subsequent response to the Report (Donnison et al., 1962) provide the first insight into Labour Party policy on these issues. Its concern was far less with the detail of the organisation of the juvenile court than with the reorganisation, rationalisation and humanisation of the social services and the creation of a family service.

Subsequently, in 1964, the Labour Party set up a committee on criminal policy under Lord Longford. The report was fairly wide-ranging and a major proposal was the abolition of the juvenile courts. The Committee´s starting point was the belief that `delinquents are to some extent a product of the society they live in and of the deficiencies in its provision for them`. It also believed that the machinery of the law was reserved for working-class youth and that those from other social classes were dealt with by other means. According to the Longford report:

> Working class youth who break windows are taken to court: at once there is the stigma of a police record. Oxbridge under- graduates who break windows are ´dealt with` by their college authorities: there is no legal or social stigma at all (1964, 6).

The Committee´s proposals, therefore, were that ´no child in early adolescence should have to face criminal proceedings: these children should receive the kind of treatment they need, without any stigma`. Criminal proceedings were felt to be ´indefensible` where the offence committed was a trivial one and, where it was serious, this was ´in itself, evidence of the child´s need for skilled help and guidance`. The causes of juvenile delin- quency and child neglect were traced by the Commit- tee to a primary source: inadequacy or breakdown in

the family for which the juvenile was not responsible.

> Anti-social behaviour in a child may arise
> from difficulties at home, from
> unhappiness at school, from physical or
> mental handicaps or maladjustment, or from
> a variety of other causes for which the
> child has no personal responsibility
> (1964, 21).

Delinquency was 'evidence of the lack of care,
guidance and opportunities to which every child is
entitled'. Accordingly, an alternative framework to
the juvenile court was proposed: a family service
in which the child, family and social worker could
discuss together what had gone wrong and what was
necessary to resolve it. The aim was to help 'every
family to provide for its children the careful
nurture and attention to individual and social needs
that the fortunate majority already enjoy' (1964,1).
Only where agreement could not be reached or where
the facts of the case were disputed was the case to
be referred to the proposed family court.
    These proposals subsequently formed the basis
of the Labour government's White Paper 'The Child,
the Family and the Young Offender' (Home Office,
1965) except that a family council consisting of
social workers and other persons selected for their
understanding and experience of juveniles replaced
the family service. There was considerable opposition to the White Paper, particularly from the
probation service, justices' clerks and magistrates,
who were primarily concerned with the protection of
the juveniles' legal rights. They also felt that
there were too many possibilities for abuse in the
proposed scheme and that it was undesirable that
decisions which might affect the liberty of the
young should be reached by social workers. The
National Association of Probation Officers, for
example, argued that:

> No action should be taken to interfere
> with the liberty of an individual on the
> grounds of his conduct, or with the rights
> of parents on allegations of their fail-
> ings, except as a result of a judicial
> assessment of the fact or allegations
> which have been regarded as justifying
> such actions (1965, 84).

Doubts were also expressed that an appearance before a family council would eradicate the stigma of criminality.

Academic commentators were also critical. Winifred Cavanagh (1966), for example, argued that the family council idea was unsound as it assumed knowledge about the causes and treatment of delinquency which did not exist. There was no evidence, she argued, to suggest that we knew how to change criminal behaviour by any acceptable means. Cavanagh was not against the idea of family councils per se, but felt that the arguments for and against such councils should be seen as distinct from attempts to deal with offenders or their criminality. There were differences, she argued, between the ´deprived` and the ´depraved`: the ´depraved` had committed an offence and it was necessary to express society´s disapproval of this. A number of lawyers made similar points. Downey (1966) complained that the White Paper proposed to abandon justice and established courts in order to follow a ´fashionable` but not well-founded theory of juvenile delinquency. (See also Fitzgerald, 1966.) Some commentators, however, were in favour of the proposals. Kahan (1966), for example, saw family councils as a natural development from the recognition that immature human beings could not be expected to make mature judgments. The proposals were, she felt, a corollary of recognising that social inadequacy was more readily improved by constructive help than by punitive disapproval.

Other factors were also relevant in the failure of the White Paper. Bottoms (1974) points to a number of considerations: civil servants in the Home Office were unsympathetic to the proposals, the Home Secretary, Roy Jenkins, shared the civil servants´ view of the proposals and, perhaps the major factor, the Labour government in 1966 only had a majority of three. Controversial legislation, therefore, was risky; and, besides, economic difficulties were the government´s main pre-occupation.

In 1968, the government produced a second White Paper ´Children in Trouble` (Home Office, 1968) which was the basis of the Chidren and Young Persons Act 1969. For this reason, it is necessary to spell out in some detail the philosophy underlying the White Paper and its proposals. The starting point in this second White Paper was the belief that:

> Juvenile delinquency has no single cause, manifestation or cure. Its origins are

79

many, and the range of behaviour which it covers is equally wide. At some points it merges almost imperceptibly with behaviour which does not contravene the law. A child's behaviour is influenced by genetic, emotional and intellectual factors, his maturity, and his family, school, neighbourhood and wider social setting. It is probably a minority of children who grow up without ever misbehaving in ways which may be contrary to the law. Frequently such behaviour is no more than an incident in the pattern of a child's normal development. But sometimes it is a response to unsatisfactory family or social circumstances, a result of boredom in and out of school, an indication of maladjustment or immaturity, or a symptom of a deviant, damaged or abnormal personality (1968, para. 33).

Consequently, the White Paper suggested that it was necessary:

to develop further our facilities for observation and assessment, and to increase the variety of facilities for continuing treatment. Increased flexibility is needed so as to make it easier to vary the treatment when changed circumstances or further diagnosis suggest the need for a different approach (1968, para. 20).

Although the juvenile court was to be retained, the White Paper proposed that all children under the age of fourteen would cease to be tried for criminal offences. Further, in an attempt to narrow down the circumstances in which court proceedings would be possible, an offence in itself was to cease to be a sufficient reason for a court appearance. 'Care and protection' proceedings were to be possible for children between the ages of ten and fourteen who committed offences, but only where it could be established that the child was not receiving such care, protection and guidance as a good parent might reasonably be expected to give. (8) Otherwise, such children were to be dealt with on an informal and voluntary basis. Juveniles between the age of fourteen and seventeen, on the other hand, could continue to be subject to criminal proceedings, but only after mandatory consultation between the police and the local authority children's department and after an application to a magistrate for a warrant to bring such proceedings. Warrants were to be issued only in exceptional circumstances; it was expected that these offenders would also, in the main, be dealt with under 'care and protection' proceedings or informally. The overall aims of the proposals were to reduce the number of cases heard in the juvenile courts and to reduce the number of cases in which the commission of an offence was a sufficient ground for intervention in itself. There was a clear preference for civil rather than criminal proceedings and for informal rather than formal action.

Thus far, the proposals appear little more than an extension of the approach suggested by the Ingleby Committee in 1960, but 'Children in Trouble' also envisaged an enlarged and significant role for local authority children's departments. In addition to mandatory consultation prior to criminal proceedings and to increased involvement with families and children on a voluntary basis, considerable power was also placed in the hands of local authorities to vary and implement some of the disposition orders made in the juvenile courts. Commitment to the care of the local authority (by means of care orders) was to replace approved school and fit person orders; (9) and implementation of the care order was to be at the discretion of the local authority rather than the magistrates. Local authorities were to develop a wide range of institutions of different types - to be called community homes - for all juveniles in need of care and approved schools were to be merged within these - to be called community homes with education on the premises. Attendance centres and detention centres were to be replaced by a new form of treatment - intermediate treatment - and the form that this would take was also to lie with the supervisor (that is, the local authority). Magistrates were no longer to be involved in detailed decisions about the kind of treatment appropriate. Supervisors, within the limits of the particular order, were to determine this. Thus, although the composition and constitution of the juvenile courts was virtually unchanged, its jurisdiction was to be radically altered.

The assumption underlying the White Papers of the late sixties was that juvenile offenders, like other juveniles in trouble, were not responsible for the circumstances which brought them before the juvenile court. The juvenile court, therefore, was to focus its attention on the status of the juvenile rather than his or her conduct and its function was to remedy this rather than punish the offence. Similar proposals were made in Scotland at the same time. The Kilbrandon Committee had been set up in 1961 with terms of reference much like those of the Ingleby Committee. Its recommendations, however, were radically different from the Ingleby Committee's and were closer to those of the two White Papers.

The Kilbrandon Committee (1964) began with the assumption that the juveniles appearing before the juvenile court - whatever the reason for the appearance - were all in fact exhibiting the varied manifestations of the same difficulties. It stated that, in terms of the juvenile's actual needs, the legal distinction between juvenile offenders and those in need of care or protection was - looking to the underlying realities - very often of little practical significance. Delinquency was described as a ´symptom of personal or environmental difficulties` (1964, para. 13) and the root of the problem was felt to be a failure to develop normally. In the subsequent words of Lord Kilbrandon (1968, 236): ´the problem is primarily one of arrested or deformed development. There has been a growth failure`. These personality problems could be explained further. The Kilbrandon Committee saw the causes as lying in ´shortcomings in the normal "bringing-up" process - in the home, in the family environment and in the schools` (1964, para. 87). The Committee stressed that the measures recommended by it - social education - were intended not to supersede the natural beneficial influence of the home and the family, but were, wherever practical, to strengthen, support and supplement them. The needs of the juvenile could not be met, it felt, ´by treating the child in isolation, but rather as a member of a family unit in a particular environment` (1964, para. 86).

Key notions in the Committee's recommendations were ´assessment`, ´diagnosis` and ´treatment`. For example, appropriate treatment measures could only be decided after an ´informed assessment of the individual child's needs` (1964, para. 12). To achieve this, the Committee hoped to establish ´a procedure which from the outset seeks to establish the individual child's needs in the light of the fullest possible information as to his circumstances, personal and environmental` (1964, para. 78). The new system, it was stated, would not work

without 'adequate machinery for early identification
and diagnosis', 'adequate facilities for assessment', and 'a flexibility of approach'.
The approach of the Kilbrandon Committee to the
causes of crime has been widely criticised (for
example, May, 1971; Morris and McIsaac, 1978) as
reflecting a medical model of delinquency. These
critics have in turn been criticised, for example,
by Martin et al., (1981, 4) who argue that the
medical analogies used by the Kilbrandon Committee
are merely illustrative and that concepts such as
'treatment' mean no more than 'management' or 'doing
something about'. To some extent this is right, but
the method of management clearly reflects notions
derived from positivist criminology: that is,
delinquency has certain causes which are identifiable and which can be eradicated. Furthermore,
even if one interprets the meaning of 'social
education', as used by the Committee, narrowly, it
was subsequently recaste by the acceptance of a
social work ideology. It was social work rather
than education departments which implemented the new
procedures. The relevant legislation was the Social
Work (Scotland) Act 1968 (our emphasis) which also
incorporated the proposals of the White Paper
'Social Work and the Community' (Scottish Education
Department et al., 1966).
Thus the proposals in both Scotland and England
and Wales were based on a similar and novel approach
to juvenile offenders. The conceptual framework of
such an approach was very different from that which
had surrounded the original juvenile courts.
Indeed, both jurisdictions explicitly rejected a
criminal justice approach. Though the proposals
differed in detail, in both countries it was assumed
that the juvenile offender was in need of measures
of care. The emphasis was on the shortcomings of
juveniles and their families, whether social or
individual. Ideas of justice or legal rights were
of secondary importance - the major aim was the
identification and diagnosis of juveniles' needs and
the provision of treatment to suit these needs. In
both countries, there was a preference for administrative and consultative decision-making dominated
by professional, primarily social-work, judgments.
Protection from the stigma of criminality was
considered essential and so informal procedures were
preferred to formal.
Why did these proposals occur at this
particular time? Was it merely the culmination of
decades of debate? What makes this question

particularly pertinent is that, at this very time, other jurisdictions, for example, the United States, were moving away from a social welfare or treatment approach. The original philosophy of the American juvenile courts was welfare oriented rather than punitive. By the 1960s, however, there was considerable concern about these courts. In the words of the President's Commission on Law Enforcement and the Administration of Justice:

> The great hopes originally held for the juvenile court have not been fulfilled. It has not succeeded significantly in rehabilitating delinquent youth, in reducing or even stemming the tide of juvenile criminality, or in bringing justice and compassion to the child offender (1967,7).

The Commission went on to identify the lack of resources as a possible reason for the juvenile court's failure, but stressed that the simple infusion of resources would not improve matters as the problem went much deeper. Basically, the Commission viewed the underlying philosophy of the juvenile justice system as 'grossly over-optimistic':

> Study and research increasingly tend to support the view that delinquency is not so much an act of individual deviancy as a pattern of behaviour produced by a multitude of pervasive societal influences well beyond the reach of the actions of any judge, probation officer, correctional counsellor, or psychiatrist (1967, 8).

Rather than help juveniles, the Commission suggested that action in the juvenile court might actually make matters worse. Research (see West, 1982 for a review) indicated that processing delinquents through the juvenile justice system was more likely to increase than reduce delinquency through, for example, the creation of a delinquent self-image in the juvenile or of negative responses to the delinquent by peers, employers and other agencies.

This disillusionment with the American juvenile courts reflects in part a disillusionment with positivist criminology - the theoretical basis for the belief in social welfare. The 1960s saw the emergence of labelling theory (with its awareness of the potentially harmful consequences of the official handling of juvenile offenders and its emphasis on discriminatory practices among the police, probation officers and judges) and radical or Marxist criminology which drew attention to structural rather than individualistic explanations of delinquent behaviour. The implications of these theories for policy was clear. (10)

First, they repudiated the notion that the delinquent was essentially different from the non-delinquent (self-report studies were prolific in the 1960s) and, secondly, they rejected the notion of individual reform. Delinquency was viewed, on the one hand, as normal and common-place and, on the other hand, as requiring fundamental social change for its eradication. The basic injunction, summed up in Schur´s (1973) words, was ´leave kids alone whenever possible´. Lemert (1971) translated the idea more pragmatically into ´judicious non-intervention`. These theories undoubtedly influenced practice. Programmes of diversion (strictly speaking keeping juveniles out of the juvenile justice system but broadened to include keeping them out of institutions) were developed and attempts were made to decriminalise minor offences (e.g. the use of marihuana) and to prevent status offenders being dealt with in the same way as those who had broken the criminal law.

The 1960s in the United States was also a period of the restatement of civil rights. Many legal reforms took place - the right to counsel and the privilege against self incrimination - but, in particular, legal reforms occurred in the juvenile court. The most important event was the intervention of the Supreme Court, which had been silent on issues raised by the juvenile court since its inception. In the words of Siegal and Senna, this intervention ´literally reshaped the constitutional and philosophical structure of the juvenile court system` (1981, 322). To sum up the situation in the United States at this time, four practices - diversion, deinstitutionalisation, decriminalisation and due process - were the hallmarks of changes in juvenile justice policy.

Understanding Change

Given what was happening in the American system of juvenile justice, how can we make sense of the nature of the changes in Great Britain? The answer, in part, relates to the influence of party politics on the formation of penal policy. As we noted, policy statements stressing juveniles´ lack of responsibility and their need for extended social services were consistently presented by socialist intellectuals and the Labour Party throughout the sixties. While presented as policies for dealing with juvenile delinquency, the Children and Young Persons Act 1969 was part of the Labour government's legislative programme to develop a more socially just society in which socialist values would be achieved. (11)

There are many different strands represented within the Labour Party but, put somewhat simply and crudely, central values are said to be equality, freedom and fellowship. 'Equality' underlies all else because it leads to social unity, social efficiency and social justice. It involves, therefore, more equal rewards and a more equal distribution of wealth. The provision of an equal chance is stressed and so Labour Party policy is against inherited wealth and favourable tax laws for the rich and is in favour of comprehensive education and a national health service. 'Freedom' means the freedom to control one's life and hence the preference for unionism and workers' participation in their working conditions. There is a belief that through government action one can redistribute freedom in much the same way as one can redistribute wealth. 'Fellowship' involves collective rather than individual responsibility and hence stresses co-operation and altruism. In policy terms, this leads to the development of nationalised industries and social security systems. The overall objective is to make capitalism bearable. The welfare state, therefore, is a means of reforming capitalism. (See George and Wilding, 1976, 62-84, for a more detailed discussion.)

The welfare state is intended to meet the needs of those unable to participate in the social reconstruction because of some disability. 'Needs', however, within the post-war setting, are not limited to material needs. Delinquency is viewed as only one of many of the expressions of 'secondary poverty' (Crosland, 1963) and as an indicator of underlying social needs which are shared with the deprived, the abused and the homeless. In a sense, the delinquent is viewed as a social casualty; the offence is unimportant. But more than this. Delinquency is not considered a distinct social problem. The real problems are family breakdown and inadequacies in society. Thus according to the Longford report:

It is a truism that a happy and secure family life is the foundation of a healthy society and the best safeguard against delinquency and anti-social behaviour (1964, 16).

A political point, however, is also made:

The values that prevail among those who dominate society may be expected to spread to all its levels. If men and women are brought up from childhood to regard personal advancement and ruthless self interest as the main considerations, material success will certainly not train them in social responsibility...It is the get-rich-quick ethos of the affluent society...that leads to a weakening of the moral fibre (1964, 5).

Indirectly then capitalism is to blame. The alternative is socialism which would ´substitute the ideal of mutual service and work towards a society in which everyone has a chance to play a full and responsible part` (1964, 5). The appropriate remedy for delinquency lies in the reconstruction of the family unit. The family is the central transmitting agency of socialist values and the main objective is, therefore, to enhance family responsibility through the expansion of the social services: thus the preference for a <u>family</u> service, <u>family</u> councils and <u>family</u> courts. By moving the debate away from the nature of the juvenile´s offence to the nature of the juvenile offender, the stage is set for a redefined role for the juvenile court.

A very different conception of social order and of the appropriate response to juvenile offenders is held by the Conservative Party. Again presenting complex issues rather simply, central Conservative values are said to be freedom, individualism and inequality. ´Freedom` requires a limited role for the government. It acts as a defender of freedom against the state and hence favours free enterprise and competition. Government intervention is viewed as wasteful, inefficient and disruptive. Conservatives accept the drift towards state involvement but do not promote it and reduce it where possible. The stress on ´individual responsibility` means one is free to act for oneself; man must be as free as possible to pursue his own interests and bear the consequences of that action. Failure is the individual's not society's fault. Equality is seen as undesirable as it would require coercion to achieve it. Man, therefore, must be free to be unequal. As Macleod put it, 'on our banners we will put opportunity, an equal opportunity for men to make themselves unequal` (1958, 14). Within this framework, the state has only a minor role to play - that of ensuring individual freedom - and only where groups or individuals are considered to be 'non-responsible` should the state take paternalistic action (Friedman, 1962, 22-36).

Thus the sterotype of the delinquent is not that of a social casualty but of a conscious law-breaker. While juvenile delinquency is viewed here, too, primarily as a personal problem, it is assumed to arise from personal iniquity rather than from social inequality. Underlying causes of crime are considered to be wide ranging: the increase in immigration, the effects of cinema and television, lack of powers in the courts, the absence of discipline in schools and families and decline in respect for the law. (See, for example, Cooper and Nicholas, 1963.) But, importantly, delinquency is exacerbated by the influence of socialist concep-tions of social reconstruction generally and of the welfare state in particular. For example, the Bow Group, in its response to the Longford Committee, wrote:

> It is clear that the authors of this pamphlet put the interests of the individ-ual offender above the protection of society. We do not accept this...there is a very real danger that the socialist attitude would hinder the progress of penal reform and delay the introduction of necessary measures (1964, 6).

The appropriate response to juvenile delin-quency, therefore, is considered to be not the prov-ision of social help, but the correction of the offender by discipline and punishment. Reform is of secondary importance: relevant only where other kinds of considerations are not appropriate. Reform is also viewed as obtainable <u>through</u> punishment. Difficulties in deciding where to draw the line of responsibility are, however, recognised, for not all children should be punished. The Bow Group's response to the Longford Committee's proposals provide one example of an attempt to draw this line:

It is easy to find excuses for children who have shown signs of anti-social behaviour, but we do feel that a child over the age of 10 is old enough to be responsible for his actions, or at least to appreciate the difference between right and wrong, and if not he should be corrected (1964, 4).

Though family responsibility is stressed, this is induced through the imposition of external controls, for example, by punishing the parents rather than by the provision of help or support. Overall, the preference is to retain the juvenile courts. These safeguard the public and defendants´ rights and represent the authority of the law. This insistence on criminal procedures (and deterrent sanctions) ultimately rests on the belief that juvenile offenders, like adults, are responsible for their actions and must be subjected to the symbolic impact of courtroom procedures. Protagonists of these views, those both professionally (for example, many magistrates and police officers) and politically interested, consistently reiterate the need for legalism in dealing with juvenile offenders; such departures as they consent to (and which have occurred) are related only to inessential features in the juvenile justice system.

Not surprisingly, the 1969 Children and Young Persons Act did not have an easy passage through Parliament; it was opposed throughout the debates by Conservative politicians (Bottoms, 1974). They argued that the Bill was the product of inadequate preparation and consultation, it was unjust (and class-biased) as between different juveniles, it gave insufficient recognition to the constructive role of the juvenile court and it interfered with police work with juveniles especially in regard to more serious offences. They also objected to state intervention in a juvenile´s life through an executive rather than a judicial body. Sir Peter Rawlinson summed up the view of the opposition when he said:

The Bill offends against the major principles of fairness; it introduces unnecessary delays and cumbersome procedures, and it is the fruit of a philosophy of penology which is unacceptable to the public (H.C. Deb. Vol. 787, col. 1290).

This stress on the importance of political ideologies per se is a necessary, but not sufficient explanation for what occurred as the first White Paper (´Child, Family and Young Offender`) with a similar philosophy to the second (´Children in Trouble`) had failed. Bottoms (1974) suggests that an explanation lies in a conjunction of interests and ideology between the Labour Party and those in key positions in social work. There are certainly clear linguistic shifts between the first and second White Paper. In the former, crime was presented as due primarily to social causes; in the latter, crime had become a symptom of maladjustment. Clarke (1980) consequently describes this change as a shift from socialism to social work. Bottoms (1974), however, admits that this, too, is not a sufficient explanation. This conjunction already existed in 1965. He speculates about the relevance of other factors.

First, there was a new Home Secretary and the government was insisting that some legislation in this area had to be carried through. It was obviously embarrassing to have to withdraw two sets of proposals. Coincidentally, a strong team of civil servants in the children´s department of the Home Office took the view that delinquency was symptomatic of maladjustment and saw the advantages of social work intervention. Social workers themselves had also matured professionally during the 1960s. There was a unified professional body - the British Association of Social Workers - which represented their interests instead of a multiplicity of small organisations. In 1968 also, the report of the Seebohm Committee urged the creation of unified local authority departments. This occurred in the Local Authority Social Services Act 1970: the probation service was excluded from this and, in the meantime, its professional body - the National Association of Probation Officers - was weakened by internal squabbles. But perhaps the most important point is that much of the sting had been taken out of the criticisms of opponents of the changes by the symbolic retention of the juvenile court. It appeared as if they had won a great victory. What magistrates and the probation service failed to realise, at this stage, was how far the traditional functions of the juvenile court had been eroded by the new framework and that the underlying philosophy of the two White Papers was very similar.

The Children and Young Persons Act 1969, however, was a compromise. It perpetuated a dual image of juvenile offenders: the full machinery of courtroom adjudication for those who saw them as responsible and an emphasis on social welfare for those who saw them as the 'non-responsible' product of social circumstances. But the spheres of influence of these two conceptions are not mutually exclusive and the people who operate the juvenile justice system are not isolated actors. This means that they collided at various stages: whether or not juveniles should be referred to the juvenile court and the nature of such proceedings, their adjudication, the determination of their disposition and the operation of the juvenile court itself.

The situation was made more complex by a change in government in the period between the passage of the Act (1969) and its implementation (January 1971). The new Conservative government announced that it would not bring into force those parts of the Act with which it disagreed. Thus criminal proceedings for offenders under fourteen were not prohibited nor were they restricted for offenders between fourteen and seventeen. Similarly the minimum age qualification for a borstal sentence was not increased from fifteen to seventeen, and detention centres and attendance centres were not phased out. In practice, the social welfare ideology underlying the 1969 Children and Young Persons Act never came to fruition.

An interesting question is how the Scots were able to implement, in 1971, their new system, given the considerable opposition to similar proposals in England and Wales. Arguably the Scottish system was even more radical than the English, for it abolished the juvenile courts and replaced them with welfare tribunals staffed by lay people. Children's hearings, as these are called, are concerned only with disposition. There is a complete separation between the judicial and disposition functions. If the juvenile or parent denies the commission of the offence, the case is referred to the sheriff court for the offence to be proved. If they object to the decision made by the children's hearing on the appropriate disposition, they can also appeal to the sheriff court. In both these instances, the parents and the juvenile are entitled to legal aid. Key figures in the new system are the reporters. It is their function to decide, on the basis of reports, whether the juvenile referred to them by the police, social worker or education department is 'in need of compulsory measures of care'. If the reporter believes that this is so, the juvenile is then referred to the children's hearing. The new system applies to juveniles under the age of sixteen, (12) although where they enter the system before sixteen they remain within it until the age of eighteen unless the children's hearing terminates its jurisdiction. The children's hearing can discharge the referral or impose a supervision order - the latter may be with or without conditions and can include residence in a List D school (that is, a former approved school). The children's hearing also has continuing jurisdiction, that is, the case must be reviewed annually by it. It has, however, no power to fine, to send the juvenile to a detention centre, or to remit the case to the sheriff's court for a custodial sentence.

This question of why the new system was implemented in Scotland becomes even more interesting when one reviews the evidence submitted to the Kilbrandon Committee: the majority of the evidence was in _favour_ of the retention of the juvenile court. Only three groups were in favour of a social welfare approach - the Howard League, the British Medical Association and the Royal Medical Psychological Society. Their memoranda, however, were highly influential. Indeed, the language of sections of the Committee's report is strikingly similar to their submissions (Morris and McIsaac, 1978).

But this does not explain the lack of impact of the critics. Certainly, opposition to the proposals was less organised in Scotland than in England. There was, for example, no equivalent to the Magistrates' Association as there was, at this time, no uniform juvenile court structure. But the police, sheriffs and probation service all expressed concerns similar to those expressed about the 1965 White Paper: the lack of procedural safeguards and the deprivation of liberty by a non-judicial body. Their attention, however, was probably diverted by the publication of a White Paper 'Social Work and the Community' (Scottish Education Department _et al._, 1966) which aimed at reorganising social services in Scotland. Sheriffs and probation officers then focused their campaign on an attempt (which failed) to retain a separate probation service for dealing with adult offenders.

Also, press reaction to the Kilbrandon Committee report was favourable. It was described as 'worth waiting for' and 'more refined than anything already in practice anywhere in the world'. This nationalism was echoed in the Parliamentary debates on the subsequent Bill. Bruce Millan, in winding up

for the government on the second reading of the
Bill, described it as 'ahead of the English'.
Another factor which may have smoothed the Bill's
passage was that, traditionally, only Scottish MPs
debate Bills which affect Scotland alone and the
majority of Scottish MPs were Labour. Further, the
Conservatives in Scotland were not united; some
were in favour of the Bill. Also, much of the
debate centred on the issue of the reorganisation
of social services which was more controversial than
the proposals to reform the juvenile justice system.

It is important to keep in mind in trying to
understand policy that the various attempts to
change juvenile justice systems and resistance to
these changes are not mere technical debates. They
are bound up with central changes occurring in the
social and economic order and with the political
debates within which that social order continually
(re)produces itself. Changes are not just responses
to perceived increases in juvenile delinquency but
rather to political ideologies which are expressed,
through the debates, in rhetoric about 'the lack of
discipline in youth', 'juvenile crime' and so on.
Clarke sums up this argument:

> What is important about this process of
> creating a state reorganisation is not
> some form of conflict between two abstract
> models of juvenile justice, but the
> rehearsal and working through of
> alternative state strategies for dealing
> with sets of problems thrown up by one
> particular historical moment (1980, 93).

The Children and Young Persons Act 1969 in Practice

If there had been agreement about the direction
of the juvenile justice system in England and Wales,
practitioners could have acted as if the legislation
was implemented. But those who disagreed with it -
and magistrates quickly realised that they did -
were free to carry on as before. A core problem in
the operation of the new system was that a common
philosophy about the appropriate way of handling
juveniles who offend did not exist among the main
professionals operating the system. While each
group may have shared a common long-term goal, for
example, the prevention of delinquent behaviour,
there was little agreement about the best method of
achieving this objective. It is not surprising,
therefore, that tension arose between the police and

magistrates. The 1969 Children and Young Persons Act can thus be represented as the operation of these different conceptions in practice. (13) The power struggle among the various interest groups for satisfaction that their values were reflected in current policy continued.
Almost as soon as the Act was implemented, it was described as a failure. The Act was blamed for 'vast increases in juvenile crime' and it was said that magistrates were powerless to deal with this. (14) Professor Winifred Cavanagh, a former chairman of the Birmingham Juvenile Magistrates Bench, for example, told a meeting of magistrates, social workers and government officials in 1973 that the position then was much worse than before the Act and that the sanctions which the community looked to the juvenile court to supply were non-existent (quoted in Berlins and Wansell, 1974, 77). They also quote the views of a magistrate's clerk on the Act:

> It is not too much to say that a blank cheque has been written for all children and young persons under the age of fifteen and that there is no effective measure of control over them...This all tends to contribute to a fast-approaching state of anarchy and the public seems totally unable to protect itself. The courts are impotent, the police seem dazed and the local authority social workers appear to relish their new-found power to over-rule the so-called reactionary ideas of the magistracy (1974, 81).

A report of the Committee of the Society of Conservative Lawyers is a typical later example of the criticisms:

> Increasing numbers of...children...commit crime with impunity...We lay the blame (for this) on the provisions of the Children and Young Persons Act 1969...The law is not effective in dealing with the hard core of delinquent children...Juvenile apprenticeships in crime must be stopped ...Magistrates are now powerless. This brings the magistrates and the law into disrespect...Children are encouraged further along the highway of crime... Public morals must, at times, be reinforced by the proclamation of legal

sanctions...The Act should be amended (1974, 6ff).

The same themes were echoed by the Magistrates' Association. For example:

> The Act sought broadly to substitute care and treatment for punishment of young offenders. For most of them this has worked quite well. For a minority of tough sophisticated young criminals (and some youths of fifteen and sixteen are strong young men) it has been disastrous. They prey on the community at will. They deride the powerlessness of the court to do anything effective. They are encouraged to become criminals. The essential problem is, therefore, to provide the courts with greater powers and facilities where they are clearly needed for persistent young offenders (Evidence to the House of Commons Expenditure Committee, 1975, 128).

Thus a 'moral panic' about the powerlessness of the juvenile courts was soon established. This focused particularly on the practice of care orders. Magistrates believed that children made the subject of care orders were not placed residentially but rather went home immediately. The extent to which this accurately reflects the state of affairs is difficult to gauge. Early attempts to defuse this 'moral panic' and to clarify these issues came from two surveys on the use of care orders for offenders undertaken by the Social Work Service Division of the Department of Health and Social Security (D.H.S.S. 1972 and 1973). After reviewing the operation of care orders in twenty local authorities in 1971 and 1972, the Department concluded that the 1969 Act had started well. It was comparatively rare for children subject to a care order to be returned home directly from the court. Nevertheless, the surveys did note that, in respect of community homes with education, 'the placing of boys took longer to achieve and in some cases...could not be achieved at all' (D.H.S.S. 1972, 6). However, the Department saw such problems as no more than teething troubles and felt that too much should not be made of 'isolated breakdowns in communication which could not be expected to be altogether avoided in the early stages of a new system' (1972, 8).

Examination of sentencing trends also fails to confirm this claimed lack of powers in the juvenile court. Table 3.1 demonstrates the pattern of sentencing (and cautioning) for juveniles who committed indictable offences in 1970 and 1979.

Table 3.1   Percentage of Juvenile Offenders Sentenced and Cautioned in 1970 and 1979 (for Indictable Offences)

	1970	1979
Cautioned	38%	50%
Conditionally discharged	13%	10%
Fined	20%	17%
Attendance Centre Order	5%	6%
Probation order/Supervision order	15%	9%
Approved school or fit person order/Care order	5%	3%
S28 remits to Crown Court	<1%	1%
Detention Centre Order	1%	3%
Other	1.5%	<1%

This kind of information, however, conceals differences in the use of measures for the different age groups and for boys and girls. Table 3.2 shows the variations in the use of the different dispositions over the same period by age and sex. Overall there was an increase in the number of juveniles referred to the juvenile court, despite the policy of diversion. This is discussed in Chapter 5. Further, the response of the juvenile court to the offenders appearing before it changed over the decade. Broadly speaking, fines, attendance centre orders and custodial sentences (i.e. detention centre orders and recommendations to the Crown Court for borstal training) were increasingly relied upon by magistrates for fourteen to seventeen year old boys at the expense of middle-range, community-based alternatives (supervision orders) and those dispositions, the precise operation of which, was left in the hands of social workers (care orders). (15) Thus between 1970 and 1979 there was an increase of 109 per cent in the number of 14-17 year old boys given attendance centre orders, an increase of 155

Table 3.2   Percentage Variations in the Sentencing
             and Cautioning of Juvenile Offenders be-
             tween 1970 and 1979 (for Indictable   and
             Triable either Way Offences) by Age   and
             Sex

	BOYS		GIRLS	
	Under 14	14-17	Under 14	14-17
Variation in number cautioned	+36%	+91%	+143%	+190%
Variation in number found guilty	-31%	+15%	-17%	+30%
Variation in number discharged	-28%	+13%	-14%	+32%
Variation in number fined	-24%	+12%	- 4%	+51%
Variation in number given attendance centre orders	- 5%	+109%	-	-
Variation in supervision orders	-44%	-14%	-28%	+ 7%
Variation in care orders	-34%	-42%	-11%	+12%
Variation in S28 remits to Crown Court (for borstal training)	-	+56%	-	+121%
Variation in detention centre orders	-	+155%	-	-

per cent in the number sent to detention centres and
a 56 per cent increase in the number of section 28
remits to the Crown Court.   In 1970, over 2,500
young persons were given detention centre orders or
remitted to the Crown Court with a recommendation
for borstal training; by 1979, this figure was more
than 6,500.   In contrast to this was the decline in
the use of supervision orders.   In 1970,
approximately one in six male fourteen to seventeen
year olds were placed on probation. By 1979, it was
less than one in ten.   The opposite to that intended
by the 1969 Act had occurred - sentencing had
become more penal than welfare orientated - and,

paradoxically, the Act was blamed for this.

The increase in the use of custodial measures could have been due to increases and changes in juvenile crime. A review by the D.H.S.S. (1981a), however, suggests rather that it was the result of a change in sentencing policy. This review showed that in 1965, one in 800 of the fourteen to seventeen year old boys referred to the juvenile court were sent to a detention centre or borstal. By 1979, the chances of that happening had substantially increased so that one in every 180 of this age group were given a custodial penalty. According to the D.H.S.S., only one-sixth of this increased use of custody could be explained on the basis of changes in juvenile crime. About a third was attributable to the more frequent use of custodial sentences for theft and about a quarter to the more frequent use of custodial penalties for burglary. For example, in 1969, 9 per cent of fourteen to seventeen year old boys sentenced or cautioned for burglary received a custodial sentence compared with 14 per cent in 1979. For robbery, the comparable figures were 27 and 43 per cent and, for offences of criminal damage, 2 and 10 per cent. Paradoxically, the proportion receiving a custodial sentence for offences of violence remained virtually the same: 5 per cent in 1969 and 7 per cent in 1979. The D.H.S.S. report also showed that throughout the 1970s, those given custodial penalties had not necessarily experienced the full range of non-custodial options which the juvenile courts had available to them. This was particularly so for boys given detention centre orders. Thus changes in the use of custody reflected changes in sentencing practice rather than changes in the nature of juvenile crime.

The D.H.S.S. report also showed that there was a shift in the pattern of removal from home. Only 7 per cent of known juvenile offenders in 1979 had sentences which required or permitted removal from home; this was, in fact, slightly less than the 1965 figure. But the balance between care orders and custodial sentences was very different. In 1965, 6.3 per cent of juveniles appearing in the juvenile court were given the equivalent of a care order and 1.3 per cent a custodial disposition. By 1979, 2.7 per cent were given care orders and 4.2 per cent custodial dispositions. Put another way, in 1965, 20 per cent of removals from home were to custodial institutions; in 1979 the comparable figure was 60 per cent. This rapid growth in the use of custodial

penalties was undoubtedly the most notable feature
of juvenile court sentencing in the 1970s - a trend,
moreover, which contrasted markedly with
developments in the sentencing of adult offenders.
As the then Home Secretary, Leon Brittan, put it in
1979:

> During the past twenty years the propor-
> tion of convicted adults received into
> custody has been more than halved. During
> the same period the proportion of juven-
> iles receiving custodial sentences...has
> been more than tripled. In 1955 an adult
> was twenty times more likely than a juven-
> ile to get a custodial sentence...now he
> is only twice as likely (quoted in Tutt,
> 1981, 254).

In part, this sentencing pattern reflects a
lack of faith on the part of magistrates in the
ability of the social welfare professions to control
delinquents. Indeed, some juvenile court magistrates
openly acknowledged that the increased use of
detention centre orders and recommendations for
borstal training was intended to show young people
that the courts did have teeth.
It is certainly clear that magistrates did not
like the way the new care order was intended to
operate. In theory, magistrates were to determine
whether or not there was sufficient ground for such
intervention and to set the limits to that intervention. Social workers were to determine the precise
operation of the order. This meant that the social
worker had power to remove juveniles from home, but
need not if he or she felt it was not in their best
interests. Magistrates, however, saw the failure of
social workers to remove juveniles from their homes
after such a disposition as an arbitrary flouting of
their wishes. For example, one juvenile court magistrate (quoted in an article in The Magistrate) said:

> We feel frustrated. We feel we have done
> the best for the children and sent them away
> from home. Then we see them walking along
> the road looking at the magistrates, shout-
> ing ´ha, ha, we´ve won, you have lost`
> (Magistrate, 1974, vol. 30, no. 11, p.168).

Moreover, magistrates believed that leaving
juveniles subject to care orders in their own homes
exacerbated their propensity to re-offend and made

them impervious to the influence of the juvenile
courts. This, they claimed, created a ´minority` of
tough sophisticated young criminals who preyed on
the community at will and derided the powerlessness
of the courts. Empirical evidence about the
operation of care orders contradicts this.

Zander´s (1975) study of a small sample of
London juveniles subject to care orders showed that,
while a high proportion of juveniles were returned
home, this was not inevitably associated with
further offences. Those juveniles placed in a
community home, in fact, committed more offences
subsequently than those placed at home (including
those for whom no residential place was available).
This was confirmed by Cawson´s research (1981).
Just over one-third of her sample committed another
offence during the nine-month period following the
making of the care order, but more than two-thirds
of them were in residential care at the time of the
offence. Very few juveniles placed at home
committed a second offence. (See also Giller and
Morris´ (1981a) research in the Inner London
boroughs and Thorpe et al.´s (1980) research in a
variety of different local authority areas.)

However, this belief of the magistrates in the
need for placement in an institution following the
imposition of a care order and in the myth that
approved school orders (which were automatically
residential) were effective in preventing absconding
and recidivism remained strong.(16) Whether mag-
istrates´ impressions were fact or fiction is
probably irrelevant; they were formed and affected
the operation of the Act.

It would be wrong to conclude from the sentencing trends over this period that there was simply a
conspiracy among juvenile court magistrates to
deprive the social work and probation professions of
access to juvenile offenders. Social work professionals themselves (both directly and indirectly)
contributed to the process whereby juvenile
offenders were not routinely considered for a wide
range of non-custodial dispositions. Practice developed whereby magistrates were given the impression
that a custodial sentence was being requested or, at
least, that a community-based disposition was not
appropriate. These practices are apparent in recommendations made by social workers, probation
officers and others within social inquiry reports
and this is considered further in Chapter 7. It is
sufficient to note for the moment Thomas´s (1982)
finding that a third of juveniles in his sample

sentenced to a detention centre had a direct recommendation for such an order in their social inquiry reports.

Social workers also appear to have made use of care orders early in a juvenile's career. For example, we (Giller and Morris, 1981a) surveyed a sample of juveniles who had received care orders for criminal offences. In the main, these orders had been made on the positive recommendation of a social worker. Rather than the care order being a remedy of 'last resort' (as was the approved school order), many of these recommendations and orders were made for first offenders. In fact, 45 per cent of the sample were given a care order on their first appearance in the juvenile court and a further 14 per cent on their second court appearance. When interviewed, the social workers commented that, while the care order was appropriate in these particular cases, the early application of care orders was generally atypical. The stereotype of the typical case for a care order for offending was the juvenile who had appeared in the juvenile court on four or more occasions and who had previously received a wide range of non-custodial penalties. Only when these measures were found to be ineffective was it believed that a recommendation for a care order should be made. But, in fact, the supposedly 'atypical' was typical.

What this and other studies have shown (e.g. Cawson, 1981; Thorpe et al., 1980) is that the stereotype of the 'typical' case had no basis in empirical evidence. The presumed 'typical' case was the exception rather than the rule. Instead, early intervention was justified on the basis of a number of 'unique' features associated with the particular case - usually not delinquency, but rather the existence of family problems or educational difficulties.

While one can understand the benign motives of those who used a care order for a juvenile who had committed an offence in order to facilitate social work ends, their contribution in producing as an unintended consequence severe responses by magistrates when the juvenile returned to the juvenile court cannot be minimised. As Thorpe et al., note:

> It is almost a matter of common sense that once a child has received a care order, subsequent offences are likely to be dealt with more severely by juvenile courts (1980, 84).

The fact that nearly half of the fifteen to seventeen year olds in borstals were or had been in care clearly illustrates this interactive effect. Moreover, the magistrates´ negative reaction to the subsequent ´failure` of the care order by the return of the juvenile to the juvenile court was not limited to the escalation of sanctions. Magistrates also saw this as failure by the social worker and, more generally, of social work to provide an effective response to juvenile delinquency. This point is valid with respect to supervision orders too. Extrapolating from Home Office statistics which showed that over 50 per cent of all supervision orders made to the probation service were on juveniles with no previous convictions, Thomas (1982) suggests that, annually, some 10,000 first offenders were placed on supervision and, of course, those who re-offended were likely to move further up the sentencing tariff, having ´failed` to respond to a non-custodial disposition.

There was also within the child care system a growth in the number of secure places. Between the passing of the 1969 Act and the end of the 1970s, this increased from sixty to over 300. (17) Researchers who investigated this expansion have clearly demonstrated that this was not merely a response to an increasing number of ´hard core` juvenile offenders with whom community resources could not cope. In comparison with juveniles who were in these facilities prior to the implementation of the 1969 Act, the research suggests that they were, in fact, a less deviant group. According to Cawson and Martell, the juveniles in secure accommodation in the 1970s:

> were less likely to have been living with both natural parents but apart from this their homes appeared more stable than formerly: parents and siblings were less likely to have criminal records or records of psychiatric treatment. There was no evidence that they were more institutionalised or presented greater behaviour problems (1979, 209).

Also, they were not found to be more serious offenders or more disturbed than their counterparts in open community homes (Millham et al., 1978; Cawson and Martell, 1979). Far more influential in the determination of whether or not a juvenile was placed in a secure facility was the willingness and ability of social workers to continue to work with him or her. (See also Morris and Wilkinson, 1983.) In other words, the expansion of secure accommodation tells us more about the inability of those running open institutions and working with juvenile offenders in the community than it does about the juveniles concerned. For Cawson and Martell, the hallmark of the system of secure accommodation was:

> The constant passing on of children to others considered more ´expert` or ´specialist`, the perpetuation of myths about ´diagnosis` and ´treatment` or ´cure` at the expense of ´care`...and the use of therapeutic euphemisms which indicate unwillingness to face the reality that children were being locked up for extended periods occasionally in solitary confinement (1979, 229).

Conclusion

The history of juvenile courts in England is a history of continuous review. The creation of the juvenile court in 1908 was not viewed by its contemporaries as a particularly significant development (Bottoms, 1985, 96) and yet, in the almost eighty years of its operation, both its improvement and abolition have been key issues in juvenile justice policy. The centrality of the appropriate role of the juvenile court in the debates is even more marked when one considers the concomitant lack of discussion about the particular form and content of interventions. For example, a major study into the effectiveness of approved school training (Cornish and Clarke, 1976) essentially demonstrated its ineffectiveness. This did not lead to a major re-evaluation of the role of residential treatment by policy makers. The decline in its use during the seventies was due primarily to magistrates' preference for more penal sanctions which also had high reconviction rates. Indeed, the last widespread political debate on the use of a particular measure for juvenile offenders seems to have been the abolition of corporal punishment (eventually achieved in 1948). (18)

Why has the juvenile court itself been the focus of such debate in the recent past? In part, it seems due to the growth in sentencing options which became available for dealing with juvenile offenders. When there were relatively few sentencing options, the area of discretion given to

sentencers was less significant. As these increased, the use of that discretion (and the power
associated with it) became more significant.
Secondly, while the juvenile court began life as an
ordinary criminal court, it acquired early on the
responsibility to have regard to the welfare of the
child. In this way, the juvenile court moved from
merely meting out penalties into a role which
assumed that the court's intervention might
encourage the juvenile to adopt a non-criminal life
style. Thus, it was the juvenile court which had
responsibility for ensuring that the 'right'
decision was made. The failure of the juvenile
justice system to produce the desired outcome - to
stop juvenile crime in general and the re-offending
of those it sentenced in particular - consequently
became integrally linked in policy-making discourse
with the failure of the juvenile court itself and,
in the 1960s, it became the focus of concern. However, the attempt to radically alter the jurisdiction of the juvenile court failed: magistrates
retained control. And, in the 1970s, they maintained this control by shifting the focus of the
debate to their powerlessness to deal with juvenile
crime. What is important about this strategy is
that concern was fostered, if not created, by the
magistrates themselves. It was an attempt to shift
the debate from their supposed failure to the fail-
ings of others. By implication, they were arguing
that a fully implemented '69 Act would have made
matters worse.

NOTES

1. An equivalent committee was set up in
Scotland: the Morton Committee (1928). The substance
of its recommendations was similar to the Molony
Committee.
2. The age of criminal responsibility was
raised from seven to eight in the Children and Young
Persons Act 1932.
3. This had been recommended by the
Departmental Committee on Corporal Punishment which
advocated instead 'some form of punishment which
will operate directly as a deterrent' (Cadogan
Committee, 1938, 49).

4. A master had recently been murdered at an approved school and this contributed to the view that the juvenile courts were increasingly dealing with difficult juveniles.

5. Reformatory and industrial schools were amalgamated under the title of schools approved by the Secretary of State in the Children and Young Persons Act 1933.

6. Care proceedings were the usual way of dealing with such children in most European jurisdictions.

7. Even this change was the result of considerable conflict and compromise in the debates in the House of Lords (Walker, 1983, 25).

8. The same double-barrelled test was to be applied to children who were exposed to moral danger, beyond parental control and neglected.

9. The juvenile courts had the power to commit to a fit person any child or young person who might otherwise be sent to an approved school. It applied to juveniles guilty of an offence or in need of care and protection.

10. For an outline of these theories, see Empey, 1978, 341-353 and 369-401.

11. Integrally linked to the Act and to these objectives was the Local Authority Social Services Act, 1970 which was the result of the recommendations of the Seebohm Committee. This had been set up in 1965 'to review the organisation and responsibilities of the local authority personal social services...and to consider what changes are desirable to secure an effective family service'. It recommended a new local authority department, providing a community based and family oriented service. This new department, according to the Committee, would:

> reach far beyond the discovery and rescue
> of social casualties; it will enable the
> greatest possible number of individuals to
> act reciprocally, giving and receiving
> services for the well-being of the whole
> community (1968, 11).

We are not suggesting that these Acts achieved or could have achieved 'a more socially just society'. Clearly they contained the potential for discriminating against and increasing state control over most working-class families.

12. It does not, however, apply to all juveniles under sixteen who commit offences. The power to prosecute juveniles in the sheriff's court has been retained in certain situations. These are:

serious offences, offences involving forfeiture or disqualification and offences committed with an adult (Crown Office Circular No. 1095 (4.8.70)).

13. Other complicating factors were that responsibility for policy for juvenile offenders within the child care system shifted from the Home Office to the Department of Health and Social Security and local government reorganisation occurred which meant both new local authority boundaries and newly created social services departments.

14. As evidence of this, magistrates produced and circulated dossiers of juveniles whom they claimed persistently committed offences and were let off. Berlins and Wansell (1974, 79-81) cite some of these.

15. Fourteen to seventeen year old girls were an exception to this pattern, but the greatest change with respect to them was in S28 remits to the Crown Court. Attendance Centres were not then available for girls as a disposition and detention centres remain unavailable.

16. In fact, approved schools had a reconviction rate of around 65 per cent and absconding from them had increased despite decreases in the approved school population.

17. The D.H.S.S. (1982) expected 522 places to be available by April 1983.

18. Although it was intended in the 1969 Act to phase out attendance centres and detention centres and to replace them with intermediate treatment, there was little discussion about the form and content of intermediate treatment. Also, although magistrates throughout the 1960s requested increased powers, these bore little relationship to intermediate treatment in its eventual form.

Chapter 4

JUVENILE JUSTICE: REVOLUTION AND COUNTER REVOLUTION

Responses to the 1969 Act

Throughout the 1970s, the magistrates and the police were consistently critical of the operation of the 1969 Act. Indicative of this was the fact that as early as 1974 a subcommittee of the House of Commons Expenditure Committee was established to review the whole area. This provided a convenient forum for the various parties to state their case and present their recommendations for the future. For example, in its evidence to the subcommittee, the Justices´ Clerks´ Society wrote:

> It (the Act) fails because it deliberately confuses the distinction between the functions of the court, the police and the local authority. It fails because it blurs what is often the very real distinction between a child in need of care and a juvenile offender. It fails because it deprives society of an important part of the courts´ criminal jurisdiction, namely to protect the public (House of Commons Expenditure Committee, 1975, vol. 11,303).

The evidence of the Magistrates´ Association and the Police Federation had much the same ring: generally they felt powerless to deal with juvenile offenders, and that juveniles could commit offences with impunity. Most of the memoranda submitted to the subcommittee agreed on one point: the inadequacy of resources. What is interesting, however, is that such inadequacies were used both to damn and to support the Act. Social workers argued for increases in manpower, social service budgets and the like. Magistrates, on the other hand, believed that ´some kind of "long stop" measure` was necessary so that young offenders would be shown that `in the last resort the law has teeth` and they pressed, more generally, for `stronger measures`, including an increase in the number of secure places (1) and sanctions for the non-payment of fines and for breaches of supervision orders. (2)   Overall, the evidence submitted fell into four broad categories: the `radical` view that the 1969 Act did not go far enough; the `crime control` view that the Act was based on unsound principles; the `child care` view which accepted the broad principles of the Act and called for full implementation; and the `crime control/child care` view which suggested that some juvenile offenders were susceptible to welfare measures, but that others required penal measures.

As a result, there were a number of alternatives available to the subcommittee. It could adopt one view at the expense of others, attempt a compromise, or rethink juvenile justice policy. The subcommittee attempted the third but, within that framework, was heavily influenced by the crime control/child care view.

While not accepting the view of the Magistrates´ Association that the Act had led to an increase in juvenile crime, the subcommittee seemed to accept that a treatment or welfare model would not reduce delinquency. Thus it proposed two new guidelines in paragraph 13: that of `satisfying society´s wish to punish the offender` and that of `preventing him for a time from committing further offences at a reasonable cost and in the most humane way`. The subcommittee, in its recommendations, was motivated less by an image of the juvenile in trouble or in need of care, and more by an image of a physically mature, often economically independent, adolescent who was a threat to established order. Thus, although the subcommittee suggested that the causes of crime lay in social deprivation, it also felt that, in addition to juveniles `who need care, welfare, better education and moral support` from society, there were some who needed `strict control` and an `element of punishment`. Also, while recognising that many juveniles grow out of delinquent behaviour, the subcommittee stated that some attempt had to be made:

> to hasten the process in the case of certain offenders to deter others from embarking on criminal activities, to contain a hard core of persistent offenders, and to

punish some offenders (House of Commons Expenditure Committee, 1975, para. 17).

The subcommittee's report contained in all forty recommendations for improving the operation of the Act. Many of these were directed towards the smooth running of the Act and involved minor administrative changes (e.g. social workers should be trained in juvenile court procedures). A few recommendations substantially reinforced the social welfare philosophy underlying the Act (e.g. the development of non-residential forms of intervention). Other recommendations marked a move from the philosophy of the 1969 Act. These recommendations were that:

1. when a care order was made, magistrates and social workers should agree in the juvenile court on what should be done with the offender;

2. when a juvenile already subject to a care order appeared before a juvenile court charged with an offence, the court should be able to place him or her in a secure establishment;

3. attendance and detention centres (with additional short periods of detention between two days and three weeks) should be retained; and

4. probation officers rather than social workers should deal with juveniles who offend.

Overall the report reflected the confusions apparent in attempts to align a crime control and a welfare approach. The subcommittee wrote:

> The major failing of the 1969 Act is that it is not wholly effective in different-iating between children who need care... and the small minority who need strict control and an element of punishment (House of Commons Expenditure Committee, 1975, para. 167).

Of course the White Paper 'Children in Trouble' (Home Office, 1968) and the Act did not attempt nor intend to distinguish between these two groups. A central tenet of its philosophy was that the underlying difficulties of such juveniles were similar and that consequently they required similar measures.

The (Labour) government responded to these recommendations in an inter-departmental White Paper in May 1976. It reaffirmed the philosophy of the 1968 Act and stated that: 'the framework provided by the Act for dealing constructively and humanely with children in trouble remains a fundamentally sound one' and that there should be within this framework 'a major shift of emphasis towards non-residential care involving supervision, intermediate treatment and fostering' (Home Office et al., 1976, paras. 3 and 10). However, also in the introduction, there are statements of equal force yet opposite intent:

> The government fully realise and share the widespread anxiety that is felt, especially by magistrates, about the continuing problem of how to cope with a small minority, among delinquent children, of serious and persistent offenders. It is in this area, as the Expenditure Committee observed, that the present measures under the Act are felt to be falling short (Home Office et al., 1976, para. 3).

The White Paper, therefore, supported the subcommittee's belief that there existed a group of juveniles identifiable by the nature of their behaviour. This struck at the root of the philosophy underlying the 1969 Act. 'Children in Trouble' had stated that disposition decisions should 'be soundly based on the best possible diagnosis of the child's needs and circumstances' (Home Office, 1968, para. 33). What the 1976 White Paper attempted to do was to create two separate systems for dealing with juvenile offenders: one based on minor or inconsequential offending and the other based on serious or persistent offending.

There is an inconsistency in this given that the White Paper also continued to accept as sound the philosophy underlying the 1969 Act. It also marks a shift in the Labour government's thinking on the appropriate response to juvenile crime. The bifurcation (3) now proposed identified a category of juvenile offenders ('the majority') for whom existing measures might still be right and a group of supposedly 'hard core' juvenile offenders ('the

minority`) for whom new powers were necessary.
Neither category, however, was defined; and, as we
noted in Chapter 3, evidence for the existence of a
`hard core` is difficult to find. (See also
Magistrates' Association et al., 1978, 5.)
Specifically, the White Paper rejected the recommendations of the subcommittee which would have
given the juvenile courts direct control over the
local authorities' discretion in care order cases
(that is the power to make residential or secure
care orders):

> A juvenile court is not, and cannot be a
> child welfare department, and it is of
> great importance that local authorities
> should accept and shoulder undivided res-
> ponsibility for looking after difficult
> and dangerous young people who have become
> their charge (Home Office et al., 1976,
> para. 25).

It proposed instead that magistrates should be able,
in cases of special concern to them, to make a recommendation to the local authority about where the
juvenile should be placed, including secure placement. It further welcomed the continuation of
detention centres and the expansion of attendance
centres indicating that, by this time, the intention
underlying the 1969 Act to phase out such dispositions was long forgotten.
Thus by the end of the 1970s, juvenile justice
policy bore little resemblance to that proposed in
the 1969 Act. The Magistrates' Association and the
police had been successful in presenting their
conception of juvenile delinquency across the whole
machinery of juvenile justice. They controlled both
those who were referred to the juvenile court and
those who were given dispositions organised by
social services. Further, magistrates and the
police were able to force social services to act
more explicitly to control juvenile offending.
Social workers also moved from a social welfare
approach to delinquents. For example, the British
Association of Social Workers issued guidelines in
1977 which emphasised the need for care orders to be
used for the so called `hard core` minority. Social
workers, therefore, were forced to state that they
could fulfil the social control function demanded by
magistrates in order that they could maintain a
credible role in dealing with delinquents.

Concerns about 'Law and Order'

The Conservative Party is seen by the electorate as more concerned about crime than the Labour Party, although more accurately its concern is with law and order. This has a long history. An obvious example is the number of motions about crime at party conferences. There are always many more motions expressing concern about crime at the Conservative than at Labour Party conferences. But the difference lies not only in number; the motions differ in content too. The majority of motions at Conservative conferences call for the reintroduction of capital or corporal punishment.

What is particularly interesting about this is the appeal that Conservative views on crime have for traditional Labour voters. Hall et al., (1978) demonstrated this in their text on mugging and it is also apparent in opinion polls which often show that working-class people favour capital and corporal punishment. When one takes into account the fact that the working class are commonly the victims of conventional crime, this correspondence between class and punishment is hardly surprising. But it does create problems for Labour politicians' agenda on crime, (4) just as it creates a favourable climate for the rhetoric (and action) of the Conservative Party.

'Law and order' was one of the central themes in the Conservative Party's strategy during the 1979 general election campaign. At the commencement of that campaign, the Conservatives released a pamphlet ('Now Is The Time to Choose') which listed six essential steps for Britain's recovery. The need for greater respect for 'law and order' was one of these. (5) The themes of 'nostalgia' and 'change for the worse' identified by Pearson (1983) are clearly visible in the pamphlet. New programmes were presented as necessary to bring about what had been lost and to prevent Britain becoming a different kind of country. In it, Mrs Thatcher wrote, 'things have happened this winter which would have been unthinkable even 10 years ago'. The next day, the 'law and order' message was made more explicit by Sir Keith Joseph: 'keep the law or take the punishment'. Sir Keith went on in his speech to say that he had once believed that deprivation was an important and contributory factor to lawlessness, but he had come to realise that this was a feeble explanation:

> If we are ever to begin to deal effect-
> ively with present crime levels we shall
> have to reverse the unfashionable notion
> that crime is the responsibility of those
> who commit it, and not of society...In the
> recent past we have diluted this idea by
> blaming crime upon ´social factors´such as
> poor housing or ´deprivation´. To continue
> doing so will be to weaken still further
> the barriers that a sensible society
> erects against violence and crime (quoted
> in The Times, 18th April, 1979).

He specifically referred to the need to amend the
1969 Children and Young Persons Act which he said
had ´removed the concept of delinquency from the
law´. He added that parents should be held responsible for their children´s behaviour but he made it
clear where the major blame lay: with ´attitudes
that have grown out of fashionable Socialist
opinion´. The Shadow Home Secretary, David Howell,
stressed the same theme. He argued that respect for
the rule of law was well down Labour´s list of
priorities (quoted in the Daily Express, 18th April,
1979).

In a speech in Birmingham on 19th April,
Margaret Thatcher made the connections even more
explicit. Labour Ministers, she said:

> ...do not seem to understand their own
> responsibilities in the unending task of
> upholding the law in a free society...Do
> they not understand that when Ministers go
> on the picket line and when Labour back-
> benchers attack the police for trying to
> do their difficult job, that gives the
> green light for lawless methods right
> throughout industry? Do they not dimly
> perceive that their silence when confron-
> ted with flying and violent pickets
> carried a louder and more deadly message
> to every lawbreaker than any speech...?
> In their muddled and different ways, the
> vandals on the picket lines and the
> muggers in our streets have got the same
> confused message - "We want our demands
> met, or else" and "get out of our way,
> give us your handbag or else" (quoted in
> Clarke and Taylor, 1980, 101).

She recalled recent criticisms made of the police at

the 1978 Labour Party Conference and continued:

> The path Labour delegates were charting on
> that occasion was the path to social dis-
> integration and decay, the path to a piti-
> less society in which ruthless might rules
> and the weak go to the wall. Across that
> path we will place a barrier of steel.
> There will be no passing that way once a
> Conservative Government is again in office
> (ibid).

The Labour Party, therefore, was presented as
anti-police, as condoning law breaking and as having
ineffective policies for crime control. While the
imagery was part of a political campaign, Mrs
Thatcher attempted to depoliticise it:

> Some people feel that law and order should
> not be an election issue. But it is not
> the politicians who have made it so. It
> is the electorate. It is the millions of
> people who are deeply frightened and
> anxious about what is going on in our
> streets and cities (ibid, 102).

The explicit plans for reducing crime were presented
by the then Deputy Leader of the Party, William
Whitelaw: 'young thugs' were to be sent to detention centres for a 'short, sharp shock', the number
of secure places for juveniles was to be increased
and 'compulsory attendance centres for hooligans'
were to be expanded. Magistrates were also to be
provided with the power to impose residential and
secure care orders.
     The gap between the two parties becomes more
apparent when we compare these claims with the views
of the then Home Secretary, Merlyn Rees, speaking at
a Labour Party press conference:

> The growth of crime has many causes
> closely related to the social and physical
> environment...It must be tackled through
> policies on housing, education, the econ-
> omy and the social services (quoted in the
> Daily Mirror, 17th April, 1979).

The then Prime Minister, James Callaghan, presented a somewhat firmer line: 'We are the resolute
enemies of the criminal and the vandals' (quoted in
the Daily Telegraph, 20th April, 1979). He went on

to list Labour's achievements in government: new pay deals with the police, stiffer penalties and better compensation for the victims of the crime.

But the irresolvable problem remained: the Conservatives' main election pledges were approved of by a majority of Labour voters and the reduction of crime was a key element in this. Tables 4.1, 4.2 and 4.3 (from The Observer, 22nd April, 1979) clearly demonstrate not only this, but also that voters believed that a Conservative government was likely to achieve its objectives. The reduction of crime was an exception to this, but 95 per cent of Labour voters interviewed for the survey felt that the next government should attempt to achieve that objective.

Clarke and Taylor (1980) analysed television coverage of 'law and order' in the 1979 election. They argue that it was skewed in favour of the Conservatives both formally and substantively. They also argue that the coverage was both qualitatively (it was within a framework of issues constructed by them) and quantitatively ('experts' tended to be from the police and judiciary) imbalanced. For example, in their analysis of I.T.N.'s News at Ten on 24th April 1979, Clarke and Taylor argue that the agenda was set in five steps: there is a general law-and-order problem, it is getting worse; 'young thugs' are among those who are primarily responsible; the Conservatives want immediate, stern penalties and the Labour and Liberal Parties have not formulated their ideas. Indeed the next day (25th April), there was no mistaking the Conservative Party's electoral message. The following information appeared as a full-page advertisement, placed by the Conservative Central Office, in major newspapers:

CRIME THE FACTS

Since the war, crime has risen twice as much under Labour Governments as under Conservative Governments.
Crime has gone up faster under this Labour Government than at any time since the war.
The increase in crime slowed substantially under the last Conservative Government.

The Conservatives won the 1979 election and the success of their campaign can be judged from the fact that the votes in their favour increased by nearly a third in comparison with 1974. The bulk of

Table 4.1

CONSERVATIVE OBJECTIVES

	Named as one of three most important issues	% saying should attempt to achieve these objectives, minus % saying should not	% saying Conservative Government would succeed in achieving these objectives, minus % saying would not
Reduce violent crime and vandalism	40	+94	-20
Reduce supplementary benefit for strikers, on the assumption that they are getting strike pay from their unions	20	+63	+42
End secondary picketing by strikers	18	+81	+ 5
Reduce income tax, especially for the higher-paid	18	+33	+49
Give council house tenants the right to buy their homes with discounts for people who have lived in them for 3 years or more	12	+61	+61
Reduce the number of civil servants	10	+58	- 1
Sell off parts of some State-owned companies	6	+31	+39

Table 4.2

LABOUR OBJECTIVES

	Named as one of three most important issues	% saying should attempt to achieve these objectives, minus % saying should not	% saying Labour Government would succeed in achieving these objectives, minus % saying would not
Bring the rate of price rises down to 5 per cent a year within 3 years	53	+92	-41
Reduce income tax, especially for the lower-paid	48	+92	+30
Achieve a long-term working understanding with the trade unions on wages	32	+89	- 3
Prevent increases in Common Market farm prices	16	+84	-29
Provide universal education and training for all 16-19 year-olds	12	+46	- 6
Control the amount of inessential goods bought from abroad	11	+71	-12
Reduce the powers of the House of Lords	3	- 8	- 8

Table 4.3

LABOUR VOTERS ON TORY AIMS

Should the next Government attempt to achieve these objectives?

	Should %	Should not %	Don't Know %
Reduce violent crime and vandalism	95	3	2
Reduce supplementary benefit for strikers, on assumption that they are getting strike pay from their unions	63	30	7
End secondary picketing by strikers	78	14	8
Reduce income tax, especially for the higher-paid	52	45	3
Give council house tenants the right to buy their homes with discounts for people who have lived in them for 3 years or more	75	20	5
Reduce the number of civil servants	70	22	8
Sell off parts of some State-owned companies	40	49	11

this increase came from skilled and semi-skilled
workers and from voters in the 18 to 24 years age
group - arguably traditional Labour supporters.
At the Conservative Party Conference of October
that year, the then Home Secretary, William Whitelaw, made good the electoral promises. Two detention centres were to have tougher regimes (6) in
which:

> Much greater emphasis will be put on hard
> and constructive activities, on discipline
> on tidiness, on self-respect, on respect
> for those in authority (quoted in the
> Daily Express, October 11, 1979).

The Emergence of the Delinquent

Subsequently, in October 1980, the Conservative
Government issued a White Paper 'Young Offenders'
(Home Office et al., 1980). The White Paper suggested further expanding police cautioning as a primary
diversionary device and, in addition, encouraging
the use of voluntary programmes of intermediate
treatment both as a preventive and diversionary
measure. Significantly, however, it was also concerned with expanding and modifying the juvenile
courts' ability to penalise those who had slipped
through the preventive or diversionary net.
Thus it proposed giving the power to juvenile
court magistrates to impose a 'residential care
order' on a juvenile offender already in the care of
the local authority who was found guilty of a
further imprisonable offence, to impose on offenders
aged fourteen to seventeen a sentence of youth
custody for a term of up to twelve months, (7) to
order a supervision order which would include a
specific programme of activities, to impose community service orders on offenders aged sixteen and to
require parents to pay the fines imposed on their
children. The White Paper also proposed increasing
the amount of financial recognisance which parents
could be ordered to forfeit if they failed to
exercise proper control over their child, retaining
attendance centres and retaining detention centres
for male offenders aged fourteen to seventeen (but
with a new minimum period of three weeks custody and
a maximum of four months).
Basically, these proposals hit at the root of
the social welfare philosophy underlying the 1969
Act. They represent a move to the political right,
and towards notions of punishment and individual

and parental responsibility. They also represent a
move from executive (social workers´) to judicial
decision-making and from the belief in the ´child in
need` to the ´juvenile criminal`, what Tutt (1981)
calls the ´rediscovery of the delinquent`. Indeed
the White Paper is noteworthy in that, throughout,
it refers to juvenile and young adult offenders as
´young offenders`.

A range of modifications to the juvenile
courts´ powers to make non-custodial penalties was
proposed as is apparent in the above list. The
intention underlying these was to expand the range
of non-custodial measures available to the juvenile
court and to promote in juvenile court magistrates a
´greater confidence in the supervision order and in
the use of intermediate treatment`. At the same
time, however, the White Paper proposed that magistrates should have new custodial powers which would
give them direct access to such sentences. Overall,
the proposals can thus be viewed as a toughening and
tightening up of the provisions of the 1969 Act. To
some extent, the child care services were presented
as an integral part of the law and order services.
There is, however, a contradiction underlying these
proposals. The White Paper recognised that appearances before the juvenile court could be harmful and
stigmatising. Hence it recommended increased use of
diversion, including voluntary programmes (Home
Office et al., 1980, para. 38). But it also recommended increased powers to impose custodial sentences which can be equally harmful and stigmatising.

The nature of the changes proposed in the White
Paper could, arguably, have been influenced by research findings on various parts of the juvenile
justice system. That this was not so stresses the
importance of the ideological value of the changes.
Farrington (1984) analysed four claims in the White
Paper and contrasted them with available research
findings. (See also McConville, 1981.) The government, for example, justified the reduction of the
minimum detention centre order to three weeks on the
ground that ´the deterrent effect of a sentence of
this kind is likely to diminish after the first few
weeks` (Home Office et al., 1980, 5). According to
Farrington (1984,91), there is ´no adequate evidence
in favour of (or against) this statement`. (8)
Also, the White Paper stated that ´one of the most
useful non-custodial penalties for young offenders
is the attendance centre order` (Home Office et al.,
1980, 2). Again, Farrington demonstrates that there
is no evidence for the effectiveness of attendance

centres, at   least in relation to reoffending (1984, 92).   The same was so with respect to the   proposals concerning community service and police cautioning. The White Paper evoked considerable   criticism. Although one finds in it statements about   the   need to expand community resources, critics believed that this was no more than rhetoric and that the emphasis was on the expansion of   custodial   resources.   The National   Association   of   Probation   Officers,   for example, said that:

> The concentration on custodial   provisions gives a distorted balance to   the   paper. Measures   should   be   taken   against   the excessive use of custody...it should   only be used as a last resort (1981,6).

Both they and   the   British   Association   of   Social Workers believed that further increases in   the   use of custody were likely on the   introduction   of   the proposed   shorter   custodial   sentences   (see   also Morris and Giller,   1981 and Rutherford,   1981)   and recommended the introduction of criteria to restrict the use of custody.   The underlying concern was that the new shorter custodial sentences would be used in those cases   in   which   previously   a   non-custodial sentence would have been imposed.   (See   also   Tutt, 1981.)

´Law and Order` Modified

The recommendation of this White   Paper   formed the basis of the Criminal Justice Act 1982.   Details of the sentencing powers of the juvenile   court   are discussed in Chapter 6.   For present purposes, it   is sufficient to note that the 1982 Act made   available to justices three   new   powers   of   disposal: youth custody,   care   orders   with   charge   and   control conditions (the equivalent of earlier proposals   for residential   care   orders)   and   community   service. Further, there were three major changes to   existing powers: shorter   periods   in   detention   centres, restrictions on activities as   part   of   supervision orders, and it was to become normal practice to fine parents rather than the juvenile. (9)

The passage of the bill through Parliament   was not particularly smooth.   In the words of Tutt (Tutt and Giller, 1983a):

> The passage of the Criminal   Justice   Bill translating   the   proposals   of   the   White

Paper "Young Offenders" into statute was by no means easy...during the passage of the Bill important new clauses were added directed at strengthening the power of the courts but also seeking to protect the rights of children within the juvenile justice system.

On the one hand, the ´secure care order` which had appeared in the Conservative Party´s election manifesto was dropped. Ministers decided that such a measure, though desired by magistrates, was too costly. Moreover, due to the opposition to it by the local authority organisations (the Association of Metropolitan Authorities and the Association of County Councils), it would have involved central government becoming more involved in the system, a move quite contrary to the government´s pledge to ´roll back the state`. On the other hand, the ´night restriction order` (curfew) was introduced as a condition in supervision orders which further strengthened magistrates´ powers.

Major inroads to curtail magistrates´ powers were made in the Act as a result of the successful intervention of a number of liberal (in the non-political sense) MPs during the Committee stage of the Bill in the House of Commons. (10) They introduced a number of elements geared to increase procedural safeguards. To understand these more fully we have to take a brief step back in time.

The Criminal Justice Act 1982 is not simply a reflection of the Conservative government´s ´law and order` campaign; it is more complex than this. There was general agreement by the early 1980s that some kind of change was necessary: first, to reverse a number of the unintended consequences of the 1969 Act and, secondly, to take account of growing demands to introduce ´justice for children`.

The unintended consequences - primarily the expansion of the use of custody - have been discussed in detail in Chapter 3. But by the end of the 1970s, the philosophy of welfare as an appropriate basis for responding to juveniles who commit offences was increasingly being questioned (Morris et al., 1980; Taylor et al., 1980). Much influenced by American writings (for example, American Bar Association, Institute of Judicial Administration, 1977), such critics argued, amongst other proposals, that the sole justification for the punishment of offenders should be the commission of a specifically defined offence, there should be proportionality between the seriousness of the crime and the penalty, penalties should be determinate in nature and of the least restrictive alternative, and the rights of juveniles (and their parents) should be protected by legal representation.

The proposals of the Black Committee (1979) in Northern Ireland, subsequently accepted by the government, reflect this thinking. It identified the premises which underlie both a welfare and a justice approach to juvenile delinquency and their respective weaknesses. From this, it developed principles which, it believed, would respond to both juveniles' needs and society's demand for protection and it identified ´key considerations` which, it believed, should determine any policy for dealing with juveniles who offend. These are explored further in Chapter 8, but correspond broadly with the adoption of a justice oriented approach to juveniles who commit offences.

More directly relevant to developments in England was the publication in 1981 of the report on young offenders of the Parliamentary All-Party Penal Affairs Group, chaired by Robert Kilroy-Silk. This group was particularly concerned about the increasing trend towards the use of custody for juveniles. Thus its main recommendations concerned attempts to reverse that trend: juveniles should be dealt with in the community so far as possible and the system of police cautioning should be extended. It did, however, accept that there were a minority of juvenile offenders who required ´an element of punishment and secure containment` (1981, 79). Overall, it argued that its proposals would lead to a ´more humane, more cost effective and more just response`, (1981, 79) to offending by juveniles. With respect to a ´more just response`, the group argued for determinate residential and custodial orders, mandatory legal representation in certain situations, statutory criteria to guide the decisions of sentencers and local authorities and the requirement to give reasons for some decisions.

Cumulatively, these publications had an impact on the content of the 1982 Act. For example, criteria were introduced into the Bill which restricted the use of care and custodial orders and also of secure placements. (11) Thus a sentence of detention centre or youth custody was to be made only if it was ´appropriate`, and the 1982 Act specified the situations in which it was:

1.   The offender is unable or unwilling to

respond to non-custodial penalties, or

2.   The custodial sentence is necessary for the protection of the public, or

3.   The offence is so serious a non-custodial sentence cannot be justified.

The juvenile court was also to obtain a social inquiry report to assist it in determining these issues and legal representation was to be offered to the juvenile. With respect to care orders for offences, two conditions had to be met: the offence must be serious and the juvenile must be in need of care or control. Here, too, the juvenile must be offered legal representation.

Thus, overall, the 1982 Act reflects not only elements of a ´law and order` strategy but also of justice. There is a recognition that hearings in the juvenile court should be adversarial in nature (for example, the right to legal representation at certain stages) and that sanctions should be both determinate (for example, a youth custody <u>sentence</u> replaced the semi-determinate borstal <u>training</u> order) and proportionate to the offence (care orders and custodial sentences are reserved for serious offences).

During the passage of the Act through Parliament, the then Home Secretary, William Whitelaw, expressed the view that by broadening and strengthening existing non-custodial measures, the courts would be able to avoid using a custodial sentence except where absolutely necessary. To what extent has the trend towards the use of custody been slowed down?

The 1982 Act in Practice

The purpose of the criteria outlined earlier was to provide safeguards against the excessive use of custodial sanctions. Comments made in the <u>Justice of the Peace</u> summarising the Act, however, indicate that they were likely to have little effect:

It may be doubted whether the new statutory restrictions upon the use of custodial sentences for young offenders add anything to the mental processes of the courts (1983, 184).

It went on to say:

> Given the lack of interest on the part of the legal profession in the law of sentencing and the inadequate opportunities for the clerks to lay magistrates to offer advice in this area, we wonder whether the statutory criteria will have much practical effect (1983, 184-185).

And by November 1983, there was already some evidence that the statutory criteria were not being successful at reducing the number of juveniles given custodial penalties.

Prior to the implementation of the Act, it had been expected that the new shorter forms of detention centre order (from the minimum of three weeks to a maximum of four months) would be frequently used. This proved not to be the case. It was the longer forms of custody available to juvenile court magistrates for the first time under the 1982 Act (youth custody orders) that increased most. Table 4.4 demonstrates this.

Table 4.4   Reception of Males (14-17 years) and Females (15-17 years) by sentence

| | | Comparison of the six-month periods May-November | | |
		1982	1983	% change
Females:	Youth Custody	25	45	+77
Males:	Detention Centre	2,630	2,250	-15
Males:	Youth Custody	570	960	+69

Source: Adapted from NACRO, 1984a, 5-6.

These trends have continued. NACRO (1984b)(12) examined sentencing patterns in the first twelve months of the Act's operation and compared them with the previous year. The number of young people in custodial institutions had continued to rise and the shift was from short detention centre orders to longer youth custody orders. A report published by the Home Office statistical branch (Home Office,

1985b) on young offenders in prison department establishments questions the increase in custodial sentences, however. The figures presented there show that the number of males aged fourteen to seventeen received into custody dropped from 6900 in 1982 to 6580 during the year ending June 1984. (13) Within these figures, the report nevertheless confirms that there has been a shift away from the detention centre order to the new youth custody sentence. Detention centre receptions of males aged fourteen to seventeen dropped by 16 per cent between 1982 and June 1984; the number of youth custody receptions of males aged fifteen to seventeen, on the other hand, was 41 per cent higher over this period.

Previously, juvenile court magistrates could not directly award long periods of custody to juvenile offenders. The procedure was for them to recommend a sentence of borstal training to the Crown Court. The Crown Court judge would then review this recommendation and, if he wished, he could substitute an alternative sentence. Some 25 per cent of all such recommendations were rejected by the Crown Court. With the abolition of borstal training and its replacement with youth custody, juvenile court magistrates now have direct access to youth custody centres without the routine check of a higher court's review. The increase in the use of youth custody since May 1983 indicates that a substantial component of this increase is due to the inclusion of juveniles who previously would have had a recommendation for custody rejected.

The Home Office's report (1985b) also showed that, despite the availability and use of short detention centre orders (the average length of such orders dropped from thirteen weeks in 1982 to ten weeks in the year following the introduction of the 1982 Act), the average period actually served remained much the same due to the reduction in remission - for this age group - from a half to a third. The average length of youth custody sentences for males fifteen to seventeen (eight months and, with remission, this means five months actually served) was, however, less than the usual eight or nine months served under a borstal order. Girls also served shorter periods on youth custody than in borstal. It is still possible, however, that a number of juvenile offenders who would have formerly received detention centre orders are now being given youth custody orders (Reynolds, 1985a). There is no evidence, therefore, which contradicts the fear that the 1982 Act would lead to an increase in the use of custody.

Indeed, the findings of Reynolds (1985a and b), Burney (1985a and b) and Whitehead and MacMillan (1985) give considerable cause for concern. Reynolds (1985b) for example, found in an examination of sentencing practice in the juvenile courts in Northamptonshire between 1982 and 1984 not only that the use of custody had increased, but that it was not related to the seriousness or persistence of the offences. Furthermore, 80 to 90 per cent of the orders, in her sample, were made in the face of a recommendation for some kind of non-custodial penalty by a probation officer or social worker.

These researchers all found that the statutory criteria to restrict the use of custody by juvenile court magistrates were commonly misused or ignored. For example, the reasons ´seriousness of the offence` and ´protection of the public` were used in cases involving trivial offences. Burney´s study involved twelve magistrates´ (including juvenile) courts in the south-east of England and in the majority of cases the courts broke the law by failing to follow the statutory sentencing formula or to record it. For example, in 60 per cent of the cases, the reasons were incomplete or invalid; in 14 per cent no reason at all was given. She argues from this that the introduction of the statutory criteria had changed nothing since ´a decision in favour of custody having been made the most appropriate statutory justification was then sought` (1985a, 287). Whitehead and MacMillan (1985), on the basis of their research in a northeast juvenile court, have gone as far as suggesting that the criteria are being used as a basis to send more juveniles into custody. They also argue that mandatory social inquiry reports have failed to discourage magistrates from using custodial penalties. In eight out of 99 reports in their survey, a clear recommendation for custody was made by the probation officer and in a further seven it was implied. In eight reports, no recommendation was made. In the remaining 76, magistrates had imposed custodial sentences despite recommendations for non-custodial disposals. However, Whitehead and MacMillan described these proposals as ´vague and unclear`. On the other other hand, in all 99 cases, legal representation had been offered and thirteen of the juveniles appealed. In six of these cases, a non-custodial penalty was substituted and in three their period of custody was reduced.

The statutory criteria for making care orders in criminal proceedings seem to have influenced the number of such care orders made. In 1985, under 500 care orders were imposed on young people aged ten to fourteen found guilty of indictable offences, considerably fewer than the 1982 figure of 1,050. About 900 care orders were made on fourteen to seventeen year olds in this category, about 1,500 less than in 1982. This may not be, however, solely the effect of the statutory criteria. As we noted in Chapter 3, a decline in the use of care orders on offence grounds has been taking place since the early seventies. Also, local authorities have changed their practices with respect to requests for care orders. This is discussed further in Chapter 7. Thirdly, economic considerations have led to a reduction in the number of places available in community homes with education on the premises within local authority areas and to an expansion of intermediate treatment (and, latterly, supervised activity) schemes as direct alternatives to care (and custody).

The inter-relationship between the decline in care orders and the increase in custodial sentences is a relatively unexplored area. Overall, care orders declined by 81 per cent between 1974 and 1985 (from 7,100 to 1,350) while the use of custody (both detention centre and borstal/youth custody) increased by 11 per cent (from 5,400 to 6,000). Table 4.5 shows the differential distribution of care orders and custodial sentences between these years for fourteen to seventeen year olds (i.e. those eligible for both care orders and custodial sentences).

While care orders declined for this age group (they also did for those under fourteen years: from 2,800 to 500: a decline of 82%), custodial sentences increased and it could be argued that some of those kinds of cases which were given care orders in 1975 are now receiving custodial sentences. If we construct a combined care and custody rate of sentencing as an indicator of the extent to which young persons have been removed from the community, little has changed in this period (15.3% were removed in 1975 and 13.0% in 1985). What is different is the kind of institution to which they are sent. It is increasingly likely to be a custodial rather than a care setting.

The use of community-based dispositions - typically supervision, intermediate treatment, supervised activities and community service - has been

Table 4.5   Number of 14 to 17 Year Olds Given Care
              or Custody Sentences in 1975 and 1985

	1975 Number sent-enced	% of all sentences for 14-17 year olds	1985 Number sent-enced	% of all sentences for 14-17 year olds
Care orders	4300	6.4%	900	17%
Detention Centre	4300	6.4%	4000	7.5%
Borstal/youth custody	1700	2.5%	2000	3.8%
TOTAL	10300	15.3%	6900	13.0%

Source: Home Office, 1986d

mixed (Tutt and Giller, 1985a). In fairness, some
of these dispositions were not immediately available
for juvenile courts to use by the implementation
date whereas the custodial provisions were immediately available. For example, community service
orders for 16-year olds could only be used by the
courts when appropriate schemes were notified to
them by the organisers (that is, the probation
service). In areas where schemes were constructed, a
six-month preparation period was usual. In many
areas, however, no provision for community service
existed for this age group. (At the end of 1983, 21
of the 56 probation areas in England and Wales had
no such provision and by the end of 1984 it was
still not available in six probation areas.) Community service orders were made on about 1,900 males
and less than 100 females aged sixteen in 1985, four
times as many as in 1983 when it first became
available.

Similar comments can be made with respect to
intermediate treatment. In February of 1983, the
Department of Health and Social Security announced a
£15 million programme to fund intermediate treatment
schemes for a three year period. Applicants for the
funding (which had to be local authorities and voluntary organisations acting together) were only to
submit schemes which were to be alternatives to care

129

or custody. The limitations (both financial and time-wise) on the fund, however, meant that many areas did not make an application. Moreover, the processing of applications meant that, in most cases, twelve months passed before any new programmes were available at a local level. In August 1986, grants had been approved in 110 such schemes.

According to NACRO´s (1984b) survey on the operation of the first year of the Act, intermediate treatment orders decreased by 10 per cent for fourteen to seventeen year olds over the year. NACRO also found that only 77 supervised activity requirements had been made in those areas surveyed. Two areas, however, accounted for over half of them and, in 24 of the 35 areas, no requirements had been imposed. More recently, the criminal statistics for 1985 (Home Office, 1986d) show that positive requirements in supervision orders (both supervised activity and intermediate treatment requirements) were used in about 2,000 cases (that is in 18 per cent of all supervision orders). Whether or not such orders were always imposed as a direct alternative to care or custody, however, remains problematic and depends upon the credibility with which local programmes are perceived by individual benches.

Table 4.6 presents information on sentencing practice in three local juvenile justice systems over a six month period in 1985 and compares the local distribution of sentences with national figures (Social Information Systems, 1986). Each of the areas had launched an intermediate treatment or supervised activity initiative since the implementation of the 1982 Act and community service schemes also operated in each area.

In area A, supervised activity orders had been designated as a direct alternative to care and custody; intermediate treatment was intended to be used as a mid-tariff option. The former were used in 6 per cent of cases and community service orders accounted for a further 4 per cent of sentences. No care orders for offences were recorded over the six month period and only 3 per cent of sentences resulted in custody. Supplementary analysis by S.I.S. showed that the characteristics of the offenders given these alternatives (based on such factors as offence type and previous convictions) indicated that in the absence of such programmes they ran a substantial risk of being removed from the community. The custodial sentences which were imposed were on offenders similar to those given one of the alternatives to custody and had occurred

Table 4.6   Distribution of Sentences (%) in Three
Local Juvenile Justice Systems over a
Six Month Period in 1985 and National
Sentencing Distribution for 1985

Sentence	A	B	C	National Distribution (1985)
Absolute/Conditional Discharge	18.2	28.6	16.2	26.8
Fine	35.4	27.5	27.0	24.0
Attendance Centre	6.5	18.0	10.0	16.2
Supervision Order	11.9	10.3	9.0	14.7
Supervision Order with Intermediate Treatment	6.8	3.3	9.0)	
Supervised Activity Order	6.0	-	6.3)	3.4
Community Service Order	4.2	2.7	5.4	3.2
Care Order	-	0.6	7.2	2.1
Detention Centre	2.6	3.1	6.3	6.4
Youth Custody	0.2	1.2	3.6	3.2
Other	8.2	4.7	-	-
TOTAL	100% N=429	100% N=582	100% N=111	

Source: Derived from Social Information Systems, 1986

despite a recommendation for an alternative in the juvenile's social inquiry report. Prior to the introduction of the alternative into this local system, some 14 per cent of juveniles were given care orders or custodial sentences over a comparable period.

In area B, the intermediate treatment initiative and community service orders were used less frequently than in area A and supervised activity requirements were not used by the juvenile courts there at all. Nevertheless, the low care and custody rate in the area (5 per cent of all sentences) is considerably below that of the national figure (12 per cent). The impact of the intermediate treatment initiative in this area had not been to reduce further the care or custody levels (which were traditionally low) or to increase the use of intermediate treatment for those not at risk of removal from home, but to increase the use of low tariff measures by effective ´gate-keeping` (especially by an increase in the proportionate use of conditional discharges) for those appearing in the juvenile courts for their first to third time.  The role of ´gate-keeping` is explained in Chapter 7.

In area C, almost 21 per cent of all sentences passed in the six months of the survey were said to be alternatives to care or custody. 17 per cent were either care orders or custodial sentences. Supplementary analysis by S.I.S. showed that there were clear differences in the two groups in terms of seriousness of offences and persistence of offending. Moreover, there was a major difference in the kinds of recommendations made to the courts. Positive recommendations for care or custody were made in the social inquiry reports in nearly half of the cases so sentenced and in only one such case was a direct alternative to care or custody recommended.

In the light of such information on variations in the use of intermediate treatment and supervised activities, evaluation of these measures will have to examine not merely their frequency of use in local systems, but also to document their impact (if any) upon care and custodial outcomes. The mere presence of a programme of alternatives to care or custody does not ensure its appropriate use.

There is clear evidence, on the other hand, that the number of fines and compensation orders imposed on parents has increased since the power to do so was enlarged. Such orders increased from 1,228 in 1982 to 9,413 in 1985: almost an eight-fold increase. This represented 26 per cent of the fines and 35 per cent of the compensation orders imposed in juvenile courts in 1985.

Conclusion

Why did such changes occur? It was said by the government to have been a response to the magistrates´ sense of powerlessness in the juvenile court. But from the information presented in the previous chapter, it is clear that much of this sense of powerlessness was unfounded. To understand the changes, we need again to consider the power of politics. The Conservative Party was never sympathetic to the philosophy and provisions of the 1969 Act; nor were the Magistrates´ Association or the Police Federation, the organisations which, to some extent, represent the interests of magistrates and the police. And both these organisations have stronger links with the Conservative than with the Labour Party.

It is certainly clear that the policy changes were not based on research information. Indeed, much research (including that done by government departments) provides evidence against the development of the new provisions. Institutions, for example, have notoriously high failure rates. One is left with the conclusion that ideological commitment dictated the changes. The 1982 Act´s objective was said to be to strengthen respect for the law and to increase the deterrent impact of the juvenile court. But it is implausible that the government believed that such changes would reduce juvenile crime and juvenile recidivism. Rather, the changes perform a symbolic function; they provide the appearance of a strong government willing to take tough measures against crime.

A good example of this is provided by the experimental introduction of the ´short, sharp shock` into detention centres. This was designed quite explicitly to deter juvenile offenders from committing further offences by imposing a rigorous regime of physical education, formal drills, parades and inspections. The Prison Department Psychology Unit carried out research on the regimes´ effectiveness (Home Office, 1984a). Not surprisingly, there were no discernible differences in terms of reconviction rates between these ´experimental` regimes and other detention centres: both remained high. More importantly, the regimes were not perceived as significantly tougher by the trainees and, in fact, some of the activities - inspections, drills and parades - were enjoyed by them. Despite these results, the ´short, sharp, shock` regime was extended to all detention centres (from March 1985).

Ministers´ reactions to the poor reconviction rates is interesting. They were described as ´hardly a surprise` (quoted in The Times 13th March 1985) and Leon Brittan, the then Home Secretary, stated that the policy on detention centres was fully justified on the merits. This seems to imply that the merits of the scheme lie elsewhere than in reducing recidivism. Farrington concludes his review of the English juvenile justice system with the words that its development reflects ´prejudices,

vested interests, and political beliefs` (1984, 92),
but the practice of juvenile justice has rarely been
otherwise.   The expansion of   the   experimental
regimes can only be viewed as   ideologically   rather
than research based.
    There is increasingly <u>less</u> differentiation   be-
tween the juvenile, the young adult   and   the   adult
offender. A recent example of   this   is   the   White
Paper `Criminal Justice Legislation` (Home   Office,
1986a)   which   discusses   suspended   sentences   of
detention centre and youth custody which would apply
to both juveniles   and   young   adult   offenders   and
which would serve much the same purpose as suspended
sentences of imprisonment for adults.   In some   ways
then, current policy discourse - with   its   emphasis
on deterrence -   reflects   a   return   to   nineteenth
century penal philosophy;   current practice reflects
the continuation of the   trend   towards   bifurcation
which began in the seventies.   What this means at   a
local level is discussed in the next three chapters.

NOTES

    1.   Grants were subsequently given by   central
government to local authorities to build secure facilities in the Children Act 1975.
    2.   The Criminal Law Act 1977 subsequently
gave magistrates power to fine   or   make   attendance
centre orders where   juveniles   breached   the   conditions of a supervision order.
    3.   Bottoms (1977) coined this phrase to   dis-
tinguish dangerous from other   offenders.   However,
according to Greenwood and Young (1980), this was   a
general feature in policy discussions throughout the
`60s and `70s.
    4.   In recent years at   Labour   Party   confer-
ences,   some   delegates   have   been   specifically
critical of   certain   policing   practices   (e.g.
policing industrial disputes) and this   has   created
further problems for the Labour Party´s response   to
crime.
    5.   The other steps were lower taxes, improved
education,   strengthening   defences,   striking   a
balance between   the   rights   and   duties   of   trade
unions and reducing government intervention.
    6.   Other measures announced were: the lifting
of restrictions on courts wishing to sentence   young

134

adult offenders to prison for periods between six months and three years, giving magistrates the power to make residential care orders and an expansion in the number of attendance centres.

7. The ´custody and control` order proposed by the Advisory Council on the Penal System in its report on ´Young Adult Offenders` (1974) formed the basis for the proposal although the Council also envisaged the abolition of detention centres and the full implementation of the Children and Young Persons Act 1969.

8. Cf. Dunlop and McCabe (1965) and Ericson (1975) both point to the trainees´ <u>dislike</u> of the first two weeks.

9. The sections of the Act dealing with juvenile offenders were implemented in two stages: sections 26, 27 and 28 which deal with financial sanctions against parents and guardians were brought into effect on 31st January 1983; sections 1 to 25 which are concerned with arrangements for custodial sentences, care orders and non-custodial penalties were implemented on 24th May 1983.

10. A number of amendments were not successful however. For example, Dr. Summerskill failed to get rid of detention centres and to replace them with something more constructive (as the Advisory Council on the Penal System (1974) and a subsequent Green Paper (Home Office, 1978) had recommended). Various more restrictive amendments also failed. For example, Sir Nicholas Benson´s attempt to get the minimum age for detention centres reduced to twelve.

11. Regulation of the use of secure accommodation for all children in care (not merely delinquents), was included to forestall an impending application to the European Court which would have challenged juveniles in care in secure facilities without a judicial review. This matter had been the subject of a D.H.S.S. working party (1981b) and the legislation substantially endorsed the proposals made there. The criteria limiting secure placement and the procedures to be followed are discussed further in Chapter 6.

12. Their information was drawn from only 35 local authority areas and was incomplete so some caution must be exercised in generalising from the survey.

13. The Criminal Statistics for 1985 confirm this (Home Office 1986d, 125). However, the proportionate use of custody for males aged fourteen to seventeen sentenced for indictable offences remains at 12 per cent.

Chapter 5

THE POLICE AND DIVERSION

Introduction

Government policy in England and Wales is to maintain diversion high on the agenda in attempts to reform juvenile justice. As the White Paper 'Young Offenders' put it:

> All the available evidence suggests that juvenile offenders who can be diverted from the criminal justice system at an early stage in their offending are less likely to re-offend than those who become involved in judicial proceedings (Home Office et al., 1980, para. 3.8).

In executing this policy, the police currently stand as the 'gatekeepers' to the juvenile court and (until recently) diversion has primarily been their responsibility. Diversion has primarily taken the form of formally cautioning juveniles rather than prosecuting them; it did not usually mean that they would be involved in some kind of programme (as is frequently the case in the United States (Sarri, 1983b)). A few police forces, however, have now developed diversion schemes which involve programmes (Giller, 1983).

One of the objectives underlying the Children and Young Persons Act 1969 was to divert juveniles from the juvenile court, and consultation between the police and other agencies (social services and education) prior to deciding on criminal proceedings for the fourteen to seventeen age group was one of the main mechanisms to achieve this. This procedure, of course, remained unimplemented (Tutt, 1981 and 1982), but this did not mean that diversion and inter-agency consultation did not take place. On

the contrary, the decade of the 1970s marked a
substantial growth in cautioning for those juveniles
brought to the notice of the police. It had, however, consequences few had anticipated. The operation of this discretionary power, its increased use
in the 1970s, its organisation within individual
police forces and its revision in the 1980s are the
subject of this chapter.

New criteria issued by the Home Office to the
police in 1985 to increase the likelihood of
diversion from formal court proceedings means that
this area of discretionary practice will undoubtedly
remain important in the juvenile justice system.
However, the monopoly of the police to prosecute
offenders has been broken with the introduction in
1986 of the Crown Prosecution Service (in the Prosecution of Offences Act 1985). The need to separate
policing and prosecution functions to counterbalance
the increase in police powers introduced in the
Police and Criminal Evidence Act 1984 and to ensure
greater consistency in the decision to prosecute
both within and between police force areas led to
proposals to introduce an additional filter into the
prosecution system. The implications of this for
the police and for diversion from the juvenile
justice system are also considered in this chapter.

Diversion

Diversion has been a dominant thrust in western
juvenile justice policy for the past 25 years
(Klein, 1984). Even prior to that, arguments in
favour of diversion appeared in embryo form in the
debates in the nineteenth century which surrounded
the establishment of separate institutions and
courts for juvenile offenders. It was believed that
these, in part, would protect juveniles from the
contaminating influence of adult offenders.

Diversion is a concept with multiple meanings
and, within any one juvenile justice system, not all
forms of diversion will necessarily be pursued (Tutt
and Giller, 1984a). Broadly speaking, three (1)
forms of diversion are discussed in the literature:

1. Diversion from crime. This is mainly assoc-
    iated with policies of crime prevention either
    directed at reducing opportunities for the
    commission of offences or targeted on partic-
    ular crime-prone groups (such as juveniles) who
    participate in certain offences.

2. Diversion from court. Here those who act as gatekeepers into the court system are given the opportunity to discontinue proceedings (entirely or conditionally) and either do nothing or substitute some kind of informal intervention.

3. Diversion from institutions. In this, community-based programmes are promoted as an alternative to institutions (welfare or penal) for those who would otherwise be removed from the community because of their offending.

In this chapter, we concentrate on diversion from the juvenile court and, in particular, on the role of the police in this. In policy terms, the police have been the main agents of diversion in England and Wales over the past twenty years (Bottoms, 1974), although, of late, attention has also been given to diverting juveniles from institutions (this is discussed in Chapter 7) and to enhancing crime prevention initiatives (see, for example, Burrows et al., 1979; Clarke, 1978). There have also been attempts recently to consider more actively diversion of young adult and adult offenders from the court (Home Office circular 14/1985) and to explore non-judicial settlement of disputes (Marshall, 1985).

Proponents of diversion claim a number of advantages for such a strategy. Diversion is believed to break the seeming inability of the juvenile court system to respond constructively to law-breaking and to avoid the negative consequences of traditional forms of intervention. Its major strength is claimed to be the circumvention of the labelling process associated with juvenile court processing. Thus it is said to avoid stigmatising offenders and to avert the development in the juvenile of a deviant self image and a sustained criminal career. Diversion, it is argued, also avoids the contagion effect on naive and inexperienced offenders when exposed to their more experienced counterparts. As Morris comments:

> Proponents of this view commonly feel that too many minor offenders appear in our juvenile courts, that many of the acts committed by children referred to juvenile courts indicate family, educational, or welfare difficulties, or difficulties of growing up. The criminal justice system, it is felt, is too heavy handed for

such offenders; the criminal law and its
processes should be a last and limited
resort (1978a, 47).

Linked with each of these points is an over-arching
argument - especially pertinent in the 1980s - that
diversion is less costly than the formal processing
of cases through the full criminal justice system
and that resources could thereby be saved or re-
allocated. Collectively, proponents of diversion
share the view which is characterised by Lemert´s
term ´judicious non-intervention`:

> Society or the local community would treat
> a great deal of deviance among the young
> as normal behaviour on the assumption that
> most youths will pass through their
> ´deviant` or ´storm and stress` stage and
> mature into reasonably law abiding adults
> (1981, 39).

An alternative body of opinion favouring
diversion, and one which has proved far more
influential elsewhere than here, is that diversion
can be a means whereby deviant juveniles (not merely
those who commit offences) can be identified at an
early stage and worked with in a range of ´treat-
ment` programmes. These programmes can involve
counselling and giving advice, but they can also
include behaviour modification, vocational training
and reparation (Klein, 1985; Sarri, 1983b). In
England, this form of diversion took the form in the
1970s of ´preventive intermediate treatment`
(Thorpe et al., 1980). By 1981, it was evident that
this use of intermediate treatment (I.T.) far out-
weighed its role in providing the juvenile courts
with a range of programmes geared to diverting
sentenced juveniles from institutions. In that year,
some 17,700 juveniles were taking part in
intermediate treatment programmes provided by social
services departments. Of those:

> 3,700 (21%) were on supervision orders
> with an I.T. requirement;
> 3,800 (21%) were on supervision orders
> without an I.T. requirement;
> 2,300 (13%) were on care orders;
> 7,900 (45%) were children who fell outside
> these categories.

Harper and Thomas (1984) analysed these figures and

found that by far the largest category of juveniles undergoing intermediate treatment were described as `at risk`. Moreover, they demonstrated that most of those involved in preventive intermediate treatment would not have been involved in either formal juvenile court processing or removal from the community. One tenth of the total cases involved children who were under ten years of age and a further 50 per cent were aged ten to fourteen. Harper and Thomas (1984, 5) found that few were 15 or older and girls were over-represented. (See also Bottoms and Pratt, 1985.)

Whether or not these schemes are real diversion is debatable. As Bullington et al., note:

> Increasing the number of programmes for juvenile offenders is incompatible with the idea of diversion from the system. New programmes, however we label them, are certainly a part of the overall system for responding to delinquency, and sending youngsters to those programmes cannot be fairly characterized as keeping them out of the system...From this perspective, the phrase diversionary programme is a contradiction. When new programmes are proposed it can only be because it is hoped that youngsters will be diverted to them, thus remaining within the overall system (1978, 66).

Such schemes, therefore, are more properly described as `minimisation of penetration` into the juvenile justice system (Cressey and McDermott, 1974). Moreover, research has shown that, in practice, this form of diversion can have a number of unintended consequences (Morris, 1978a; Bullington et al., 1978; Klein, 1979; Sarri, 1983b). Among those most frequently documented are:

1. the tendency to bring more juveniles into the ambit of networks of control than would have hitherto been the case - the `net widening` phenomenon;

2. the production of a new range of potentially stigmatising labels which can be applied to the juveniles involved (e.g. `persons in need of supervision`, `at risk cases`, `pre-delinquents`);

3. the possible infringement of legal rights
    by pressure being put on juveniles and their
    parents to admit guilt and to participate in
    the diversion programme in order to avoid a
    juvenile court appearance;

4. the possibility that involvement in a diversion
    programme will be for longer and be more
    incursive than the order which the juvenile
    would have received if referred to the juvenile
    court;

5. the danger that professionals running diversion
    programmes employ discriminatory selection
    criteria and practices which are subject to
    neither public scrutiny nor control;

6. the risk that failure of the juvenile on or
    after participation in a diversion programme
    will lead to greater intervention by
    the juvenile court on a subsequent appearance.

These criticisms, while traditionally voiced by
academics and the liberal left, have also recently
been advanced by those involved in the practice of
the system, for example, justices' clerks and
magistrates (McKittrick and Eysenck, 1984).

In an English context, diversion has centred
around the issue of police cautioning and has not,
as in other jurisdictions, formally involved a range
of ancillary agencies providing services. As we
shall see, however, even within the restricted forms
of diversion which developed throughout the 1970s,
some of the criticisms identified by researchers
elsewhere are pertinent.

The Inheritance of the 1970s

There was without doubt a substantial expansion
in the number of children and young persons cautioned by the police during the 1970s. In 1970, 35 per
cent of known juvenile offenders were cautioned by
the police for indictable offences; by 1979, the
proportion had reached 50 per cent and, by 1985, it
had reached 60 per cent. In absolute terms this
meant that, in 1970, 53,000 children and young
persons received a formal caution, in 1979, 82,000
and, in 1985, 112,500.

Traditionally, children are more likely to
receive formal cautions than fourteen to seventeen
year olds and girls are more likely to receive
cautions than boys. Table 5.1 shows this.

Table 5.1   Offenders Cautioned for Indictable Offences as a Percentage of Offenders Found Guilty or Cautioned by Age and Sex

Year	Males		Females	
	Aged 10 and under 14	Aged 14 and under 17	Aged 10 and under 14	Aged 14 and under 17
1975	63	33	83	57
1976	63	32	81	55
1977	67	35	85	58
1978	64	34	85	57
1979	66	35	85	59
1980	65	34	85	58
1981	68	35	87	60
1982	70	38	88	65
1983	74	42	90	68
1984	75	45	91	71
1985	79	68	93	78

Source: Home Office, 1986d

Such discrepancies in police decision-making are not solely explained on the basis of juveniles' differential degree of involvement in crime (Riley, 1986b). The willingness of the police to caution children and girls is well documented in this and other jurisdictions (Alder and Polk, 1982). With respect to children, this is likely to be related to the minor nature of the offences they commit, the absence of previous offence histories and the fact that they do not represent the challenge to social order which the stereotypical image of the older offender does. With respect to girls, these factors are probably also relevant (Carey, 1979). In addition, the so-called 'chivalry hypothesis' is said to explain the police's reluctance to prosecute girls (Simon, 1975), but this does not appear to extend to all girls. It extends only to those whose offences are consistent with the expectations of appropriate sex-role behaviour which are held by those who operate the juvenile justice system (Terry, 1965). Hence, the police may be willing to caution girls arrested for 'traditional' offences such as shoplifting or handling stolen property, but reluctant to do so where burglary or offences of violence are involved. Also, in view of the social-isation of girls which encourages them to be outwardly (but not violently) emotional, the will-ingness of girls to express their emotions and remorse for their offending may be a crucial factor in the decision to caution (Gelsthorpe, 1984).

The growth in police cautioning during the 1970s was not accompanied by an immediate direct reduction in the overall number of juveniles who were dealt with in the juvenile courts. In 1970, some 74,387 juveniles were referred to the juvenile courts; in 1979, the figure was 82,000. These over-all figures do, of course, mask differences between the two age groups. For example, for boys under the age of 14 years, the marked increase in cautions was accompanied by a substantial decrease in the number dealt with in the juvenile court (a decrease of 30 per cent between 1970 and 1979); a similar, although smaller, decrease occurred with respect to girls in this age group (a decline of 17 per cent over the decade). However, for the older age group, there was an increase in the number of referrals to the juvenile court for both sexes: an increase of 15 per cent for boys and of 30 per cent for girls.

It was acknowledged early in the 1970s that a paradox had developed in this area of juvenile justice practice: an increase in the use of a measure intended to divert juvenile offenders from the juvenile courts was not, in fact, having the effect of reducing the number of juveniles entering that system (a feature well documented at the time in the United States; for a review, see Morris, 1978a). Rather than operating as real diversion, the cautioning procedure was said to be 'widening the net' of available labelled delinquents.

An early and influential report on this point was by John Ditchfield (1976). He showed that those police force areas with the greatest increase in the number of cautions in the early 1970s were also the areas with the largest increase in the known offend-er population. However, those police force areas with the greatest increase in cautioning rates (the proportion of those cautioned of all offenders caut-ioned or convicted) showed the largest increase in the proportion of juveniles to adults in the known offender population. These increases were much larger than could reasonably be accounted for by changes in the age structure of the population.

Ditchfield concluded that this process of ´net widening` occurred ´because changes in police practice brought about by the 1969 Act have resulted in a number of juveniles being officially cautioned, when previously they would have been dealt with by informal warning or no further action` (1976, 12). (2)

Farrington and Bennett´s (1981) study of the Metropolitan Police District figures similarly showed a rapid increase in cautioning in the early 1970s. For example, between 1968 and 1970, the arrest rate for those under the age of fourteen increased by 85 per cent and for fourteen to seventeen year olds by 44 per cent. Farrington and Bennett argue that this increase over such a short period, not replicated in subsequent periods, was influential evidence of the ´widening of the net` phenomenon. They do note, however, that the major impact of the negative aspects of this process (an appearance in the juvenile court on a subsequent referral to the police) was more marked with respect to young persons than children.

Responsibility for ´net widening`, however, is not necessarily only that of the police officers who process juvenile cases. As Mott (1983) has shown, the opportunities for offenders to be directly discovered or apprehended by the police at or near the scene of an offence vary considerably (between 4 per cent and 43 per cent of boys aged fourteen to seventeen in Mott´s sample of six police forces were so apprehended) and such apprehensions seem unrelated to the recorded crime rates in different police force areas (Burrows, 1982). More influential in determining the number of juveniles referred to the police is the way in which the police, as a locally based organisation, approach the general public or particular schools or youth clubs to encourage referral to them of disputes involving juveniles (Taylor, 1971). Indeed, these individuals or agencies may themselves decide to refer juveniles to the police (for example, shopkeepers may insist upon the prosecution of shoplifters).

Commentators are divided as to whether ´net widening` is a phenomenon uniquely related to the early and mid 1970s or is a continuing feature of current diversion practice (Tutt, 1984). By the early 1980s, for example, although there were more juveniles involved in the juvenile justice system, fewer juveniles were appearing in the juvenile courts. In 1985, 175,600 juveniles came within the system compared with 164,000 in 1979. But only

63,100 juveniles were dealt with in the juvenile courts compared with 82,000 in 1979, a decrease of 23 per cent. It is not easy to explain this. One possibility is that the eligible population of potential juvenile offenders is declining. Pratt (1985a) has shown, using the O.P.C.S. statistics on the number of ten to seventeen year olds in the population, that between 1977 and 1984 there was a 9 per cent decline in this age group (see also Riley, 1986a). This overall figure masks a different rate of decline in the two age groups: ten to fourteen and fourteen to seventeen. The population declined by 15 per cent for ten to fourteen year old boys but only 2 per cent for fourteen to seventeen year old boys. Thus the largest decrease was in the age-group least likely to be referred to the juvenile court and so demographic changes per se are not likely to sufficiently explain the decrease in the juvenile court population.

Another possibility is that, in part as a response to earlier criticisms, police practices in the administration of cautions have changed so that diversion from the juvenile court if not from the juvenile justice system is now taking place. Certainly in the 1980s, the police became more willing to experiment with different forms of administering cautions and of selecting juveniles for cautions. This is discussed further later in this chapter.

Criteria for Diversion

Criteria for applying cautions, although not mentioned in the 1969 Act, were quickly established in police forces in the early 1970s. There were three main criteria, subsequently embodied in a Home Office circular of 1978 (70/1978):

1. the evidence against the juvenile must be sufficient to support a prosecution;

2. the juvenile must admit the offence;

3. the parents or guardian of the juvenile must agree to the caution being administered.

Once these primary criteria were satisfied, police forces then looked at a range of 'second tier' considerations which included the circumstances and seriousness of the offence, the wishes of the aggrieved persons and, frequently but not invariably, the recommendation made by the social services department or allied agencies (Home Office circular 70/1978, Home Office 1984b). The precise application of these criteria varied considerably depending upon the wording of local force orders (Laycock and Tarling, 1984). Moreover, research has demonstrated that their application was considerably influenced by the biases of and selection procedures employed by officers dealing with the juveniles concerned. This is best documented in the American literature. (See Rutter and Giller, 1983, 20 for a review.) Its overall conclusion was that police decisions to arrest were most strongly influenced by the seriousness of the offence, whether or not the suspect was a first offender, the attitude and demeanour of the suspect and the role of the victim. Thereafter, factors such as race and socio-economic status were also found to have a bearing on the decision.

The findings of Landau's (1981) study of the Metropolitan Police's decisions to directly charge (i.e. prosecute) or to refer juveniles to the juvenile bureaux (in which case a caution was a _possible_ outcome) were similar. He found that the primary decision was related to the type of offence involved and the previous criminal record of the juvenile. Superimposed on these, however, were the age and race of the offender. Older juveniles were more likely to be directly charged than younger, and black juveniles were more likely to be directly charged than white when apprehended for offences of violence, burglary and 'public disorder and other offences'. Variations were also related to where the offence was committed. Crimes of violence and public disorder were more likely to result in the juvenile being charged in run-down inner city areas, whereas burglary was more likely to lead to the juvenile being charged when committed in more prosperous suburban areas. Subsequently, Landau and Nathan (1983) went on to investigate the variables operating within the juvenile bureaux when deciding on cases referred to them. They found that while legal variables (previous record and type of offence) played a major role in the decision-making process, non-legal variables (age, area, ethnic group and parental control) also had a significant impact on the eventual outcome. Importantly, they concluded that the chances of black juveniles being cautioned were considerably lower than their white counterparts, especially when charged with a serious offence and where they were assessed as having a

problematic family background.
Landau and Nathan's statistical analysis must,
of course, be read alongside the more recent claims
of the Policy Studies Institute on the <u>Police and
People in London</u> (Smith <u>et al</u>., 1983), which were
referred to in Chapter 2. Observational data of
police encounters with young black people indicate
the existence of racial prejudice in the police (see
especially Smith and Gray, 1983, 137-150; Scraton,
1982). In particular, the police stereotype of the
West Indian family as disorganised led to assessments of family backgrounds as 'problematic'; these,
in turn, informed the decision whether or not to
caution (Smith and Gray, 1983, 163). The reports
also highlight young blacks' feelings of repression
by the police. As Smith and Gray note, however,
general attitudes of prejudice can be mediated in
specific instances, although they form an important
context to policing:

> Young people of West Indian origin tend to
> be hostile to the police in general terms
> but often assess their behaviour favour-
> ably in specific instances. In a comple-
> mentary way, we found from our observa-
> tional research that police tend to be
> hostile to black people in general terms,
> and certainly indulge in much racialist
> talk, but often have friendly and relaxed
> relations with individual black people in
> specific instances (1983; 334).

Earlier findings on the significance of the
seriousness of the offence and age as determinants
of police decision making in London were reported by
Bennett (1979) and Farrington and Bennett (1981).
In addition, they found some evidence that middle-
class juveniles were more likely than working-class
juveniles to be cautioned for serious offences and
that the level of co-operation received by the
police from the juveniles and their parents was also
significant. This was seen as an indication on the
part of the parents that they would exercise greater
control over the juvenile and that the juvenile recognised his or her culpability. Such findings were
replicated by Fisher and Mawby (1982) in a study of
the West Yorkshire police.

<u>The Organisation of Police Decision-Making</u>

Given the eclectic nature of the criteria of

police decision-making, incorporating both 'substantive and discriminatory judgments' (Landau and Nathan, 1983), it is not surprising that the use of the formal caution varies considerably among police forces. (3) Table 5.2 shows that, in 1985, for male juveniles the proportion formally cautioned (of all those cautioned or prosecuted) varied between 48 per cent in Humberside and 84 per cent in Northamptonshire. These variations do not solely reflect the differential crime rates of different police force areas. For example, the West Midlands police cautioned slightly more males (67 per cent) than the national average whereas the Greater Manchester police, with a broadly similar crime rate, cautioned considerably less (52 per cent). Moreover, neither the different criteria for cautioning contained in police force area orders nor variables related to the offender explain this variation. Laycock and Tarling (1984) have shown that while the proportion of first offenders (those most likely to receive a caution) in a particular police force has a bearing on the overall cautioning rate, it cannot account for the range of diversity. As Table 5.3 shows, whereas just under half of all those coming to the notice of the police in the Metropolitan area and in the Nottinghamshire area were first offenders (Column B), the overall cautioning rate was 37.3 per cent in the former and 60 per cent in the latter (Column A).

Understanding the reasons for these variations is further complicated by the fact that, in addition to the differential application of formal and informal criteria, there exist very different structural arrangements within police forces for decision-making (Tutt and Giller, 1983b). In the late 1960s, in view of the impending implementation of section 5 of the Children and Young Persons Act 1969, many police forces established special procedures and departments (frequently called 'juvenile bureau' or 'juvenile liaison offices') (4) to deal with referrals of juveniles to the police (including those referred for non-offence reasons). The Metropolitan Police District juvenile bureaux (Oliver 1978) was frequently used as the archetype for the organisational structure subsequently developed in other police forces in England and Wales. The organisation of this approach to police decision-making is illustrated in Figure 5.1.

Table 5.2 Males 10-17 years cautioned as a percentage of 10-17 year old males
found guilty or cautioned by Police force Area for England and Wales

%	
85	-
84	- Northamptonshire
	-
	-
	-
80	-
	-
	-
	-
75	-
	-
	-
	-
71	- Devon & Cornwall, Lincolnshire
70	- Bedfordshire, Cumbria, Thames Valley
69	- Wiltshire
68	- Suffolk, West Mercia
67	- Hertfordshire, West Midlands, Dyfed-Powys
66	-
65	- Northumbria
64	- Kent, Norfolk, Warwickshire
63	- Hampshire
62	-
61	- Nottinghamshire, North Wales
60	- Derbyshire, Leicestershire, Sussex
59	- Avon & Somerset, Essex, Gloucestershire, Merseyside, Metropolitan
58	- Durham, North Yorkshire
57	- Surrey
56	- Cambridgeshire, Lancashire
55	- Gwent
54	- Cheshire
53	- South Wales
52	- Cleveland, Greater Manchester, South Yorkshire, Staffordshire
51	- Dorset
50	- West Yorkshire
49	-
48	- Humberside

<u>Males</u>

National Average: England =   60%
                   Wales   =   56%

Source: Home Office 1986d

Table 5.3 Proportion of Juveniles Cautioned and Proportion of First Offenders and Recidivists Cautioned in Selected Police Forces

Police Force	Proportion of offenders cautioned	Proportion of offenders who were first offenders	Proportion of first offenders cautioned	Proportion of recidivists cautioned
	per cent A	per cent B	per cent C	per cent D
Norfolk	67.5	68.2	84.2	31.7
Suffolk	62.5	76.4	73.0	28.3
Nottinghamshire	60.1	46.2	94.1	30.0
Essex	59.7	60.3	88.6	18.9
Hampshire	56.3	61.9	81.3	15.7
Greater Manchester	48.3	56.0	77.4	11.2
Merseyside	46.6	52.8	69.9	20.5
Cheshire	45.0	54.2	69.0	16.6
Metropolitan Police	37.3	47.1	70.9	7.5

Source: Home Office, 1984b, 46.

Figure 5.1

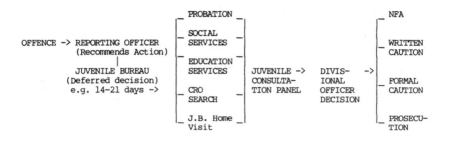

In this structure, the arresting or reporting
officer has little or no part in the decision-
making. On apprehension, the case is passed for
processing to a distinct group of police officers
dealing specifically with juvenile matters. These
officers have a broad range of responsibilities for
work with juveniles, including investigation of
cases of non-accidental injury, liaison with schools
and the community and dealing with juvenile delinquency. In deciding about a juvenile reported for an
offence, the bureau officers notify the various
social service agencies of the fact that the
juvenile has been apprehended, thereby providing
them with the opportunity to participate in the
decision if they have past or present contact with
the juveniles and their family. In some parts of
the country, police officers and social workers
actually work together on these investigations. For
example, the Exeter Joint Youth Support Team, established in 1979, brought together seconded police
officers, social workers and probation officers in
order to undertake joint investigations of juveniles
referred by the police for offences (Marshall,
1985). In other areas which have adopted this
structure, the bureau officers undertake a criminal
record search to see if the juvenile is previously
known to the police and visit the juvenile's home to
see if, in their opinion, the family environment
indicates a need for the juvenile to be separated
from it either voluntarily or compulsorily. The
police investigation, together with reports from the
other agencies, would then form the basis of a joint
discussion in an ad hoc consultative panel. This
panel makes (as in Exeter) or endorses (as in the

151

Metropolitan Police District) a recommendation for no further action, a caution or prosecution which is subsequently sent to a senior police officer for his approval. The senior police officer usually has the ultimate responsibility for decision-making in this structure; he must resolve disagreements between participants in the consultative panel and can reverse the decisions of the panel if there are special circumstances (for example, concern about the frequency of a particular type of offence in the area). Within this decision-making structure, it is not unusual for the process to take three to four weeks before a decision is taken.

Such a structure is by no means universal and many police forces have retained a more traditional organisation. This is illustrated in Figure 5.2.

Figure 5.2

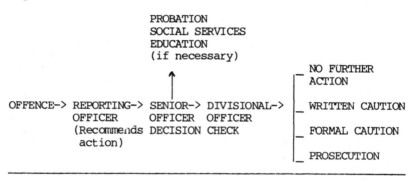

In this structure, the arresting or reporting officer has a major role in processing the juvenile offender, not dissimilar to the usual system of processing an adult offender. A recommendation for action by the reporting officer goes directly to a senior officer who is responsible for the decision at station level. His decision is usually made on the basis of police force orders on cautioning and does not necessarily demand prior consultation with other agencies or a home visit (unless further evidence is needed from the juvenile about the alleged offence). The senior officer may inform social service agencies of the juvenile's apprehension, but they are afforded no formal role in the decision-making structure and must instigate consultation themselves if they wish to bring matters concerning the juvenile or his or her family to the notice of the police. The senior officer´s decision is usually checked and endorsed by an officer with divisional responsibility before the decision is notified to the juvenile. Within this framework, decisions can be made in seven days or less. Such a procedure would, of course, have been impossible if section 5 of the Children and Young Persons Act 1969 had been implemented.

While these broad descriptions of the organisation of police decision-making became well established during the 1970s, more recent events have caused some rethinking to take place. Manpower constraints dictated by the escalating cost of police work and the growing demand for a more visible, accessible and hence decentralised police force have led many constabularies to review the appropriateness of existing decision-making structures for dealing with juveniles (Hough and Heal, 1982). Whatever the precise organisational structure now in operation, a large proportion of first-time offenders coming to the notice of the police received a formal caution (see column C, Table 5.3; Mott, 1983). This consistent finding has raised questions about the purpose of undertaking protracted and costly investigations by the police (or by other agencies) on the apprehension of a juvenile for a first offence. Moreover, to the extent that investigations into background factors can exacerbate the potential for discriminatory decision-making, limitations on the amount of ´soft´ information generated on a first referral is beneficial to the juvenile in reducing the labelling potential of the full application of the juvenile justice process (Farrington, 1977). The impact of these arguments is apparent in the emergence over the past six years of the procedure adopted by a variety of police forces of the ´instant´ or ´immediate´ caution.

Under this procedure, a juvenile arrested for a minor offence is taken to the police station, a criminal record check is made, the juvenile´s parents are informed and if the force criteria for cautioning are met, an instant caution is administered within hours of the arrest. This procedure was initially developed by Hampshire Police and led to the dismantling of the existing elaborate bureaux structures in favour of what was primarily promoted at the time as a manpower and cost-saving exercise. It has now been introduced in over thirty police forces (including the Metropolitan Police District), often alongside the traditional bureaux or liaison

structures which remain in operation for the investigation of cases outside the instant cautioning
criteria or for those juveniles who return to the
notice of the police after a formal caution.

Taken together, variation in the formal and
informal criteria employed by the police in their
decision-making and diversity in organisation,
policy and practice mean that disparities in
cautioning rates are not unexpected. In the late
1960s, the question was 'how can local juvenile
justice systems achieve a greater measure of
diversion?' Now, the question is 'how can we ensure
that juveniles committing similar offences in different police force areas have a similar likelihood
of receiving a caution even if the methods by which
they are processed are different?'

Rethinking Cautioning Policy and Practice

As the White Paper 'Young Offenders' (Home
Office et al., 1980, para. 3.8) made clear, the
government are in favour of expanding cautioning.
In 1981, the report of the Parliamentary All-Party
Penal Affairs group also stressed the need to
improve diversion in light of the practice of the
1970s. It made three recommendations:

1. The use of the caution should be sanc-
   tioned in legislation and attention
   should be given to achieving greater
   consistency in cautioning practice
   throughout the country.

2. All first time minor offenders under
   seventeen who admit guilt should be
   cautioned, and this should be the
   normal practice in regard to those who
   commit a second minor offence.

3. Formal cautions should not be administered where there is insufficient evidence for prosecution (1981, 10). (5)

At around the same time, the Royal Commission on
Criminal Procedure (1981) drew attention to incon-
sistencies in police prosecution practices and urged
the government to introduce the caution in legislative form and to put it on a more consistent basis.

The government's response to these proposals
was not to introduce legislation, but to establish a
working group of Home Office officials and Chief

Officers of Police to 'recommend a basis for more
consistent and effective police cautioning practice'
for both juveniles and adults (Home Office, 1984b).
The working party produced a consultative document
in 1984 and a circular implementing many of its
proposals was published in February, 1985 (Home
Office circular 14/1985; for a discussion, see
Giller, 1985a). (6)
The consultative document unequivocally recognised the potential of cautioning as a real diversionary strategy:

> There is no rule which says offenders
> must always be prosecuted; on the contrary
> the rule is that offenders should gener-
> ally only be prosecuted where there is
> sufficient evidence to do so and when the
> public interest requires it (1984b, 10).

Moreover, the harmful consequences of the criminal
justice process were fully acknowledged:

> It is recognised that there may be
> positive advantages for the individual and
> society, particularly in the case of
> juveniles, in using prosecution as a final
> resort: delay in the entry of a juvenile
> to the criminal justice system may prevent
> his entry altogether (1984b, 10).

The consultative document went on to argue that an
increase in cautioning could lead to greater
efficiency in the use of the courts. Other
advantages claimed were the expansion of the role of
social services and probation in consultation prior
to cautioning and, for the police, administrative
advantages and 'an enhancement in public confidence
in the way the criminal law is applied'. Draft
guidelines were contained in the consultative document and it was these, substantially modified and
expanded, which were published in Home Office
circular 14/1985.
The circular has three major policy intentions:

1) to expand offenders' opportunities of
real diversion by means of police
cautioning;

2) to encourage inter-agency liaison, in
favour of cautioning;

3) to develop greater consistency in cautioning decision-making.

To achieve the first aim, the circular warns of the dangers of ´widening the net`:

> A formal caution may be used and the juvenile thus brought within the fringes of the criminal justice system when less formal action may have been more appropriate and it should not follow that simply because a juvenile is brought to the police station formal action [a caution] is required, as against a decision to take less formal action, or no further action at all (14/1985, para. 7).

To avoid this, the circular states ´as a general principle in the case of first time juvenile offenders where the offence is not serious it is unlikely that prosecution will be a justifiable course`. Matters to be taken into account in determining ´seriousness` include ´whether significant harm has been done to a person, substantial damage has been done or property of substantial value has been stolen`. Offences of homicide, rape, arson, endangering life and serious public disorder are cited as examples of ´very serious` offences and as inappropriate for cautioning. The existence of previous cautions or convictions, however, is not to preclude subsequent cautions: ´a second or subsequent caution would only be precluded where the offence is so serious as to require prosecution`. This implies that each offence referral should be evaluated on its merits thereby intending to increase the proportion of recidivists cautioned, which traditionally has been a small number (see column D, Table 5.3). The significance of offence-related matters is reinforced by the statement that ´specifically it will not be right to prosecute a juvenile solely to secure access to the welfare powers of the court`. In the past, the views of the aggrieved party were major considerations in reaching a decision (Mott, 1983); but, under the circular, ´the interests of the victim, although a most important factor which needs to be weighed in deciding whether the public interest points to prosecution or to a caution, cannot be paramount`.

With these considerations in mind, three formal criteria must be satisfied before a caution is given:

(a) The evidence available must comply with the Attorney General's guidelines on criteria for prosecution, i.e. a conviction should be more likely than an acquittal. Cautioning should not be used as a substitute for a weak prosecution case.

(b) The juvenile must admit the offence, but, unlike the previous position, the juvenile must not only admit the facts which constitute the offence; he must recognise his <u>guilt</u>. If there is no such admission in circumstances in which otherwise there would have been a caution, the proper course is to take no further action.

(c) The parents or guardian must consent to the caution being issued, but parental consent should only be sought after it has been decided to caution the juvenile.

Inter-agency discussions, which can take place at any stage in the police decision-making process, are particularly encouraged by the circular where an immediate cautioning decision is not made, even though a prosecution is being contemplated.

At the time of writing, police forces are assimilating the circular into police force orders and it remains to be seen whether or not a greater degree of consistency in cautioning practice will be achieved by the application of the guidelines. In particular, evaluations of whether the guidelines produce ´real diversion` is essential, if somewhat complicated. Evaluations will need to look not only at the use of the formal caution as a measure of diversion but also at other outcomes, for example, whether or not ´no further action` decisions are used in some police force areas, not merely where the evidence is insufficient to bring a formal prosecution (as has traditionally been the case), but as a positive diversionary outcome.

Recent research on the operation of the first two years´ work of the juvenile liaison bureau in Northampton town (Crook, 1986) has done this. Following the lead of Wellingborough and Corby (Northamptonshire County Council, 1984), an inter-agency bureau comprising of teachers, social workers, police, youth workers and probation officers was established in 1984 to deal with all referrals of juvenile offenders with the intention, whenever possible, of diverting them from the juvenile court. In the year prior to the establishment of the bureau, 24 per cent of juvenile offenders in Northampton were prosecuted, 72 per cent were cautioned and 4 per cent were the subject of `no further action`. During the first year of the operation of the new scheme, 13 per cent of referrals were prosecuted, 64 per cent were cautioned and 23 per cent were the subject of `no further action`. Many of the `no further action` decisions (all of which were made after the juveniles admitted their guilt) involved the juveniles making an apology to their victim or returning the property stolen. In the second year of the scheme, however, `no further action` decisions declined to 14 per cent while cautions increased to 70 per cent and prosecutions to 16 per cent.

In other parts of the country, police forces in association with local social services departments and probation services are providing various schemes (involving befriending, activities and forms of reparation) for juveniles given a second or subsequent caution. In Kent, for example, pilot projects were established by the police in 1985 to provide activities for those given a second or subsequent caution. An earlier initiative for cautioning second-time offenders was that provided by the Cheshire police in its `Juvenile Volunteers Scheme` (Giller, 1983). (7) Under this scheme, the police linked volunteer `Aunts and Uncles` to juvenile offenders who had been cautioned for the purposes of providing help, guidance or advice. In some parts of the country (for example, in certain London boroughs), however, social services departments and allied agencies have refused to participate with the police in such initiatives because of the perceived dangers of the unintended consequences of `net widening` and labelling, while in others (such as Hampshire and Newcastle) the police themselves have not wished to enter inter-agency arrangements to provide diversion programmes for the same reasons.

Significant in any future evaluation of diversion will be an assessment not only of the role of the police, but also of the new `gatekeepers` to the court process, the Crown Prosecution Service. The Prosecution Service has the equivalent role in the processing of juvenile court referrals to that in adult cases and it remains to be seen precisely what impact, if any, this agency will have as a further 'filter' in the diversion of juveniles from juvenile court hearings. Instructions from the office of the Director of Public Prosecutions indicate that the prosecutors are to aim at consistency across their region in the practice of cautioning and prosecution and that inter-regional consistency will be a matter for review. What is equally clear, however, is that the Crown Prosecution Service will not be negotiating or bargaining with defendants, legal representatives or those offering diversion services as an alternative to prosecution in individual cases. The prosecutor's decision to discontinue a case ends proceedings there and then, leaving the police to determine in future whether to divert such cases rather than refer them for prosecution. While some have argued that the pattern of prosecution is unlikely to change radically with the introduction of the new service (Sanders, 1985), the experience of other jurisdictions, especially the United States, would suggest the contrary (Rubin, 1980).

In the United Kingdom, there is a precedent for a prosecutor playing a role in diversion in the Scottish children's hearing system (McCabe and Treitel, 1984; Martin et al., 1981; Morris and McIsaac, 1978). All applications for juveniles to be made the subject of compulsory measures of care in Scotland (from the police, procurator fiscal, social work department, education department or others) are made through the reporter. Such referrals are reviewed by the reporter to determine whether or not such compulsion is warranted and, if it is not, the case is dealt with other than by referral to the hearing. In 1984, some 23,715 offence referrals were made to the reporters of which 49 per cent were dealt with by a 'no action' decision, 6 per cent were referred back to the police for an informal warning and 3 per cent were referred to the social work department for some other form of intervention. Despite the welfare philosophy ostensibly underpinning the Scottish system, research suggests that the characteristics of the offence and the number of offences committed have a fundamental bearing on the reporters' decisions (Morris and McIsaac, 1978; Martin et al., 1981). Nevertheless, over the fourteen years of the operation of the Scottish system, the reporters' diversionary role has been consistently claimed to be a major strength of that system (Martin et al., 1981; McCabe and Treitel, 1984). But it is not as clear cut as this. The police in England caution and the reporters in Scotland take no action in roughly the same proportion of juvenile cases. The paradox is that the police are often criticised for 'net widening' and the reporters are often praised for diverting. To determine what is actually happening we need further information. For example, we need to know the rate of referral to the reporters and to the procurator fiscals per 1,000 of the population and their rate of referral to the children's hearings and to the courts. We need then to contrast these figures with the rates of cautioning and prosecution per 1,000 of the population in England. In the absence of such information, therefore, reporters may be doing no more in Scotland than the police do in England.

Whether or not the English prosecutor will have an impact on rates of diversion remains to be seen. If they do, it will be of interest to see whether or not <u>police</u> initiated diversion will fall to the level currently operating in Scotland. There, only 20 per cent of juveniles referred to the police in 1983 received a formal warning directly from them. Their open dislike and distrust of the Social Work (Scotland) Act 1968 has meant that, over the years, they have referred proportionately fewer juvenile offenders to the reporter. In 1983, they referred only 50 per cent of their cases directly to the reporter (McCabe and Treitel, 1984, 36). The remainder were sent to the procurator fiscal to be processed in the Sheriff's Court which can also deal with juvenile offenders. Confidence in the children's hearing system on the part of the procurator fiscals meant that they in turn referred many of these cases back to the reporter. (8) But the point remains. The police attempt to avoid in many instances the jurisdiction of the hearing.

Conclusion

It is unarguable that diversion from the juvenile court will remain a key issue in both English policy and practice. The arrangements for diversion within local systems are likely to continue to be diverse and involve a wide variety of programmes and agencies. In the face of this, there is a need to continue to evaluate the variety of organisational arrangements which are intended to produce diversion and to ensure that the criteria for diversion are consistently applied across local juvenile justice systems.

NOTES

1. Some describe removing juveniles from formal court proceedings and dealing with them in welfare tribunals (as in Scotland) as a form of diversion. Such arrangements, however, are essentially a substitution of one set of control networks for another (Morris, 1978a, 54-9).

2. It is difficult, however, to assess at any one time or in any one place precisely what proportion of juveniles were, arguably, `inappropriately` cautioned as information on cautioned offenders is poorly recorded. As a result, some have questioned whether `net widening` is a useful concept (Binder and Geis, 1984).

3. Variations in practice are also a feature within police force areas operating the same force orders.

4. Such schemes had existed in some police forces prior to that time (Mack, 1963). One should note that, within the police culture, such speciallist departments are not regarded as `real` police work, which is primarily categorised as crime control and detection (Smith and Gray, 1983; Lemert, 1981). Many remarks are made in jest about juvenile bureau officers. One description heard by one of us was as `Gurkhas` because their regimental motto is `We take no prisoners`. This marginal status within police culture has a long pedigree (Cain, 1968). As a consequence, officers seeking rapid advancement within the police have not sought these positions and the work has traditionally attracted little kudos.

5. Similar proposals were contained in the Black Committee's (1979) recommendations with respect to young offenders in Northern Ireland.

6. Legislation was rejected by the working party on the grounds that `this would not in itself bring about greater consistency in cautioning practice` and that `there would be a danger of imposing damaging rigidity on what is essentially a flexible system capable of adaption to both the circumstances of the individual offender and offences and to the wider requirements of the local community` (Home Office, 1984b, 7).

7. Within a short time of the scheme's inception, however, the criteria for entry changed and the initiative rapidly moved from a diversionary to a preventive programme (including the befriending of children under the age of criminal responsibility). The dangers of `net widening` and shifting criteria

for entry into diversion programmes make it vital for routine evaluation of schemes to take place.

8. In 1978, 1,639 juveniles were prosecuted in the Sheriff's Court (1 in 5 of those referred to the fiscal), whereas in 1982 only 667 juveniles were prosecuted (1 in 14).

Chapter 6

INSIDE THE JUVENILE COURT

Introduction

The juvenile court, its powers, procedures, participants and decision-making processes are the focal
point of recent debates on juvenile justice. In
this chapter, we provide a description of the
personnel of the juvenile court, an examination of
the adjudication process and an overview of the
range of dispositional powers available to the court
and the frequency of their use. We also explore the
main issues and themes which have been raised by
research into the operation of the juvenile court
and outline recent practice developments.

There have been a number of changes in the juvenile courts in the past fifteen years, changes in
policy, powers and personnel. In the 1960s, for
example, it was unusual for juveniles to be legally
represented; now it is relatively common. The
frequency of such representation, however, says
nothing of its content, style or effectiveness and,
as we shall see, each of these elements varies
depending on the context within which it occurs.
Similarly, the juvenile court traditionally relied
on a small group of probation officers to provide it
with background information on offenders. This has
been superseded by the introduction in the early
1970s of local authority social workers. These
welfare professionals also have a representational
role which, like their legal counterparts, must be
negotiated within a particular practice setting.

Juvenile Court Personnel

Juvenile courts in the 1980s look much as
they did at their inception in 1908. Very few juvenile courts are in buildings separate from the

magistrates' court although changes in architecture, building materials and design have made courtrooms somewhat less austere than their Victorian counterparts. A panel of magistrates drawn from the bench of each petty sessional division because of their experience or interest in juveniles are appointed to the juvenile court. This panel deals with both the criminal and civil aspects of the juvenile court's jurisdiction. Such sittings, however, usually form only a part of the magistrates' wider duties. In the Inner London area there is a distinct juvenile court bench.

Ordinarily, three magistrates sit in a juvenile case, at least one of whom must be a woman and one a man. It is not uncommon to find a preponderance of female magistrates on juvenile court panels. Similarly, younger magistrates are also encouraged to take on these responsibilities. Juvenile court magistrates can serve until they are sixty-five years of age, (1) although they can continue to sit in the magistrates' court until their seventieth birthday. While magistrates are lay people who are intended to represent the character of the local community, the selection process is such that they tend to be from the professional and social classes which have the time to undertake this type of public work (Baldwin, 1976). The Lord Chancellor's Department has attempted to broaden their base, but little change has occurred.

Induction training is now provided to all those appointed to the juvenile panel, as are refresher courses for longer serving magistrates and special courses for chairmen. Such training includes summaries of the law, practice developments, sentencing exercises and recent policy initiatives from both central and local government. Contributions are usually made by justices' clerks, social workers, probation officers, police officers and, occasionally, academics.

Magistrates sitting in the juvenile court in its criminal jurisdiction have two principal functions - to adjudicate guilt in contested cases and to impose the appropriate sentence after a finding or admission of guilt. In both these tasks, magistrates are assisted by the clerk to the court. The clerk, who is usually professionally trained in the law or undergoing such training, should have up to date information on the criminal law and on sentencing policy and practice. In addition to advising the magistrates on these matters, the clerk has a key role in ensuring the smooth administration of the court (for example, organising the rota of sittings for magistrates, constructing the listing of cases, separating contested and non-contested cases, organising adjournments for further hearings or reports). As McCabe and Treitel put it:

> The clerk is the closest of the magistrate´s confederates in the work of the court; indeed, he can be, and often is, the master of the whole proceedings (1984, 22).

Because of this, the clerk can make a particular contribution to setting the tone of the proceedings (either formal or informal) by allowing or denying the parties a participatory role and can control the flow of information which is used by the court (for example, the type of reports submitted to the bench and their distribution (Ball, 1984)).

The clerk´s influence also extends beyond the courtroom setting itself, in that the clerk usually controls the flow of general information to magistrates (for example, circulars from the Home Office, D.H.S.S. or local agencies) and frequently chairs meetings at which magistrates meet with others working in the juvenile justice system. Some clerks are eager to encourage magistrates to become directly involved in local initiatives dealing with juvenile offenders, for example, by sitting on management committees of community homes or intermediate treatment programmes. Others have resisted such involvement seeing it as a blurring of the boundaries between sentence makers and sentence providers. But communication between different agencies and the bench is becoming increasingly important due to an awareness that they are participating in a local juvenile justice system which is inter-dependent upon its constituent parts (Feeney, 1985) and which is enhanced by sharing information about the resources available (Pullinger, 1985).

Integral to providing resources to the juvenile court are the respective roles of the probation service and local authority social services department. The traditional connection between magistrates and the probation service was somewhat disrupted by the introduction of the 1969 Children and Young Persons Act which placed the primary responsibility for providing the juvenile courts with information (through social inquiry reports) and with community-based sentences in the hands of local social services departments. In practice, these responsibilities are frequently shared between the two agencies, with young persons being the responsibility of the probation service unless they are previously known (directly or through their family) to the social services department. Recently these arrangements have been reviewed and some probation services, in light of the Home Office statement of national objectives and priorities (Home Office, 1984c), (2) are now considering whether or not to withdraw their services from the juvenile court.

During the 1970S, much was made of the different abilities of the two services to provide what was seen by magistrates as credible support to the juvenile court. Magistrates frequently viewed probation officers as providing a better quality of service, both in terms of the reports they produced and the control which they exercised over the juvenile while on supervision. Thus magistrates lobbied central government to reinstate the probation service as the main service provider in the juvenile court (House of Commons Expenditure Committee, 1975, para. 39). Social services departments, at that time, were seen as nascent (or naive) and, being newly established, as untutored in the demands and expectations of the magistrates. Much was made of the lack of faith which magistrates had in social workers' administration of supervision and care orders, although the reason underlying these expressions of dissatisfaction was more likely to have been a perceived loss of power among magistrates rather than changes in actual practices (Morris and Giller, 1978). This contrast between probation officers and social workers is surprising, however, since both share a common professional training. Differences in practice, therefore, are likely to reflect the organisational context of their work rather than its theoretical orientation. Undoubtedly, the contact which magistrates had with the probation service through their work in the magistrates' courts and through serving on local probation committees sharpened the contrast. Magistrates met infrequently with social services departments.

In the 1980s, magistrates seem to be more accepting of social workers and the services they provide (McCabe and Treitel, 1984; Tutt and Giller, 1985a and b). Certainly the return of responsibility for juvenile matters to the probation service is now acknowledged to be politically unacceptable and social services departments are developing a range of strategies whereby magistrates are better informed of policy and practice initiatives with juvenile offenders through regular liaison meetings, invitations to magistrates to join management committees of intermediate treatment centres and the like. As between social workers and probation officers, however, there continue to be differences of perspective both as to the value of work in the juvenile court and the appropriate response to juvenile offenders. There also exist differences between probation officers and social workers about the use of various dispositions available to the juvenile courts. Whereas social workers increasingly question the value of supervision orders (without conditions) and seek to restrict their use to a mid-tariff disposition (that is, after two or three court appearances), probation officers frequently see supervision as a non-tariff measure and, as such, make recommendations for such orders early in an offender´s career. The implications of these different perspectives for sentencing are discussed in Chapter 7.

Finally, and increasingly frequently, legal representatives are present in juvenile courts, even in non-contested cases. For the prosecution, the police officer as a prosecutor or the prosecuting solicitor acting on behalf of the police has been replaced by the Crown Prosecution Service. This increased involvement of legal professionals in the prosecution system has been matched in recent years by an increase in the number of defendants legally represented. Whereas, in 1969, only 3 per cent of juveniles appearing in the juvenile court were represented with legal aid support, by 1984 the figure had reached 40 per cent. These figures do not include those cases in which representation has been privately financed and research suggests that, in some courts, over 70 per cent of juvenile defendants are represented in delinquency matters (Parker et al., 1981). This increased presence of lawyers is an important dimension in the day-to-day working of the juvenile court. Indeed, it may signify a fracturing of the traditional view that the juvenile courts´ decision-making is inexorably linked to the promotion of the welfare of the child. (This is discussed further in Chapter 8.)

In part, the increase in legal representation reflects the current policy that an adversarial forum is the most appropriate location for determining issues related to delinquency. This is apparent in various provisions of the Criminal Justice Act

1982 which extended the situations in which legal representation must be offered to juveniles, even when the juvenile court is considering the application of what were traditionally viewed as ´welfare´ measures.

Historically, proceedings in the juvenile court, even in delinquency cases, were viewed as non-adversarial; the juvenile´s interests were assumed to be identical with those of the state which sought to promote their welfare not their punishment. Legal representation, therefore, was thought to be not only unnecessary, but undesirable and even retrogressive. The spirit of this can be seen in the Kilbrandon Committee´s report (1964), which formed the basis of the Scottish children´s hearing system. In arguing for a welfare rather than a legal tribunal, Lord Kilbrandon, in a subsequent address, rejected legal representation in the following manner:

> The doctrine is a concomitant to the accusatorial or adversary system of criminal procedure. Certainly we hear nothing about "due process" in the nursery or the schoolroom where it would be totally out of place (1968, 2).

At the same time in England, the appropriateness of an adversarial forum and the right of delinquents to legal representation was one of the most fiercely fought battles in the formulation of juvenile justice policy (Morris and Giller, 1978). Threatened with proposals which would have abolished the juvenile court and substituted a family service or council, magistrates and others strongly argued that such proceedings would erode civil liberties and substantially disadvantage working-class children and their families. They claimed that the tribunal´s investigation of ´needs´ as a basis for intervention would lead to the imposition of more incursive measures than would be merited on the basis of proof of the offence and an assessment of the culpability of the offender. Although the juvenile court was retained in the 1969 Children and Young Persons Act, it operated during the 1970s with two philosophies: welfare and criminal justice. Magistrates were able to choose a welfare approach for some cases and a more traditional approach for others.

Given these two philosophies, it was not surprising that researchers found a wide variety of operational styles both between benches and within benches when dealing with ostensibly similar cases (Priestley et al., 1977; Parker et al., 1981; Anderson, 1978). Hence the role which legal representatives could play within the juvenile court and the impact they had on the decision-making process depended not only on their professional skills but, more importantly, on the particular orientation or ethos which the juvenile court adopted. As Morris has written:

> Certainly one cannot talk about the system, nor can one talk about the role of the lawyer or the effect of legal representation. These must vary to suit the demands, indeed the idiosyncrasies, of individual benches (1983, 131 emphasis in the original).

This is discussed further in Chapter 7.

Since juvenile courts' operational styles vary widely, there is little consensus as to the 'appropriate' role of legal representatives and, consequently, there is considerable potential for role confusion. Three possible roles or approaches to representation are documented in the literature (Giller and Maidment, 1984). First the amicus curiae approach, where the representative acts as an intermediary between the various participants and produces, presents and clarifies information to the juvenile court for the magistrates to make a decision 'in the best interests of the child'. This role implies that even information seemingly prejudicial to the juvenile should be put before the court if believed relevant to the decision. Secondly, there is the 'guardianship' approach where representatives make their own assessment of the juvenile's 'best interests' and present the plea and programme best calculated to achieve that end. Thirdly, there is the advocacy approach in which representatives act in a fully adversarial capacity to protect the interests of the juvenile as perceived by the juvenile. Here representatives represent their clients, in the words of the American Bar Association, 'zealously within the bounds of the law', by protecting the client's rights or, more emotively, working to 'beat the rap'. (3)

While these outlines of styles over-simplify some of the styles of representation actually used, they do delineate the broad terrain upon which the juvenile courts operate. At the present state of law and practice, there can be no definitive statement as to which form of representation is 'appropriate'. Consequently, often different styles of representation are used in similar cases, depending upon the representative's knowledge of the local juvenile court's ethos. More significantly, however, different representational styles may be used at different stages of the same case (for example, advocacy at the adjudication stage and 'guardianship' at the dispositional stage).

Evidence of role confusion has been more frequently documented in research on civil proceedings in juvenile courts than in criminal proceedings (Hilgendorf, 1981; Dingwall <u>et al</u>., 1983). Although civil proceedings are said to be essentially 'non-adversarial', there has been a considerable increase in the use of legal representation there due to recent changes in practice and legislation. (4) Rather than enhancing the process of testing the evidence of those applying to the juvenile court for compulsory intervention, however, research suggests that bargaining or negotiating cases has occurred out of court prior to the hearing. The court thus becomes relegated to a reviewing tribunal (Dingwall <u>et al</u>., 1983; Giller, 1985b). The danger of this, as Hilgendorf has noted, is that:

> The independence of the court is in jeopardy if the procedures are not followed... if the solicitors pre-empt the decision of the court...or if the case is not thoroughly presented or tested (1981,153).

Moreover, in civil proceedings as in criminal cases, the confusion relates primarily to the appropriate role which representatives should adopt in the juvenile court itself. In such circumstances, therefore, a quantitative increase in the amount of legal representation may have only a marginal impact on juvenile court decision-making, unless the content of representation is understood and accepted by all the participants involved. As one American commentator has put it:

> To advocate representation without delineating the nature or mode of that representation may be to advocate a hollow right (Bersoff, 1976, 34).

Due Process and Adjudication

The adjudication process is a relatively neglected field for research. Research on the disposition process, on the other hand, has produced a considerable body of knowledge, both in terms of the determinants of decision-making and of the impact which sentencing outcomes can have on developments or changes in juvenile justice policy. (This is discussed further in Chapter 7.) Several reasons lie behind this neglect of the adjudication process.

First, the majority of juveniles plead guilty. While an admission of guilt may be the result of negotiation between various officials in the juvenile court and the defendant, the routinised nature of most adjudication proceedings has led researchers to turn their attention towards the disposition process as a more fruitful and interesting topic for study. Secondly, because of the frequency of admissions, it is unusual for points of law or procedure to be contested in cases in which juveniles are involved. While particular rules do exist governing the assessment of a child's responsibility for criminal conduct (the doli capax principle), the dangers of relying on the uncorroborated testimony of juveniles and the protection of juveniles from publicity in juvenile court proceedings, in the main, the legal principles and procedures applied at the adjudication stage are substantially the same in the juvenile court as in the magistrate's court (Moore and Wilkinson, 1984). The third, and most important reason, for the lack of interest and research in adjudication is that the juvenile court in its origin was a tribunal of twin functions: adjudicating innocence or guilt and determining dispositions for juvenile offenders. As practice developed, the ´problematic` nature of this duality emerged. This was particularly so as the mechanisms for bringing welfare considerations to the notice of the juvenile court expanded (through the provision of reports) and the availability and range of welfare services increased. The way in which these two roles operate, mediated by magistrates making case-by-case decisions usually without giving reasons, means that, in practice, these seemingly distinct functions frequently become conflated and their underlying basis becomes obscured.

In theory, the operation of due process provides a procedure which tests the legal correctness of the case alleged against the offender. In

171

practice, research (Parker et al., 1981) shows that due process is an organisational construct which is open to re-definition by court personnel. In substantiating this claim, researchers have highlighted certain features of the operation of the juvenile court which question the neutrality of the concept of due process. First among these features is the physical setting of the juvenile court itself. McCabe and Treitel offer this (not atypical) observational account of a juvenile court-room layout:

> The court was arranged like a schoolroom. (5) The magistrates sat on a fairly high platform at one end of the room. In front of them, also on a raised platform, but slightly lower than the magistrates, sat the clerk and his assistant. In the first series of rows sat the prosecuting and defending solicitors. Others sat behind. At the back of the room sat two small defendants with their parents. The magistrates had a poor view of the defendants. They certainly could not have spoken to them over the distance that separated them. Questions were addressed to and answered by the legal representatives (1984, 20).

Within such a setting it is easy to see how the defendants and their parents gradually assume the mantle of the objects of the proceedings rather than its subjects. This process begins with the usher ´herding` the juvenile and his or her parents into the court, to quote Parker et al., ´with the verbal help of the clerk pushing and ordering them into their restricted space: "Parents behind their son,the defendant standing," then re-ordering them to fit into the order of the names on the charge sheet` (1981, 83). As the proceedings begin, so technical legal language comes into operation which further hampers the ability to foster dialogue between those administering the due process and those receiving it (Badham et al., 1984; Fears, 1977). With respect to entering a plea, for example, the clerk, after reading the charge to the defendant asks: ´Do you admit that?`. As Priestley et al., note, however, for the juvenile:

> The problem lies in the starkness of the options between which they must choose. If the accused wishes to introduce the

question of motive it must seem logical to
him to do it when the charge is put. (But)
technically he is expected to deny the
charge in such circumstances (1977, 879).

If legal representatives are involved then the possibility of foreclosing direct dialogue between the
bench and the defendant is all the greater. But the
presence of a lawyer can enable the defendant and
his or her parents to legitimately question the
nature of the charge or the prosecution's account of
the evidence in a way which does not fracture the
formal requirements of due process or backfire on
the defendant in the sense of throwing moral censure
on the questioner as direct, but inappropriate, dialogue might (Emerson, 1969).
   Research has claimed that legal representation
can ensure that justice is, at least, seen to be
done. Such a contribution, however, is not necessarily in the juveniles' interests. Parker et al.,
(1981), in describing the role of lawyers in the
legally-oriented 'City' court, record that one of
their major contributions was to negotiate and
bargain, both in and out of court, in order to
assist the procedural efficiency of the courts.
These negotiations covered matters frequently at the
heart of due process - the precise nature of the
charge or waiving 'not guilty' pleas for bind overs.
Whereas Parker et al., did not note a trend whereby this interpretation was more often than not to
the defendant's advantage' (1981, 55, emphasis in
the original), it is, at least, a situation which is
open to abuse. Also, during the adjudication
process itself, Parker et al., found that lawyers
were readily co-opted into the ideological framework
set by the bench and only rarely challenged it:

   The legal representative in City courts
   would try to produce a version of a
   previous event in terms of his interpretation of the 'way the bench thinks'. He,
   unlike the juvenile, is less concerned
   with what actually happened or indeed may
   try to avoid stating what actually
   happened...Their primary goal (is to)
   maintaining credibility with both court
   and client... (1981, 57-8).

Such strategic practice may provide the appearance
rather than the reality of due process.
   It is not only the formality of the language

used which questions the validity of due process, but also its content. The content of language alludes us to what frequently underpins the proceedings - the moral evaluation of the parties. (6) At one level, this moral evaluation is squarely directed at the defendants themselves. For example, at the adjucation stage, magistrates frequently seek evidence of remorse from defendants as an indicator of their potential for redemption and of their submission to the authority of the juvenile court and the law. Priestley et al., illustrate this process in the following observations:

> When the police case has been presented... magistrates often ask supplementary questions about the offence events and invite comments from the juvenile. A typical opening in such exchanges is a neutral, "Is there anything you wish to say?" Most children say nothing or mutter inaudibly at this point. A few express conventional regret: "I´m sorry I did it and for all the trouble I´ve caused. It won´t happen again". If there is no reply or an attempted justification is made, the bench may openly request that contrition be shown (1977, 89).

Questioning from the bench is not necessarily a neutral fact-finding exercise. The responses proffered by defendants as ´explanations` can be used by magistrates as confirming previously suspected dubious moral character. Parker et al., demonstrate this point in the following exchange:

> In interrogating a boy as to what he did when truanting from school a senior magistrate was told, "We play footie, go places, go to the cinema if I´ve got money". The reply from the bench was crisp: "Ah! You muck around all day and con your mother" (1981, 90).

Moral evaluations are made not only of defendants, however; questions routinely encompass parental competence in controlling their offspring and the quality of parental support in the home. This, of course, is most readily assessed by magistrates by the presence or absence of parents at the court hearing. In one court observed by Parker et al.:

Officials wanted to know, before the finding of guilt, whether they were dealing with a single parent family, or whether the father was in prison or even in bed. For when both parents were present the clerk often referred only to one of them, not necessarily the father. The father's presence was apparently not as necessary as his absence was unacceptable. Only the working father was not chastised in and for his absence (1981, 83-4).

Evaluations of parental competence relate not only to the parents' immediate reaction to the offence itself (the punishment or otherwise of the juvenile prior to the court appearance (Priestley et al., 1977, 91)), but also to the nature and character of the family. Given that the majority of the defendants appearing in the juvenile court are working-class, the investigation tends to concentrate on whether they fall into the category of a 'respectable' or 'criminal' family. The magistrates' previous acquaintance with the family through the sentencing of another child of the family or of the mother or father assists in this assessment. However, even unknown families can attract negative assessments by 'inappropriate' challenges of police evidence, questioning court officials or making statements which are felt to be attempts to 'con' the court.

How overt the issue of moral evaluation is in any particular court does, of course, vary. As Parker et al., (1981) have shown, the ideological ethos of a bench can differ markedly even in neighbouring petty sessional divisions. In a study of two neighbouring courts, Parker et al., found that one, 'Countryside', through the removal of the safeguards of due process got close to a simple refusal of justice. Conversely, Parker et al.'s other court, 'City', extended civility to defendants, rigorously respected due process through the use of legal representation and utilized a fully graduated tariff range of interventions to produce a 'rational response to the reality of urban crime' (1981, 75). In spite of these contrasting styles, however, at the heart of decision-making lies moral evaluations. While different criteria may be used and different conclusions drawn, the offence as charged is merely the medium through which evaluations are made and presumptions tested, countered or confirmed. Donzelot has referred to this process as the 'dematerialisation of the offence`:

> There is a dematerialisation of the off-
> ence which places the minor in a mechanism
> of interminable investigation, of perpet-
> ual judgment. The break between the
> investigation and the decision is obliter-
> ated. The spirit of the laws...requires
> that more consideration be given to the
> symptomal value of the actions of which
> the minor is accused, to what they reveal
> concerning his temperament and the value
> of his native milieu, than to their mater-
> iality. The investigation is meant to
> serve more as a means of access to the
> minor's personality than as a means of
> establishing the facts (1979, 110-11,
> emphasis in the original).

As Donzelot intimates, within such an all-embracing
investigation, the adjudication process becomes an
inexorable part of the sentencing process. The
moral evaluations made by the bench (whatever their
cultural or contextual expectancies) at the adjudication stage are derived from an investigation of
the same determinants which later inform the sentencing decision (Emerson, 1969).

Consumer Views of the Juvenile Court

Thus far, the problems identified with the
adjudication process have been approached from the
view-point of the outside observer or analyst. What
of the clients of the juvenile court system? Are
the confusions identified in both the philosophy and
practice of juvenile justice decision-making communicated to them?

Consumers' views of the juvenile court process
have, until recently, been an under-researched area
(Parker, 1978). Work which preceded the partial
implementation of the Children and Young Persons Act
1969 (Scott, 1959; Voelcker, 1960) suggested that
children and parents saw the juvenile court
primarily as a retributive tribunal. More recent
work tried to ascertain the clients' perspectives in
light of the (presumed) movement of the juvenile
court towards a social welfare or reformist ideology, and, in particular, tried to ascertain whether
or not the views of clients had changed ((Morris and
Giller, 1977; Parker et al., 1981).

This research suggests that the formalism of the juvenile courtroom creates an alien world for those appearing before it. (7) The researchers found that the organisation of the juvenile court was negatively evaluated (for example, consumers disliked the lack of an appointment system) and that the respective roles of key personnel were inadequately communicated to, and hence frequently misunderstood by, parents and their children. For example, the important distinction between the roles of the magistrates and the justices' clerk was often not understood by them. Also the assorted individuals who often sit in the juvenile court while a case is being heard but who are not associated with it (social workers, probation officers, education welfare officers) were frequently assumed to be participating in the decision-making process.

Given the physical setting of the juvenile court, it is not surprising that effective communication between the participants is problematic. For example, the social distance between the adjudicators and the adjudged can lead to a lack of comprehension about what is going on or what is being asked. Fears (1977) has demonstrated that the elaborate language codes of the former (usually middle-class) are not familiar to the latter (usually working-class). The initial making of the plea to the charge, for example, with the choice of 'admitting' or 'denying' the offence can pose problems for juveniles. These are not the words they expect to hear; they are accustomed rather to notions of 'guilty' and 'not guilty'. Attempts to simplify the language (as introduced in the Children and Young Persons Act 1933) confused rather than clarified the question. Moreover, once evidence of the offence is laid, there is sometimes expressed a feeling that the police cannot be challenged and that such an advantage is (mis)used to 'bump up' the nature of the charges and to 'criminalise' and 'decontextualise' a complicated series of events (Parker et al., 1981, 109; Morris and Giller, 1977). Of course, such elaborations not only have an impact on the adjudication process; they may also affect how magistrates view the offence for the purposes of determining a disposition. Not surprisingly, therefore, juveniles frequently see the juvenile court as 'a confusing, remote and primarily punitive agency' (Morris and Giller, 1977).

In such an alienating environment, parents and children, on the whole, value the contributions of the lawyers who represent them. This is so even though by objective standards the quality of legal representation in the juvenile court is not of the highest order (Morris, 1983). For example, Parker et al., (1981) recorded that the solicitors they observed were ill-prepared, confused, indifferent and often encouraged their clients to enter guilty pleas in order to assist the juvenile court in its smooth-running. Nevertheless, the majority of the juveniles and their parents interviewed by Parker et al., reported satisfaction with the quality of the legal representation they received. The reasons Parker et al., cite for this are that the lawyers were frequently the only ones who unequivocally showed themselves to be on the side of the defendant and who actively prepared the juvenile and his or her parents for what might happen. The parents and children also tended to over-estimate what would happen to them in terms of disposition and thus they believed that the representatives had influenced the eventual outcome. As Parker et al., comment, their perceptions of lawyers can be:

> explained by the lack of analytic and com-
> parative knowledge defendants have with
> which to judge the performance of their
> legal representatives (1981, 126). (8)

Some commentators (for example, Martin et al., 1981, 234) have contrasted parents´ and children´s satisfaction with the children´s hearings in Scotland with their dissatisfaction of the adjudication process in England. But, as Bottoms notes:

> The Scottish system of children´s hearings
> tends to score with parents and children
> especially in its procedural aspects - the
> proceedings are more comprehensible, less
> confusing, and there is a valued sense of
> participation. The English consumer
> studies´ apparent support for a ´justice
> model` approach derives not so much from
> procedure as from the final dispositions -
> children and their parents favour disposi-
> tions based upon offence rather than wel-
> fare criteria. Thus the two sets of
> results relate to different aspects of the
> work of juvenile tribunals and are not
> necessarily incompatible (1985, 106).

We shall discuss parents´ and children´s views of dispositions in Chapter 7. Now we outline the dispositions available to the juvenile court.

Disposition Powers in the Juvenile Court

In this section, we describe the powers of disposition available to the juvenile court. These
have been substantially changed with the introduction of the Criminal Justice Act 1982 (Tutt and
Giller, 1983a). In part, as we noted in Chapter 4,
the intention of this legislation was to provide the
magistrates with an increased and strengthened range
of non-custodial penalties for dealing with juvenile offenders. However, the Act also provided them
with increased custodial powers. Our description of
dispositions starts with those involving the least
intervention with the juvenile's life through to the
custodial sanctions. Further detailed information
on these powers can be obtained in the handbook 'The
Sentence of the Court' (Home Office, 1986b; see
also Moore and Wilkinson, 1984; Ashworth, 1983).

Bind-Over (Recognisance)

The juvenile court can order a juvenile to
undertake to pay a fixed sum of money if he or she
subsequently misbehaves over a period of up to three
years. As such, a bind-over resembles a suspended
fine. A bind-over can be made in addition to or
instead of another disposition and it is not limited
to those against whom there has been a finding of
guilt or admission. It can be imposed on any person
involved in the offence including the complainant.
A bind-over can also be made up to the sum of £500
against a parent or guardian, as a way of making
them exercise proper control over their child. The
party must agree to the imposition of a bind-over.
If later 'misbehaviour' takes place, the juvenile
court can order that all or part of the original sum
be paid over. Bind-overs are not widely used in the
juvenile court and are most frequently made in minor
and public order offences.

Absolute Discharge

This is generally considered to be the most
lenient penalty which the juvenile court can impose
and it is usually imposed in situations in which the
magistrates believe that no penalty is justified,
for example, where the breach of the criminal law
was technical. It is infrequently used and, in part,
this is due to the willingness of the police to

caution juveniles for minor offences. There are some indications that in areas with a low rate of cautioning absolute discharges are used more frequently than elsewhere. As Ashworth notes:

> A court will generally reserve the absolute discharge for a case where there is little moral guilt in the offence, where mitigating factors are overwhelmingly strong...or in other cases where it is thought inexpedient to punish, and indeed in some cases where the court thinks it wrong a prosecution should have been brought (1983, 3).

Conditional Discharge

A conditional discharge means that the offender will be discharged if he or she commits no further offence within a period of up to three years. If the offender is convicted of another offence within the period specified, then he or she may be sentenced for both the new offence and the original offence. Conditional discharges are a popular measure in juvenile courts and accounted for over 20 per cent of sentences in 1984. In the main, they are imposed on those appearing in the juvenile court for the first time.

Compensation Orders

Section 67 of the Criminal Justice Act 1982 changed the juvenile courts' powers to make compensation orders. Previously such orders could only be made in addition to some other penalty (usually a fine). Compensation orders are now penalties in their own right. Magistrates can award up to £1,000 for any one offence. The magistrates can also make an order against the parent or guardian. This power is discussed further in the section on fines.

Fines

Fines are the most frequently used disposition in the juvenile court and accounted for nearly 25 per cent of sentences in 1985. For children, the upper limit of a fine is £100 and, for young persons, it is £400. While fines are often imposed upon those appearing in the juvenile court for the first time, they are also used for minor offences even where more severe dispositions (including care orders and custodial sentences) have been used previously. Failure to pay a financial penalty can lead to an attendance centre order being imposed on the juvenile.

Significant changes in the power to fine (and to award costs and compensation orders against) parents were introduced by sections 26 to 28 of the 1982 Criminal Justice Act. The juvenile court now has a duty to impose these financial orders against the parents or guardian of the juvenile rather than the offender unless the court is satisfied that:

> the parent or guardian cannot be found; or it would be unreasonable to make an order for payment, having regard to the circumstances of the case.

The parents or guardian have a right to be heard before such orders are imposed and they are given distinctive rights of appeal to the Crown Court and subsequently to the Court of Appeal against such orders. The power to enforce fines and other financial awards against parents is the same as that in other courts (that is, ultimately, imprisonment). In 1985, some 26 per cent of fines and 35 per cent of compensation orders imposed on juveniles were 'parents to pay' orders (Home Office, 1986d). The intention behind this change in the law was to make parents more accountable for the delinquent acts of their offspring (Home Office et al., 1980). Research indicates, however, that there are practical difficulties in realistically expecting parents to control the day-to-day activities of their children (Shaw, 1986; Riley and Shaw, 1985; Wright, 1983; Parliamentary All-Party Affairs Group, 1981, para. 91). Wilson (1982) argues that juveniles from strict homes who become delinquent will have done so without their parents' knowledge or, at least, against their parents' advice. In such circumstances, she claims that 'it would be unjust and unwise to require parents...to answer for the acts of their children by paying their fines' (1982, 31). Juveniles from homes where there is some degree of supervision may also have drifted into delinquency without their parents' knowledge. Whether these parents would be encouraged to take greater control over their children by being fined is, according to Wilson, questionable. She goes on:

> In homes where discipline is lax the youngsters who become delinquent will

typically see themselves as independent persons who have been given free rein by their parents at an early stage. The (fine) would probably be received with some anger by their parents, who would consider these measures as quite inappropriate, especially for the over 14s, whereas the youngsters may welcome the shift of punishment with mirth. Parents who are lax in handling their children are not necessarily negligent towards them... many lax parents live under considerable stress. Debts, rent arrears, unemployment, sickness, invalidity and other adverse conditions are not conducive to good child-rearing practices, and the imposition of the payment of their children's fines on such parents would not lead to better parenting methods (1982, 32).

Attendance Centre Orders

Attendance Centres were introduced by the 1948 Criminal Justice Act as a "short, sharp, shock" to deprive offenders of their leisure time at weekends. The 1969 Children and Young Persons Act intended to replace attendance centres with schemes of intermediate treatment but this policy has now been reversed. There are currently 109 junior attendance centres in England and Wales (89 for boys, seven for girls and thirteen for both sexes). Orders last for up to twelve hours for ten to fourteen year olds and for between twelve and twenty-four hours for fourteen to seventeen year olds. In 1985, 20 per cent of children and 15 per cent of young persons were made the subject of attendance centre orders.

The majority of attendance centres are run by the police (a few are run by social services departments, education departments or the probation service) and occupy schools or similar public buildings for two to three hours on a Saturday afternoon. Police officers working in the centres do so as civilians and are assisted by staff with particular skills - teachers or instructors. The activities at the centre usually combine physical exercise with some handicrafts training, but some attendance centres include social skills, remedial education and counselling.

Research (Gelsthorpe and Tutt, 1986) suggests that juvenile courts' use of attendance centres is dependent upon local conditions. Some appear to use them as a direct alternative to fines and discharges while others use them as an alternative to supervision orders (with or without conditions). Nearly half of the attendance centre orders made are imposed on those who have no previous sentences and such orders are rarely made on those with three or more previous convictions (Gelsthorpe and Tutt, 1986; Tutt, 1985; Gelsthorpe and Morris, 1983; Dunlop, 1980). An offender who fails to attend when ordered, or who breaks the rules of the centre can be returned to the juvenile court and sentenced for the original offence.

Supervision Orders

Supervision orders place the juvenile under the supervision of a supervising officer for a period of up to three years. Supervision is usually undertaken by a social worker in the local social services department, although it can be undertaken by the local probation service. (9) The nature and content of supervision is at the discretion of the supervising officer, but research suggests that practice is fairly routine (Giller and Morris, 1978; Jones, 1983). Frequently it takes the form of weekly meetings during the first three to six months of the order and then tapers to monthly or less regular meetings. Research also suggests that probation officers tend to insist on a series of office-based reporting interviews and that social workers tend to pay more visits to the juvenile´s home (Harris and Webb, 1983; Parker et al., 1981). Both professional groups, however, express a degree of uncertainty as to the purpose of supervision orders without conditions (Webb and Harris, 1984). (10) The lack of agreement about the content of supervision was a major criticism of supervision from its introduction in the 1969 Children and Young Persons Act. Consequently, there was a steady decline in its use. In 1970, 24 per cent of juvenile court dispositions were supervision orders while, in 1984, it was 18 per cent.

Proportionately more supervision orders are made on girls (22 per cent for children and 20 per cent for young persons) than boys (18 per cent for children and 17 per cent for young persons). Recently Webb (1984) argued that such practices reflect discrimination against female offenders. He showed that girls recommended for and made the subject of supervision orders included a higher proportion of girls who had committed minor offences or

183

who had no criminal history. For example, 30 per cent of boys on supervision orders had committed minor offences compared with 39 per cent of girls. More dramatically, 46 per cent of boys and 75 per cent of girls given supervision orders were appearing in court for the first time. Walker (1985) has questioned Webb´s conclusion because a greater proportion of all girls appearing in the juvenile court are minor or first offenders. Hence, she argues, discriminatory practices cannot be determined on the basis of supervision order figures alone. However, if sex is not a relevant variable in the decision-making of report writers and juvenile courts one would expect female minor and first offenders to receive discharges or low fines.

In order to increase the use of supervision orders by magistrates, a number of conditions can be attached to the order. These are:

Intermediate Treatment. A requirement can be added to a supervision order which enables the supervisor to direct the supervised person to participate in activities for a period of up to ninety days. These provisions were intended to replace attendance centres, detention centres and borstal training for juvenile offenders. However, in practice, they were little used in the 1970s. Intermediate treatment was viewed then as lacking a coherent philosophy and strategy (Thorpe et al., 1980). Moreover, when intermediate treatment requirements were imposed, implementation was at the discretion of the supervisor and this could mean that little was in fact done (Webb and Harris, 1984).

A new financial initiative to develop intermediate treatment as a direct alternative to care and custody was launched by the D.H.S.S. in 1983 (circular LAC, 1983 (3)). Research indicates that in some local juvenile justice systems this has reduced the number of juveniles being removed from the community (Tutt and Giller, 1985b; Social Information Systems, 1986). The term ´intermediate treatment`, however, is still used by social workers and others to describe a wide range of programmes and projects directed at non-delinquent, disadvantaged juveniles or those said to be ´at risk` of delinquency. Attempts have been made recently, on the other hand, to reserve intermediate treatment for those juveniles sentenced by the courts as an alternative to care or custody (John, 1986). These revisions have taken the form of confronting juveniles with their delinquent behaviour through individual and group-work exercises and developing with them alternative strategies for dealing with opportunities to offend (Denman, 1982). Such programmes can be linked to victim-offender or community-based reparation schemes, activity groups and discussions of social problems, (for example, youth unemployment, and solvent and drug abuse (Rutherford, 1986, 138-147).

Supervised Activity Requirements. Newly introduced in the Criminal Justice Act 1982 (11) to strengthen magistrates' confidence in supervision as a community-based alternative to care and custody, these requirements are the same in form as the intermediate treatment requirements except that it is for the juvenile court magistrates, rather than the supervisor, to determine the nature of the activity programme in which the juvenile must participate and the duration of the requirement (up to ninety days). Supervised activity requirements cannot be imposed in addition to intermediate treatment requirements.

The respective positions of intermediate treatment and supervised activity requirements in the tariff is not clear. In some areas, supervised activities have been used explicitly as alternatives to care and custody with intermediate treatment being used earlier in the tariff. In other areas, however, the opposite has occurred and, in still others, the juvenile courts do not appear to have differentiated between the two (Social Information Systems, 1986).

Night Restriction Requirements (Curfew). These were also introduced in the Criminal Justice Act 1982. (12) The juvenile court can now attach to a supervision order a requirement which orders the juvenile to remain in the place he or she lives for ten hours between 6 p.m. and 6 a.m. for a maximum period of thirty days within the first three months of a supervision order. The original intention was that this would be a sentence in its own right. During the Committee stage of the Criminal Justice Bill, however, it was adopted as a condition of supervision. Opposition by social work professionals to this condition and difficulties in its enforcement have meant that it is not widely used (Tildesley and Bullock, 1983).

Refraining Conditions. Since the implementation of of the 1982 Act, (13) the juvenile court can also

now order a supervised person to refrain from participating in certain activities specified in the
order for certain days or for the whole of the supervision order. No definition of ´activities` was
included in the Act but, presumably, this could
include requiring the juvenile to refrain from
attending football matches, discos and other such
activities associated with his or her offending.

All the new conditions require magistrates to
consult with the proposed supervisor as to: the
offender´s circumstances, the feasibility of securing compliance with the requirements, and the
necessity of the requirements to secure the good
conduct of the juvenile or for preventing a repet-
ition by him or her of the same offence or the
commission of other offences. The supervised person
or, if a child, his or her parents or guardian,
must consent to the inclusion of the requirement in
the supervision order.

In 1985, less than twenty requirements of night
restriction and refraining conditions were recorded
as having been imposed on juveniles. There were
positive requirements for activities recorded in
2,100 cases, that is 18 per cent of all supervision
orders (Home Office 1986d, 11. Breach of a
supervision order can lead to the juvenile being
returned to the juvenile court. The court then has
the power to fine him or her up to £100, make an
attendance centre order or substitute a care order
for the supervision order. Recent government
proposals have suggested that the juvenile courts be
given wider powers to deal with the breach of
supervision orders, especially where the order is
made with requirements which are intended to be a
direct alternative to custody (Home Office, 1986a,
para. 22). Non-compliance with a supervision order
in the future could lead to the imposition of a care
order or custodial sentence for the original
offence.

Community Service Orders

Schedule 12 of the Criminal Justice Act 1982
introduced the community service order for juveniles
of sixteen years or more where such a scheme is
available to the juvenile court. Such schemes are
organised and administered by the probation service
and the orders can be for any period up to 120
hours. Provision for community service is now
available in all of the 56 probation areas in
England and Wales and in 1985 was used for 1,900

males and 100 females, that is 6 per cent of sentences imposed on sixteen year olds (Home Office, 1986d). In practice, distinctive schemes have not been developed for sixteen year olds and community work is undertaken alongside young adult and adult offenders. Failure to carry out work under a community service order can lead to the juvenile being returned to the juvenile court to be dealt with in any way in which he or she could have been dealt with by the court making the original order.

Care Orders

Care orders for offending (14) place parental rights over the juvenile into the hands of the local authority until the age of eighteen years (or until nineteen if the order is made when the young person is sixteen years or above). The order gives discretion to the local authority social services department to place the juvenile wherever it is thought appropriate, including returning the juvenile to his or her natural parents. Social workers' practice with respect to care orders on offenders came under severe criticism from magistrates and others during the 1970s (Thorpe et al., 1980; Giller and Morris, 1981a and b). Magistrates believed that when a care order was made social workers exercised no effective control over the juvenile and merely returned them to their own homes where they would continue to offend. Academics, on the other hand, criticised social workers' use of such orders early in an offender's criminal career and for minor offending. (These issues were discussed in Chapter 3.) Section 23 of the Criminal Justice Act 1982 introduced new criteria which must be satisfied before care orders can be made in criminal proceedings. These are where: it is appropriate because of the seriousness of the offence; and the child or young person is in need of care or control which he or she is unlikely to receive unless the court makes the order. In addition, section 24 of the Act introduced the right to legal representation before such an order is made. In 1985, under 1,500 care orders were made on the basis of offences, that is less than 3 per cent of all sentences on juveniles. This decline of over two-thirds from the number of such orders made in 1975 is due not so much to the introduction of the new statutory criteria (which post-date the decline in the use of care orders), but to an increasing awareness of the unintended consequences of such orders (this is discussed in Chapter 7) and to a decline in the availability of residential provision for this age group.

Care Orders with Charge and Control Conditions

Following magistrates' demands in the 1970s to have more control over the placing of juveniles subject to care orders for offences, the 1982 Criminal Justice Act (section 22) introduced a new power which enables the juvenile court to restrict, in certain circumstances, the 'charge and control' of the juvenile from specified 'parents, guardians, relatives or friends'. Thus where a juvenile is already on a care order for an offence, and he or she commits a further offence, the juvenile court can make a care order which restricts the charge and control of the juvenile for a period of up to six months. (15) Before doing this, the juvenile court must be satisfied that the condition is necessary because of the seriousness of the offence and that no other method of dealing with the juvenile is appropriate. It must also give the juvenile the opportunity of legal representation. Both the juvenile and the local authority social services department can appeal to the Crown Court against the imposition of a 'charge and control condition'. They can also (as can the parent or guardian of the juvenile) apply to the juvenile court for a revocation or variation of the condition. Despite the long history of demands for such a provision by the Magistrates' Association only seventy 'charge and control conditions' were attached to care orders in 1985, that is 5 per cent of all care orders (Home Office, 1986d).

Secure Accommodation

Section 25 of the Criminal Justice Act 1982 introduced for the first time a judicial review of local authorities' use of secure accommodation for juveniles in their care, irrespective of whether or not offending was the reason for entry into care. The provision of secure accommodation increased dramatically throughout the 1970s (Millham et al., 1978; Cawson and Martell, 1979). Its use was, however, previously simply an administrative act. The juvenile so placed had no judicial or statutory safeguards. Proposals for review in the juvenile court of the use of secure places were made by the D.H.S.S. in 1981 and the 1982 Act introduced new procedures. (16) Regulations made under the Act

(Secure Accommodation (No. 2) Regulations 1983) allow a local authority to detain a juvenile in their care in secure accommodation approved by the Secretary of State for up to 72 hours (over a period of 28 days) if they are satisfied that the juvenile has a history of absconding and is likely to abscond and, if he or she absconds, it is likely that his or her physical, mental or moral welfare will be at risk or that, if he or she is kept in any other accommodation, he or she is likely to injure himself or herself or other persons. If detention in secure accommodation is required beyond 72 hours, the local authority must apply to the juvenile court for an order demonstrating that the above conditions continue to apply. The court can, if satisfied, order an extension of the use of the secure placement for up to three months on a first application and, thereafter, if satisfied that the conditions continue to exist, for further periods of up to six months. The juvenile has a right to legal represen- tation at these hearings and a right of appeal against the orders to the Crown Court.

Since the implementation of these regulations, the number of secure places approved by the Secretary of State has declined. Table 6.1 demonstrates this.

Table 6.1:   Secure Accommodation in Community Homes, Approved for Use at 31 December

England and Wales	1982	1983	1984
Places in secure units in			
- Observation and			
Assessment Centres	231	213	199
- Community Homes with			
Education	200	158	171
Secure Separation Rooms	54	22	12
TOTAL	485	393	382

Source: House of Commons, 1985.

This has been matched by a decline in the number of juveniles placed in secure accommodation (Tutt and Stewart, 1986). As a recent Report from the

Secretary of State for Social Services put it:

> On 31 March 1984 there were 364 approved
> secure places in community homes of which
> 241 were occupied (196 boys and 45 girls).
> The majority of children (170) had been in
> secure accommodation for less than three
> months; 27 for between three and six
> months; 28 for between six and twelve
> months, and sixteen in excess of one year
> ...The data for 31 March 1984 suggests
> that, when compared with a survey on the
> use made of secure accommodation in 1980,
> there has been a marked reduction in the
> number of children spending longer periods
> in security since the introduction of new
> legislation governing such placements
> (House of Commons, 1985, 26).

Detention Centre Orders

Detention centre orders can be made on boys
aged between fourteen and seventeen years and, since
the implementation of the Criminal Justice Act 1982,
these orders can be for a minimum period of 21 days
to a maximum period of four months. Periods of
remand in custody (but not remands in care) prior to
the making of the order are deducted from the time
to be served and one-third remission is deducted for
good conduct in the detention centre. On release,
the detention centre trainee is on supervision for
three months. This can be undertaken by the
probation service or the social services department.
Failure to comply with the conditions of supervision
on release is punishable by way of a fine (of up to
£200) or by a further thirty days in custody.

In 1985, 4,000 male young persons were given
detention centre sentences, that is 8 per cent of
sentences on this age group. This represents a
decline in the use of detention centres (especially
from 1981 when over 6,000 such orders were made),
although the proportionate use of the sentence is
similar (10 per cent in 1981). The reason for this
decrease seems to be related not so much to the
impact of the statutory criteria contained in the
1982 Criminal Justice Act but to the increased use
of youth custody. Indeed, the recent White Paper on
`Criminal Justice Legislation` (Home Office, 1986a)
proposes that those sentenced to short periods
of youth custody should serve their sentences
in detention centres in order to make use of
vacancies there. (17)

Youth Custody Sentences

Section 6 of the Criminal Justice Act 1982 introduced youth custody for juvenile offenders (male and female) aged fifteen to seventeen years. The minimum period is four months and the maximum is six months (or twelve months where there are two or more offences triable 'either way'). The magistrates can still refer the case to the Crown Court for sentence if they feel that their own powers of punishment are inadequate, although the Crown Court can only impose a youth custody sentence of a maximum of twelve months where the offender is under the age of seventeen years. Periods of remand in custody (but not care) are deducted from the sentence to be served and one-third remission for good conduct is allowed. Supervision on release (to either the probation service or the social services department) lasts for a period of three months. Failure to comply with the conditions of supervision on release is punishable by way of a fine (of up to £200) or by a further thirty days in custody.

In 1985, 2,000 offenders (of whom just under 100 were girls), were given youth custody sentences. (18) Proposals made in the recent White Paper (Home Office, 1986a) suggest that both detention centre and youth custody sentences could be subject to a power of suspension (see also, Home Office 1986c). (19) This proposal has been criticised in that it could lead to suspended forms of custody being substituted for non-custodial sentences which would then be activated on a subsequent, albeit minor, offence. Moreover, its introduction for fourteen to seventeen year olds would break with the past and signify, further, the amalgamation in the sentencing systems of young persons and young adult offenders. (This is discussed further in Chapter 8.) The government is also considering whether the current twelve month maximum for youth custody is 'sufficiently high to enable the courts to deal adequately with offences which are of a serious character' (Home Office 1986b, para, 21 and c).

Deferment of Sentence

The juvenile court has power to defer sentence for any period up to six months. Deferment should not be used as a test of treatment, for example, to test a young person's suitability for an intermediate treatment programme, but it can be used to see if the circumstances of the offender change within the designated period, for example, by making reparation to the victim. The court should make clear to the defendant what the purposes of the deferment are and what is expected of him during the period of deferment (R v George, 1984, CLR 504 and Home Office, 1986b, 14-15).

A Note on Juveniles Remanded in Custody

Juveniles can be remanded in custody to a Prison Department establishment to await trial or sentence from a juvenile court. (20) In 1984, 1,192 juveniles were so remanded; of those, nearly one half were either subsequently acquitted or received non-custodial sentences.

Concern over the number of juveniles remanded in custody, particularly on certificates of unruli-ness to await trial, has been a major feature of juvenile justice debates in recent years. In the early 1970s, over 3,000 certificates of unruliness were issued annually. The sub-committee of the House of Commons Expenditure Committee reviewing the operation of the 1969 Children and Young Persons Act stated:

> We condemn in the strongest possible terms the use of certificates of unruliness as a means of achieving secure accommodation. We recommend that the practice of remand-ing young persons to adult prisons should cease forthwith; alternative arrangements must be made (1975, para. 23).

Since that recommendation, a number of changes have been introduced restricting the type of young person who may be made the subject of a certificate of un-ruliness and the criteria whereby such certificates may be granted. In 1977, the Certificate of Unruly Character (Conditions) Order was introduced setting out the new criteria.

Now, only males aged fifteen years and above can be made the subject of such an order. In all other instances, if a secure remand is needed, the juvenile is placed in local authority secure accomm-odation. Certificates of unruliness can also now only be made if the juvenile is charged with an offence punishable in the case of an adult with imprisonment of fourteen years or more or with an offence of violence, has been found guilty on a previous occasion of a violent offence or has persistently absconded from or seriously disrupted the running of a community home. In addition, the juvenile court has to be satisfied on the basis of a written report from the local authority that no suitable accommodation is available for the young person in a community home unless, in the case of the first two categories mentioned above, the court is remanding the young person for the first time in the proceedings and is satisfied that there has not been time to obtain such a report.

Since the introduction of these changes, the number of young people remanded on certificates of unruliness has declined, although the daily average population has remained similar as Table 6.2 shows:

Table 6.2: Juveniles Remanded to Prison Department Establishments

England and Wales	1982	1983	1984
Number of Unruliness Certificates made (1)	2,270	1,831	1,678
Average daily population of untried juveniles accommodated in prison department establishments (2)	86	74	85

Notes: 1. An unruliness certificate is normally for seven days. Several unruliness certificates may thus be made on one juvenile during the course of a single remand.

2. Statistics are collected on the last day of each month. The figures in this table are the average of these.

Source: House of Commons, 1985.

However, a recent interpretation of the statutory instrument relating to unruly certificates (R v Leicester City Juvenile Justices ex parte Capenhurst (1985, 149, J.P., 409)) has once again thrown this area of the law into confusion. There the High Court determined that a local authority's report that alternative accommodation to custody was available for a juvenile charged with offences which would have allowed the granting of a certificate of unruliness was not conclusive. The juvenile court had the ultimate decision as to whether or not the certificate should be granted and the views of the local authority, although influential, could not pre-empt this. Since this case, a number of local authorities have indicated that juvenile courts are willing to grant certificates of unruliness in the absence of a positive request by the local authorities to do so. In the Leicester case, the local authority had no secure accommodation in which to confine the juvenile. It remains to be seen whether or not the judgment means that a certificate of unruliness can be made by the juvenile court in the face of a positive request by the local authority that a juvenile be detained in its own secure accommodation.

In August 1984, the Home Secretary announced that further restrictions on the use of unruly certificates were to be introduced with respect to fifteen and sixteen year olds. In particular, it was proposed that they should be confined to cases in which the boy has been charged with murder, attempted murder, rape or attempted rape (House of Commons, 1985). At present, these proposals are under discussion (Guardian, 29th March, 1986 and 4th April, 1986) and they are likely to be introduced in the near future.

Conclusion

In describing the procedures, personnel and powers of the juvenile court, we have intentionally presented a static picture of the juvenile court. For those unfamiliar with the juvenile court it should provide a baseline from which actual practice can be assessed. However, the hallmark of juvenile court decision-making is the eclectic nature of its application. The decision-making process and its outcome varies from case to case and from court to court. Indeed, how the personnel described in this chapter come together to negotiate procedures leading to the use of the powers outlined is a critical determinant of whether or not justice is actually administered in the juvenile court. It is to these issues that we turn next.

NOTES

1. Local arrangements differ on the precise length of service. Some benches insist on retirement from the panel after a three-year period of service with the opportunity of re-appointment at a later date.

2. The 'Statement of National Objectives and Priorities for the Probation Service' (Home Office, 1984c) was the Home Office's view of the purpose of the probation service in the 1980s, the specific tasks the service should undertake and the broad order of priorities which it should follow. Each probation area was asked to construct local object-ives and priorities in the light of the national statement and plan and manage the deployment of re-sources in the light of such a strategy.

3. These representational styles are not limited to lawyers. A range of other juvenile court personnel (e.g. social workers, guardians ad litem, independent report writers) can adopt one or more of these approaches (Anderson, 1978; Giller, 1985b).

4. Such changes include the right of parents to be separately represented in contested child care cases, the introduction of guardians ad litem to act for the child where there is perceived to be a conflict of interest between the parents and the child and the use of independent social inquiry reports in disputed child care cases (see D.H.S.S., 1985; Murch, 1984; Giller and Morris, 1982).

5. The observation that the arrangement of the court is like a schoolroom is in itself interesting. Several commentators, most notably Foucault (1977) and Donzelot (1979), have argued at length the case for the comparability of courts with other elements in the disciplinary network which apply to juveniles. Moreover, with respect to schools, the norms inculcated in that setting are only a part of a broader framework for the discipline and surveil-lance exercised by the juvenile court.

6. Such moral evaluations of the deviant and deviance are not limited to courtroom settings (McHugh, 1970). Similar evaluations have been shown to operate in social workers' decision-making (Giller and Morris, 1981a) and in pre-court screen-ing processes (Pratt and Grimshaw, 1985). Moreover, given that the evaluation of the deviant is broader than that of the criminal, such assessments can be made with respect to a wide range of juveniles who are in conflict with a variety of legal regulations

(Packman et al., 1985; Pratt and Grimshaw, 1985).

7. Research from Scotland (Martin et al., 1981) presents evidence which suggests a different level of understanding and participation on the part of children and parents in the proceedings. This is discussed in Chapter 8.

8. In one Canadian study (Catton and Erickson, 1975), some juveniles represented did not know that they had a lawyer. Others who did know that they were represented did not think the lawyer was there to assist them.

9. Customarily the probation service have supervised those of fourteen years and above who are not known to the social services department, although a higher age split (for example, sixteen years) has been agreed in some areas.

10. In Chapter 7 we discuss further the differences in perspective between probation officers and social workers.

11. This created a new section 12(3C)(a) to the Children and Young Persons Act 1969.

12. This created a new section 12(3C)(b) to the Children and Young Persons Act 1969.

13. This created a new section 12(3C)(c) to the Children and Young Persons Act 1969.

14. These can be made under section 7(7) of the Children and Young Persons Act 1969 in criminal proceedings or under section 1(2)(f) in civil proceedings.

15. Further orders can also be imposed if the juvenile offends again.

16. If no change had taken place it is likely that the administrative practices would have been challenged in the European Court.

17. Currently, on the basis of figures prepared annually by the Prison Department, 72 per cent of young persons leaving detention centres are reconvicted within the following two years (Home Office, 1985c).

18. Currently, 80 per cent of males and 60 per cent of females are reconvicted within two years of release (Home Office, 1985c).

19. Power existed prior to the implementation of the 1982 Act to impose a period of suspended imprisonment on a young adult offender.

20. The juvenile court's power to remand juveniles is contained in Section 23 of the Children and Young Persons Act 1969. This enables the court to certify that a young person is so unruly a character that he cannot be committed to the care of a local authority and should be committed to a

remand centre, or, if no remand centre is available, to a prison, for a period of up to eight days. Section 30 of the Magistrates' Court Act 1980 enables a juvenile court to remand a convicted juvenile to custody for a maximum of three weeks prior to sentence. For a further discussion, see Moore and Wilkinson (1984).

Chapter 7

DETERMINANTS OF DECISION-MAKING

> It is the essence of magistrates´ justice
> that it is commonsense justice which seeks
> to resolve the tension between formal
> legal rationality and individual human
> troubles (Dingwall et al., 1983, 239).

The Disposition Process

In England and Wales and in the United States, the
quality of justice dispensed in the juvenile courts
has come under increasing criticism in recent years.
Studies in both jurisdictions have demonstrated variations in the use of the dispositions and that the
full range of dispositions is not used in any
methodical and graduated way. As Freeman notes: ´One
of the most unsatisfactory features of juvenile
justice is that in reality there is very little
justice` (1983, 210).

In part, criticism of the unclear basis of
decision-making reflects the confused theoretical
foundations of the juvenile court which we referred
to earlier. On the one hand, the court is a legal
tribunal bound by rules, principles and procedures
which seek to protect the rights of the individual.
At the same time, it is encouraged to provide
´individualised` justice which de-emphasises the
strictly ´legal proceeding and purposefully expands
its inquiry beyond and away from the provoking
incident in order to determine the root of the
child´s trouble and consider appropriate alternative
responses` (Feeley, 1979, 284).

These contradictory orientations produce many
tensions and confusions. Firstly, they place (and
it is assumed appropriate to place) considerable
reliance on the quality of judgments exercised by
decision-makers. Little in the way of guidance is,

however, provided for decision-makers. How decisions are made, therefore, is an important yet problematic issue in its own right.

Matza's (1964) seminal analysis of decision-making in the juvenile courts in the United States clearly illustrated that, faced with competing philosophies, decision-makers were forced to compromise. The wide ranging discretion to make decisions on the merits of the case rather than in accordance with formal principles - Matza likens this to Kadi justice - sits uneasily with the pressing practical problems of court management, volume of work, maintaining good public relations and ensuring inter-agency co-operation.

For Matza, the compromise reached by decision-makers was to re-instate the principles of the offence sub rosa. The significance of the offence might be qualified by such factors as parental support and availability of resources, but the offence provided some benchmark against which primary assessments could be made. As Matza notes, whether a juvenile is removed from the community or not:

> depends first, on the traditional rule of thumb assessment of the total risk of danger and thus scandal evident in the juvenile's current offence and prior record of offences; this...is then qualified by an assessment of the potentialities of (community) supervision and the guarantee against scandal inherent in the willingness and ability of the parents or surrogates to sponsor the child. If the reckoning of danger and...scandal is extremely high no amount of...sponsorship will result in a (community-based disposition)...If the reckoning of danger is moderate, the decision will turn on an assessment of the presence, the amount, the quality and the dependability of the parental sponsorship (1964, 125).

Matza goes on to show how this compromised basis of decision-making was rarely exposed to the 'clients' of the system. The language of individualised justice and treatment continued to obfuscate the underlying basis of the decisions. Nevertheless, Matza argues, the compromise reached was the only one available to achieve what was otherwise an unattainable philosophy.

Matza's analysis alludes to several vitally important features in juvenile court decision-making. For example, how juvenile courts respond to delinquents and delinquency seems to depend as much on how people and events are depicted as upon some objective assessment of the quality of the acts which juveniles commit. In Matza's terms, attempts at 'reckoning of danger and scandal' are likely to lead to variable conclusions. Assessments will depend not only on the views of the individual judge or magistrate, but also on the degree of public and community concern and on the quality of the evidence given by the police, prosecutors and others. Similarly, an assessment of the juvenile and his parents and the quality of 'sponsorship' they provide will depend very much upon how information is presented on these issues and who presents it. This evidence and the emphasis given to its component parts are what Emerson (1969) has called establishing the 'moral character' of the case. These assessments are inherent in the adjudication process, but are not limited to it. They spill over into the disposition stage, especially since the decision-makers are the same in both parts of the proceedings.

The establishment of a particular 'moral character' and the subsequent disposition decision does not necessarily mean that all who participate in the disposition process share the same aims and objectives. Indeed, the way in which information provided to the juvenile court by the various participants can be co-opted by sentencers to produce disparate outcomes is a hallmark of juvenile court decision-making.

The Basis of the Disposition Decision

Since the partial implementation of the 1969 Children and Young Persons Act, much attention has been given to the basis of disposition decisions. In particular, researchers have focused on whether the welfare philosophy underpinning the Act was, in fact, translated into action.

The first major study in the 1970s was by Priestley et al., (1977) who examined the sentencing practice of two juvenile courts in the south-west of England. They found that, despite the intention of the legislators, the traditional determinants of sentencing - age, type of offence and number of previous offences - continued to determine outcomes. Whilst Priestley et al. found disparities in the two areas in the distribution of the various outcomes (for example, variations in the use of fines and conditional discharges), these, in the main, could be accounted for by the way in which key facts on offenders and their offences varied. The new welfare measures introduced by the 1969 Act - care and supervision orders - were little used in the two areas; rather reliance was placed upon the traditional penal powers which had remained available to the juvenile courts. The application of these was dependent upon the presence of the key variables mentioned earlier, so that a form of tariff sentencing continued to operate. Thus the more serious the offence, the more severe the outcome.

The work of Parker et al., (1981) into neighbouring ´City` and ´Countryside` juvenile courts took further our understanding of this discrepancy between rhetoric and practice by stressing the existence of discrete local juvenile justice systems (see also Anderson, 1978; Thorpe et al., 1980). Like Priestley et al., Parker et al., found that age, offence and previous record were key determinants in disposition outcomes. However, they found that they could not be used predictively. Indeed, using these factors, Parker et al., guessed the outcomes incorrectly in the ´City` court in 50 per cent of cases, erring on the side of over estimating sentencing, while in ´Countryside` court they guessed wrongly in 70 per cent of the cases, grossly under estimating the punitive nature of sentencing there.

If juvenile justice systems are discrete local systems, does this mean that one cannot talk of a tariff system but only of local tariff systems? This issue was recently addressed by researchers in the Home Office Research and Planning Unit. Moxon et al., (1985) examined the sentences of male juvenile offenders imposed in 1978 in nine juvenile courts - three of the courts used custody more than average, three close to average and three less than average. The analysis distinguished between children and young persons, as the cautioning rate is higher for the younger age group and the disposals available for them are limited. For the younger age group, no clear-cut tariff progression could be discerned on the basis of either the offence charged or the number of previous convictions. Discharges, fines, attendance centre orders and supervision orders seemed to be used inter-changeably although the last two orders were more frequently used where the juvenile had one previous conviction. The most common use of care orders was for offenders with two previous sentences: however, re-offending after the imposition of a care order was most frequently dealt with by a conditional discharge. Moreover, 60 per cent of those discharged who had three or more previous convictions had previously been subject to a care order. Both of these examples illustrate that, for this age group, tariff sentencing was not always uni-directional (Jones 1983).

For the older age group, a much clearer picture of progression through the tariff emerged. According to Moxon et al.:

> Courts often gave a discharge to a first offender, but use declined sharply for those with previous convictions. For the rest, courts generally chose between a fine, supervision and an attendance centre for those with two or fewer previous convictions. There was a steady increase in the use of care orders as the number of previous convictions rose, but they were not used to any great extent for this age group. Custodial sentences, and particularly borstal sentences, only came to be used in a large proportion of cases for those with three or more previous convictions (1985, 8).

They did note one major exception to this where the charge was either burglary or robbery. In those circumstances, there was a substantial increase in the likelihood of a custodial sentence for those with two previous convictions.

Within this overall tariff range, however, major variations in sentencing practice in the nine courts were found by Moxon et al.. For example, with respect to burglary and robbery:

> For offenders with no previous convictions the high custody courts gave twice as many custodial sentences as the low custody courts; for those with three or more previous convictions the high custody courts used custody in some 72 per cent of cases compared with 41 per cent in the case of low custody courts (1985, 13).

Similarly, low custody courts used non-custodial sentences for those with up to three previous convictions whereas high custody courts made substantially less use of non-custodial options after a

second conviction. Such findings show not only in-
consistencies in sentencing practice, but also the
considerable impact that variations in cautioning
can have on young people. As Moxon et al. note:

> The most important variable in this
> context was found to be the number of
> previous convictions that the court toler-
> ated before resorting to custody. Half
> the juveniles given custodial sentences in
> 1978 had no more than two previous convic-
> tions. This would have not been the case
> if the level of custodial sentencing in
> the low custody courts had been applied
> more widely. (1985, 14).

One important implication from Moxon et al.'s
research is that a reduction in the use of custodial
sentences could have been achieved without a change
in legislation. Giller has also shown that while
the national average for the use of care orders and
custodial sentence in juvenile courts was 12 per
cent in 1985, this ranged from 3 to 17 per cent of
sentences depending on the area (Social Information
Systems, 1986). Such variations cannot be accounted
for on the basis of variations in 'intake factors'
related to offenders or their offences (Moxon et
al., 1985). (1) Whether greater consistency in
sentencing practice will reduce the use of custody,
as Moxon et al. suggest, however, is open to
question.
First, assuming that magistrates are influenced
by empirical evidence, it is as possible that low
custody courts would become high custody users as is
the opposite which is presumed by Moxon et al.
Secondly, as Parker et al., have shown in their
analysis of decision-making in 'Countyside' court,
sentencing juvenile offenders can contain a political message which is not informed or influenced by
research. Thirdly, and most importantly, the ways
in which information is assimilated, ordered and
used by decision-makers, what Asquith (1983a) calls
their 'frames of relevance', may be deeply-rooted in
tradition, custom and practice and not easily open
to examination or change.
In Asquith's (1983a) study of the different
decision-making frameworks of Scottish panel members
and English juvenile court magistrates, little difference was found between the two groups on the
expressed importance given to a variety of information relating not only to offenders, their offences

and their offending histories but also to their families, education and social welfare. What did distinguish the two groups was the way in which the information was used. Magistrates were said to make reference more frequently to issues of responsibility and fault for the purposes of determining whether or not the juvenile merited punishment. Panel members, on the other hand, were said to make greater use of welfare and family-oriented factors and, when offence related issues were considered, to use them to determine the need for compulsory measures of care rather than punishment (see also Martin et al., 1981). Hence both panel members and magistrates agreed on the type of information used in decision-making but, according to Asquith, its actual use was mediated by the ethos and organization of the system within which the decision-makers operated:

> Panel members have to resolve the conceptual ambiguity inherent in dealing with offenders by welfare measures within a system based, at least theoretically, on a conceptual framework of determinism. This does not mean however that they are not concerned at all with traditional considerations such as deterrence or social protection. Magistrates employ a more overtly 'judicial' orientation in which intent and responsibility are central features and in which punishment is a legitimate product of their deliberations. Again, however, this does not mean that they are not concerned with the welfare of children. But the difference between the panel and court system is that whereas panel members have to reconcile a welfare philosophy within a system for dealing with offenders where they are not concerned with punishment or with questions of criminal intent, magistrates are able to formally distinguish cases requiring welfare measures and those in which children can justly be punished (1983a, 179).

While Asquith's concept of 'frames of relevance' is an important contribution to our understanding of the decision-making process, his research findings are limited in that they are based on an investigation of one juvenile court bench.

Asquith assumes that the choices those magistrates
made would have been made by English juvenile court
magistrates generally. What is clear from Parker
et al´s work, however, is that different courts
draw the punishment/welfare line at different points
for similar cases. In addition, the degree and
severity of the punishment imposed varies markedly
depending upon the political orientation of the
bench. Thus while the concept of a tariff is
useful, what precisely the tariff is within a
local system depends as much on the individual ethos
of the bench, availability of resources and
magistrates´ faith in particular measures as on
´hard data` relating to offenders and their
offences.

Local systems´responses to the various tariff
options have not been uniform. Some systems operate
a welfare tariff, others a punitive tariff and yet
others make use of a combination of the two (Jones,
1983). Hence the number of measures used locally
varies as does the timing of their application in a
juvenile´s court career. This was recently illustrated by Gelsthorpe and Tutt (1986) in their study
of the use of attendance centre orders in six local
juvenile justice systems. They found that the
proportionate use of attendance centre orders over a
six month period varied from 6.6 per cent in one
system to 21.2 per cent in another. While overall
nearly half of those sentenced to attendance
centres had no previous sentences, this ranged from
33 per cent in one area to 60 per cent in another.
Moreover, a small minority had previously received
either care, detention centre or youth custody
orders. No particular offence was frequently found
among those made the subject of attendance centre
orders.

Similar, and more frequently documented, variations can be seen in the style and use of intermediate treatment programmes in the 1970s (Bottoms
and Sheffield, 1980; Thorpe, 1983). This is partly
explained by a lack of clarity in the appropriate
role of intermediate treatment and so it was used as
both a pre- and in-court resource. It is also
explained by the fact that intermediate treatment
co-existed alongside traditional measures which were
intended to be phased out. Thus a ´vertical inte-
gration` of the two systems - welfare and penal -
took place. As Thorpe et al., explain:

The new system has been deployed with the
younger age groups and has adopted a

preventive` policy. The concept of children `at risk` is involved in the identification of a new population for whom social work intervention is appropriate prior to confrontation with the courts. Once such children begin to appear in court, however, they are fairly rapidly phased into the penal system (1980, 23).

In the 1980s, the `strengthened` range of supervision orders introduced in the Criminal Justice Act 1982 and the financial incentives provided by the D.H.S.S. to make intermediate treatment a direct and credible alternative to care and custody was intended to fracture this `vertical integration`. But the impact of intermediate treatment continues to vary and it is not clear that an expansion in its use will inevitably lead to a reduction in the proportion of juveniles who eventually enter care or custody (Social Information Systems, 1986).

Further complicating sentencing outcomes in local systems are such factors as the extent to which the providers of services to the juvenile courts `tout` for clients (Tutt and Giller, 1985a) in a situation in which the number of available juveniles is decreasing. The need for practitioners to bring new services (such as intermediate treatment programmes) to the attention of magistrates when they are introduced locally is essential if they wish to encourage magistrates to use them (NACRO, 1986). But such public-relations work is not limited to encouraging the juvenile courts to use new and, hence, untried services. This strategy can also be seen in response to the recent decline in the use of junior detention centres. A report on the half-full Kirklevington Grange Detention Centre in <u>Th Observer</u> (February 16, 1986) quoted the Governor as saying, `Give us a nice write up...and we`ll get more customers`. The article went on to report an office who made a similar pitch, albeit in a more subtle way:

> By the time they come here these lads have worked the system. They know it like the back of their hands. They`ve been to court four or five times. They`ve been fined, conditionally discharged, let off, put on supervision and care orders and sent to attendance centres. By the time they come here most of them are so deeply entrenched in their ways its too late to

> change their minds anyway. Give us a lad
> on his first or second offence and he´ll
> not come back.

In fact, the profile of the junior detention centre trainee has radically changed over the past decade so that nearly half are first or second time offenders (Home Office, 1984a). But that does not matter in promoting this strategy. The need to retain a viable role in the local juvenile justice system by having a sufficient number of ´clients` is the primary concern. The resistance to change of those who operate traditional services, especially in the institutional sector, is well-documented in the United States (Rutherford, 1986).

In contrast to Matza´s claims about decision-making in American juvenile courts, decision-makers in the English juvenile courts seem to more readily and legitimately utilise the juvenile´s offence as a basis for sentencing and to develop a tariff of responses accordingly. Historically, the commitment of the English juvenile court to a welfare orientation has been equivocal. The basis of their decision-making has thus depended in practice on a localised set of arrangements which encompasses such issues as the ethos of the bench (reflecting, at the extremes, punitive or welfare philosophies), availability of resources and the bench´s faith in particular measures. However, these are not the only matters which influence the outcome. Frequently, defendants are represented in the disposition process and magistrates receive a range of reports and other items of information which seek to contribute to and influence their decisions. We will now discuss the form and impact of such assistance.

Representation

Research and practice suggests that the concept of ´representation` is more useful than concentrating on assumed distinctions in the roles of lawyers, social workers, teachers or other professionals who claim to act on behalf of a juvenile. Lawyers and social work representatives are the most common participants in the disposition process in the juvenile court and, as Anderson (1978) has shown, both share a common function. First, they ease the strain for the defendant inherent in the court-room drama by acting as mediators of the experience. Secondly, they act as an aid to the efficient processing of cases through the system. In this latter role, they both assist and contribute to the decision-making process and, on the making of the disposition, explain its implications to the juvenile and any obligations which it may involve him or her in.

The extent to which representatives assist and justify contribute to the decision-making process in any particular case, however, does not depend solely on their professional skill, ability and expertise. Equally, if not more important is the ethos of the decision-making forum within which they practise. In this respect, the precise contribution and impact of the representative - lawyer or social worker - varies with the prevailing bench ethos. This point is well illustrated by Anderson (1978) in his study of two very different juvenile courts.

In court A, a legally oriented bench, Anderson found that lawyers made a substantial contribution to and had an impact on the disposition process because the primary criterion for decisions in this setting was an assessment of the defendant's culpability. Lawyers could, therefore, use their traditional skills of clarifying the facts of the offence and advancing mitigation in an attempt to normalise the situational context in which the offence took place. The appropriateness of legal representation was appreciated by the magistrates, juveniles and their parents alike (Anderson, 1978, 39-40). Conversely, social workers and, to a lesser extent, probation officers occupied a more marginal role; their classification of the circumstances of the case (in a social inquiry report) may have been seen as assisting in the clarification of the facts of the offence, but frequently much of the social background material presented on defendants and their families was seen as 'judgmental, subjective and inclined to be emotionally entangled in the client's case' (Anderson, 1978, 41).

In court B, a welfare oriented court, Anderson found that the roles of the professional representatives were reversed. Social workers and probation officers were seen by the bench as integral to the decision-making process and the traditional skills of lawyers were viewed as, at best, marginal or, at worst, redundant. The basis of dispositional decision-making was not the offence; this was viewed as merely the event which had occasioned the inquiry. More relevant in determining the outcome was the juvenile's personality and psychological development and the contribution of the family both as the source of any dysfunction and as a basis for any therapeutic intervention (1978, 27). As Anderson writes, in court B:

> the line between the court´s interest and
> that of the client is blurred, the terms
> of argument are altered in favour of the
> social worker, the solicitor is perhaps
> not so sure against whom he is protecting
> the client´s interest when all those
> around him seem to be so demonstrably
> concerned with it (1978, 42).

Hence, magistrates in court B often questioned the utility of legal representation. In the words of one such magistrate:

> The lawyer´s position in court is very
> difficult. Frankly, I find them on the
> whole a bit of a nuisance. I find they
> didn´t really understand what the juvenile
> court is all about. They haven´t really
> any training for juvenile court procedure.
> [Often]...they make impassioned pleas not
> to punish when it is the last thing we
> have in mind anyway (quoted in Anderson,
> 1978, 40).

In these circumstances, lawyers merely recited phrases from the social inquiry report in an attempt to have some input into a decision-making process which would otherwise have excluded them. Rather than enhancing the contribution of lawyers, however, such strategies served further to alienate the bench and social work representatives.

Results on the impact of legal representation are equally equivocal. In Anderson´s (1978) sample, some 27 per cent of those represented in court A - the legally oriented court - and a further 9 per cent not represented received a detention centre order or a recommendation for borstal training. In court B, while no custodial sentences were recorded on either the represented or the unrepresented group, those not represented were more likely to receive a care or supervision order than those represented. However, given the lack of data on the correlation between offence, offender and court variables and the small number of juveniles legally represented, it is impossible to draw firm conclusions from this study on the impact of representation on outcome.

There has been much more research in the United States on the impact of legal representation but the conclusions are both variable and contradictory. (2) Some research has shown that legal representation led to cases being dismissed more frequently than unrepresented cases, but it also found that those represented were more likely to be committed to the care of the state authority (Lemert, 1970; Platt et al., 1968). This disparity can probably be explained by the fact that lawyers were likely to be consulted and used mainly where the juvenile had committed a serious offence or had a prior record and ran the risk of a severe penalty. But other researchers have found that juveniles who were legally represented were likely to be dealt with severely even where the offence which the juvenile had committed was minor. They did not, however, consider the impact on the disposition of the juvenile´s prior record (Duffee and Siegal, 1971).

The most thorough research in this area (by Stapleton and Teitelbaum, 1972) compared representation in two areas, ´Gotham` and ´Zenith`. They found that representation in ´Gotham` had little effect (other than to <u>increase</u> the juveniles chances of detention), but that representation in ´Zenith` led to favourable dispositions. Stapleton and Teitelbaum attempted to explain this by reference to a number of factors (such as the identity of the judges, the experience and ability of individual lawyers, the age, sex, race, prior record, offence and home situation of the juveniles appearing in the two areas), but none of these factors provided a satisfactory explanation. It seemed that it was something <u>in the courts themselves</u> which accounted for the different impact of representation. In ´Gotham`, the juvenile courts adhered to a social welfare philosophy and resisted attempts by lawyers to introduce elements of justice or due process. Consequently, the lawyers were prevented from acting <u>as lawyers</u>.

Clarke and Koch (1980) confirmed Stapleton and Teitelbaum´s findings, but they raised a further issue: the extent to which the participation of lawyers in the juvenile court may be largely a <u>formality</u>. Admission rates in the juvenile court are high; this sharply limits the role of counsel. Lawyers could still, however, attempt to influence the court´s disposition by, for example, presenting arguments in favour of alternatives to institutions. But here, too, Clarke and Koch found that counsel were generally ineffective and may even have been detrimental. Juveniles <u>without counsel</u> were less likely to be committed to institutions, especially if they were in what Clarke and Koch call the 'intermediate risk group'. This remained so even after taking into account prior record, seriousness of the alleged offence and other factors commonly associated with dispositions. One explanation offered by Clarke and Koch is that the juvenile courts regarded lawyers as an impediment; they maintained only token compliance with the constitutional requirement of the provision of counsel and continued to function much as they had before the Gault case. Further, they suggested that the advent of the lawyer in the process may have made it more difficult for courts to be lenient.

Taken together, American research suggests that increased representation does not necessarily influence decision-makers. The Criminal Justice Act 1982 increased the situations in which juveniles are offered legal representation, in particular where care orders or custodial sentences are being considered. Research (Burney, 1985b) indicates that few juveniles are given a custodial sentence without representation. However, Burney makes the point that it is the quality rather than the quantity of legal assistance which is important in safeguarding rights. She cites brief discussions with clients and a lack of preparation of cases as frequent occurrences. From the research we presented earlier (Burney, 1985a and b; Reynolds, 1985a; Whitehead and Macmillan, 1985), it is also apparent that lawyers have not been active in challenging the use of statutory criteria to restrict custody. Burney concludes that the legal protection currently provided is 'very fragile' (1985b, 74).

Social Inquiry and Other Reports

We noted in Chapter 4 that sentencing became more penal during the 1970s. The conclusion often drawn from these trends is that magistrates were responsible in that they reacted against the welfare ethos embodied in the 1969 Act and, as an act of defiance, made marginal the role of social workers and probation officers (Morris and Giller, 1978; Clarke, 1985). It is, however, equally important to appreciate that sentencing does not take place within an informational vacuum and, hence, some assessment must be made of the contribution of information providers to such outcomes.

The sentencing decision is made after a process of interaction between those who must make the decision and those who provide the sentencers with

information. An example of the latter is the social
inquiry report writer, be they social worker or
probation officer (Reynolds, 1982), and, while the
information they provide may not always be incorporated by sentencers, their information can have an
important bearing on the outcome of cases. This can
occur not only in cases where the report contains a
positive recommendation, but also where no recommendation is made or where an unclear or contradictory
message is given. For example, Millichamp et al.´s
work (1985) on reports on boys sentenced to Whatton
Detention Centre in Nottinghamshire showed that, in
40 per cent of those written by social workers and
in 28 per cent of those written by probation
officers, the report either contained no recommendation, a positive recommendation for custody or an
implied recommendation for custody (see also Duncan,
1985). Giller and Morris (1981a), in their research
on social workers´ decision-making in care order
cases, reached a similar conclusion. In a study of
79 juveniles made the subject of care orders for
offences, over 80 per cent of the orders were made
on the positive recommendation of a social worker.
Moreover, since social inquiry reports are prepared
in some two-thirds to three-quarters of all cases
involving juveniles (excluding traffic matters, this
comes to between 46,000 and 52,000 reports per
year), it is vital to assess the role and content of
such reports.
      The role of social inquiry reports in criminal
proceedings in the juvenile court has, until
recently, been a relatively unexplored area of
practice. Early writers (Perry, 1975; White, 1973;
Thorpe, 1979), tended not to differentiate in their
discussions between reports prepared for the juvenile and magistrates´ courts. As such, they largely
concentrated on the issue of content, and, in particular, on whether or not the reports should
contain a recommendation from the author and whether
or not they influenced sentencers. This latter
issue is particularly problematic. For example,
overall, about 50 per cent of recommendations contained in social inquiry reports in the juvenile
courts are taken up by the bench, but congruence
between recommendations and outcomes varies considerably depending on the type of sentence being
recommended. High levels of congruence exist on
high tariff options (care orders and custodial
sentences) and on low tariff options (discharges and
fines), whereas mid-tariff recommendations (supervision orders and supervision orders with conditions

of intermediate treatment) have a much lower congruence rate. However, a low level of congruence does not necessarily indicate dysfunction if, for example, the social inquiry report writers are attempting to avoid making recommendations for care or custody and the dissensus reflects a working-out between the social workers and magistrates of the appropriate use of a variety of mid-tariff options. Conversely, high congruence between report writers' recommendations and outcomes does not necessarily indicate real agreement; it may merely reflect 'second-guessing' on the part of the report writer. Or it may mean that a similar outcome has been reached by both parties but for different reasons. For example, in our study of care orders in criminal proceedings (Giller and Morris, 1981a), over 80 per cent of the orders were made after a positive recommendation to that effect from the report writer. However, whilst the bench probably granted the care order in response to the nature of the offence charged, the report writers frequently ignored the significance of the offence in making their recommendations. The care order was used as a device to meet the welfare needs of the juvenile and his or her family. Congruence, in other words, does not necessarily imply concordance.

The provision of reports to the juvenile court has a long history. The Molony Committee in 1927, for example, stressed the need for full background information on the juvenile offender. While subsequent legislation and juvenile court rules have provided for the production of such reports, there has been little guidance as to their content.

Currently, the provision of such reports to juvenile courts is governed by section 9(1) of the Children and Young Persons Act 1969, which states:

> Where a local authority or a local educa-
> tion authority brings proceedings under
> s.1 of this Act or proceedings for an
> offence alleged to have been committed by
> a young person or are notified that any
> such proceedings are being brought, it
> shall be the duty of the authority, unless
> they are of the opinion that it is unnece-
> ssary to do so, to make such investiga-
> tions and provide the court before which
> the proceedings are heard with such infor-
> mation relating to the home surroundings,
> school record, health and character of the
> person in respect of whom the proceedings

213

are brought as appear to the authority likely to assist the court.

Similar provisions for reports to be prepared by the probation service are in section 34(3) of the Act. Rule 10(a) of the Magistrates' Courts (Children and Young Persons) Rules 1970 provides further, limited, advice on the content of such reports:

> The court shall take into consideration such information as to the general conduct, home surroundings, school record and medical history of the child or young person as may be necessary to enable it to deal with the case in his best interests.

Recently two Home Office circulars (17/1983, 18/1983), issued as precursors to the implementation of the 1982 Criminal Justice Act, gave some further guidance. They reiterated and expanded the recommendation of the Streatfield Committee (1961) which suggested that the following matters should be covered in social inquiry reports:

> an assessment of the offender's personality, character and family and social background which is relevant to the court's assessment of his culpability; information about the offender and his surroundings which is relevant to the court's consideration of how his criminal career might be checked; his employment or prospects of obtaining employment; information about the circumstances of the offence in question and the offender's attitude towards it; and opinion of the likely effect on the offender's criminal career of probation or some specified sentence.

While these circulars were primarily directed towards the probation service and hence the magistrates' courts, they have been adopted by social services departments and probation services operating in the juvenile courts to guide the practice of writing social inquiry reports. However, since there are no <u>specific</u> regulations as to the appropriate form and content of social inquiry reports local practice varies widely.

First, the volume of reports produced in juvenile cases varies substantially both between and within areas. The proportion of cases in which reports are prepared can vary from over 90 per cent in one area to as low as 30 per cent in another (Tutt and Giller, 1985a). Similarly, within a geographical area (such as a county), the number of cases in which a report has been prepared can vary from over 80 per cent to under 50 per cent (Tutt and Giller, 1985a). Such variations are not dependent upon the seriousness of the offence with which the juvenile is charged.

Secondly, when reports are prepared there are substantial variations in the recommendations made by report writers in similar cases. For example, Tutt and Giller (1985a) have shown that frequently there is a divergence between social workers´ and probation officers´ recommendations in similar cases within the same area. Typically, for first or second time court appearances, social workers made recommendations for conditional discharges and fines, whereas probation officers recommended supervision and attendance centre orders. While this may have had something to do with age differences between the clients of the two services, it is likely also to reflect the different ethos of the two agencies. For the probation service, the supervision order is the major and traditional means through which officers have contact with juvenile offenders. In the social services, the value of supervision orders (without conditions) for offenders has been seriously doubted (Webb and Harris, 1984; Jones, 1983) and the imposition of other kinds of orders does not necessarily remove the possibility of the social work department working with the juveniles or their families in some other context (for example, through voluntary intermediate treatment, a parenting group or one-to-one counselling).

A similar difference in emphasis between the two services was found by Reynolds (1985b) in her study of juveniles sentenced to custody in Northamptonshire between 1982 and 1984. Reynolds reported that the social services department was more prepared than the probation service to argue for alternatives to custody over a longer period in the juvenile´s court career. However, the statistical basis for her conclusion is not clear-cut, as both agencies recommended positive alternatives to custody in 27-28 per cent of the cases, both made no clear recommendations in about 20 per cent and in 20 per cent both made positive recommendations for custody. The main difference lay in the proportion of cases in which custody was <u>implied</u>. This occurred in almost half of the probation reports, but in less than a third of social services reports. An alternative interpretation, therefore, is that the two report writing agencies shared a common perspective on avoiding custody where possible. However, the earlier use of supervision in probation officers' tariff, coupled with an older clientele, led to the earlier imposition of a custodial sentence in their cases.

The impact that different recommendation practices can have on the bench is important. If, for example, a juvenile court which is dealing with two similar cases receives a report from one agency which seems to treat the matter more seriously by recommending a mid-tariff rather than a low-tariff option, the strategy adopted by the other agency is likely to be defeated as cases may be moved up the tariff in accordance with the tariff range used by the first agency.

The lack of guidance on the appropriate content of social inquiry reports has also meant that, in the main, they have reflected the professional ideologies of report writers and their agencies (Hardiker, 1977; Osborne, 1984). In particular, they have traditionally reflected faith in the rehabilitative potential of sentences and have included a plethora of personal and social background information. (See, for example, Perry 1975.) This information is then presumed to lead the writer and reader alike to the `best` decision in the case.

In this approach, the social inquiry report becomes the diagnostic tool par excellence of the welfare model for dealing with delinquents. As Sutton (1983) notes, however, the selection and analysis of what is deemed `relevant` information in this approach has tended to personalise the causes of delinquent behaviour. Information is sought only at the `psycho-social level`, that is from behavioural, psychodynamic and social sources `at a level directed to explaining individual subjects' thinking and behaviour as functions of immediate social forces acting upon them (chiefly the family) and their emotional reactions to these` (Sutton 1983, 139). But such an understanding of individual development, motivation and action is now discredited (Sutton 1981). In relation to crime causation, we know that offending has as much, if not more, to do with the situationally specific opportunities to offend than it does with predispositional or motivational states (Rutter and Giller, 1983). In Sutton's words:

> At a technical level we simply do not know the empirical facts, never mind the mechanisms, to understand how background and upbringing interact with such extra-personal matters as opportunity, police presence etc., to produce acts construed as anti-social or criminal (1983, 139).

Such investigations and material may be legitimate in a report compiled for a social work purpose. But, in this context, social inquiry reports are compiled for an outside audience - the magistrates - and for a specific purpose - sentencing the offender. As Millichamp et al., have stated:

> While not denying the value of such material, say within the context of a case conference, one perhaps could question whether its detailed disclosure to a court is in the best interests of the juvenile. If courts are informed, for example, "that the mother suffers from depression", "that other siblings have experienced custody or care", and "that the present cohabitation is unstable", they could very easily take the view that such a background is hardly supportive to behavioural or attitudinal change and therefore began to look at other ways, namely custody, to change behaviour (1985, 27).

In practice, reports which present traditional psycho-social investigations have meant that forms of intervention not merited on the basis of the nature of the offence alone are imposed on the juvenile (Giller and Morris, 1981a).

In an attempt to redress some of the problems associated with this approach several social services and probation departments have begun to reassess the role and function of reports to courts and to develop strategies which are aimed at avoiding some of the unintended effects of previous practice. These revisions have, to a greater or lesser extent, addressed three issues: individual report writing practices, the organisational context within which reports are produced and the systems' context within which reports are received (Tutt and Giller, 1984b).

Individual Report Writing Practices

Changes in individual report writing practice have come from two distinct sources: one theoretical, the other statutory. The theoretical basis stems from Bottoms and Mcwilliams' (1979) seminal paper on the development of a 'non treatment paradigm for probation practice'. In that paper, they argued for a redirection of the probation service in the light of what they termed 'the collapse of treatment'. They posit four primary aims for a revised probation service: the provision of appropriate help for offenders, the statutory supervision of offenders, diverting appropriate offenders from custodial sentences and the reduction of crime. Within these aims, they argued for 'a complete reconceptualisation of practice in social inquiry work' (1979, 187). Although social inquiry reports are only briefly discussed in the paper, Bottoms and McWilliams suggested that probation officers should move away from the language of implied moral judgments and should develop practices which 'simultaneously aim to present appropriate social information to the court, to help offenders and to develop appropriate diversion strategies to prevent imprisonment' (1979, 185). Peter Raynor (1980 and 1985) has developed this element of their paper further. Within a 'non treatment' perspective, Raynor has argued that social inquiry reports should be offence focused and should concentrate upon two primary issues: an assessment of the moral culpability of the offender and the provision of a basis for 'contractual sentencing' (1980, 83, see also Tutt and Giller, 1984b).

With respect to culpability, Raynor suggests that reports should document the constraints and influences which affect the choices and actions of the offender so that the court may assess their place:

> along a continuum from 'he almost couldn't help acting as he did' to 'he acted in full knowledge of what he was doing, with calculated indifference to the harm done to others, after long and careful planning to maximize gain and minimize risk to himself' (1980, 81).

Clearly, it is highly unlikely that any one case would exhibit either of the polar extremes. Hence the social inquiry reports would, in the first instance, present contextual information so that the offender could be appropriately located on this continuum prior to the disposition decision being reached. While the presentation of this kind of information is relatively new to report writers, it is not unusual within an adversarial court setting; for example, the police, in giving evidence about the offence, often provide a context to the formal legal charge. Indeed Parker <u>et al</u>., (1981), in documenting the language used by police officers in such circumstances, refer to the way in which such evidence, by inference and inuendo, may be used to ´bump up´ the seriousness of the incident. The absence of such information from other sources leaves the magistrates with only one ´reading´ of the case. Raynor´s proposals, therefore, envisage the social inquiry report providing details of the offender´s role in the offence, his or her degree of participation, the extent to which such involvement is usual for the offender and the extent of the offender´s appreciation of the consequences of his or her actions.

Such an approach does not preclude reference to other factors. As Home Office circular 17/1983 notes, ´the offender´s personality, character, family and social background´ may be relevant to the court in assessing culpability. Hence family background information, details of personal history, school performance, peer relations and broader sociological and areal information can be included, but <u>only</u> to the extent that it is relevant to understanding the conduct of the juvenile. This means, therefore, that the information must be focused on the reason for the juvenile´s court appearance and not presented, as has traditionally been the case, as a free-floating catalogue of pathology. Where such links are not made, the writer of the report leaves open the possibility of the juvenile being sentenced twice - once on the basis of the offence and once on the basis of his or her pathological problem and potential for future deviance.

Implicit in such a change is the need for more investigative reports which analyse and assess important factors in the offence, but it questions the need for routine information on, for example, school attendance and attainment in circumstances in which the offence took place out of school hours and in the company of associates who are not at the same school. Such an approach would also encompass the inclusion of material relevant to the offender, what Pratt terms ´a phenomenology of the client`. He writes:

> The approach...might allow the reporter to
> include such matters as local unemployment
> rates, a child´s perception of schooling
> and the quality of education currently
> being offered to him/her, the local sig-
> nificance of the `behaviour and so on
> (1985b, 15).

Unlike traditional reports which assumed a theoretical `explanation` of the offender´s behaviour,
these revised reports are naturalistic documents
about offenders and their circumstances.

With respect to advancing contractual (non-
tariff) sentencing, Raynor (1980) suggests that the
report should document what the offender is prepared
to do, what the contribution of the service providing agency is to be and an agreed agenda of
initiatives on these matters. Once again, this is
intended to be focused and specific. Precise
programmes of intervention, therefore, are to be
constructed with details of their duration, intens-
ity and content, and a description of how the
content relates to the reason for the juvenile´s
current court appearance. A particular form of
intervention, for example, intermediate treatment,
may not prevent re-offending by the juvenile, but
the proposed programme should document what is
intended to be achieved and demonstrate how it would
be less harmful than other forms of intervention.
The objective is to minimise the possibility of
exposing the juvenile and the agency to `failure`
based on unrealistic criteria. (3)

The requirement of greater specificity and
focus in social inquiry reports is supported by the
statutory criteria introduced in the 1982 Criminal
Justice Act. These were referred to in Chapter 6.
For example, specific information from a social
inquiry report is required by section 1 of the 1982
Act if a custodial sentence is being considered by
the court. (4) One would expect this report to
address the issues raised in the criteria set out in
the Act to determine whether or not such dispositions are `appropriate`. Thus information on the
context of the offence and the offender´s culpability would assist the court in determining whether
a custodial sentence is `appropriate` because of the
seriousness of the offence or the need to protect
the public. The report could also consider specific
alternative forms of intervention and the offender´s

ability and willingness to participate in them.
While it seems that magistrates´ decision-making is
not invariably constrained by the existence of such
criteria (Burney, 1985a and b; Reynolds, 1985a),
they may nevertheless be influential in leading to a
revision of the content of social inquiry reports.

The Organisational Context of Report Production

To ensure consistency with respect to the
content of social inquiry reports and their recommendations (both intra- and inter-agency) and to
avoid the unintended consequences of the exercise of
uncontrolled professional discretion, some revision
of the organisational context of report writing has
taken place over the past five years. In
particular, three issues have dominated thinking in
this area: the appropriateness of routinely producing social inquiry reports, the reduction of
disparities in recommendations and the development
of strategies to ensure that the full range of
tariff options are considered and used.
Questioning the appropriateness of producing
social inquiry reports routinely in cases being sentenced in the juvenile court is primarily related to
research which has emerged since 1980 which shows
that reports may have led to juvenile offenders
moving rapidly through the tariff system. The
probation service in Greater Manchester, for
example, found that in the absence of social inquiry
reports, magistrates were likely to spontaneously
sentence a juvenile on a first court appearance to a
fine or a conditional discharge. When such cases
were accompanied by a report, the juveniles tended
to receive mid-tariff sentences (i.e. supervision
orders) (Baldwin, 1982). More recent research (Tutt
and Giller, 1985a) found similar results in three
different areas: area A, a shire county, area B, a
London borough, and area C, a metropolitan
authority. Figure 7.1 demonstrates the disparities.
In area A, 71 per cent of those sentenced for the
first time without a social inquiry report received
a fine or less compared with 52 per cent when a
report was produced. In area B, the respective
figures were 83 per cent and 25 per cent and, in
area C, 91 per cent and 36 per cent. Further
analysis failed to account for these differences on
the basis of the nature of the offence charged.
Such findings are, perhaps, not surprising
given the ´inculpatory` nature of much of the infor-
mation contained in a traditional social inquiry

Figure 7.1 Outcomes For First Time Court Appearance With and Without a Social Inquiry Report in Three Areas

Social Inquiry Reports	A None	A Reports	B None	B Reports	C None	C Reports
Withdrawn/ Dismiss	8	2	13	–	–	–
Absolute Discharge	2	–	–	–	–	–
Conditional Discharge	12	46	9	3	5	22
Bound Over	–	–	–	–	1	–
Compensation	1	2	–	1	1	–
Fine	32	29	31	2	24	15
Attendance Centre Order	21	34	5	4	2	29
Supervision Order	1	30	1	7	–	28
Supervision Order + IT	–	3	–	1	–	3
Deferred Sentence	–	1	1	2	–	1
C.S.O.	–	2	–	1	–	–
Care Order	–	1	1	2	–	2
Detention Centre	–	2	2	1	1	3
Youth Custody	–	–	1	–	–	–
Total	77	152	64	24	34	103

report. A number of social services departments and probation services have now withdrawn social inquiry reports for most juveniles appearing before the courts for the first time (as they have the discretion to do under section 9 of the 1969 Act) and only provide such reports, on adjournment, after a positive request is made for them by the bench. Freed from producing reports routinely, report writers can then undertake more detailed investigations and, arguably, produce better quality reports for those cases which run a real risk of custodial penalty.

The second organisational change directed towards producing greater consistency in the content of reports is the development of notes of guidance to report writers (Tutt and Giller, 1984b). Frequently these documents outline the agency's philosophy towards juvenile offenders, lay out the implications of the change in legislation introduced by the 1982 Criminal Justice Act, present the case for offence-focused social inquiry reports and detail the types of information which should (and should not) be included in them. Often they are accompanied by descriptions of the various dispositions which can be recommended to the courts and diagrams of the local sentencing tariff as it is applied to typical cases. In some areas these documents have been issued as joint statements of policy by the local social services department and the probation service.

Supplementing these notes of guidance are organisational arrangements to review the content and recommendations made in the new style reports, frequently called 'gatekeeping', by senior officers prior to the submission of the report to the juvenile court (Giller and Tutt, 1985). In some areas, report writers are required to refer the case to a 'gatekeeper' before the report is written, or, in certain circumstances (for example, when a care order or custodial sentence is likely), to hold a case conference on the report in order to ensure that all avenues or alternative programmes have been explored. One such 'gatekeeping' arrangement for a social services department in a metropolitan authority is presented in Figure 7.2. In this area, no social inquiry reports are produced on a first court appearance or on a second court appearance if agreed by a senior social worker or above. Where reports are written, they are discussed with a designated 'team gatekeeper' who reviews the content and recommendation of the report in the light of

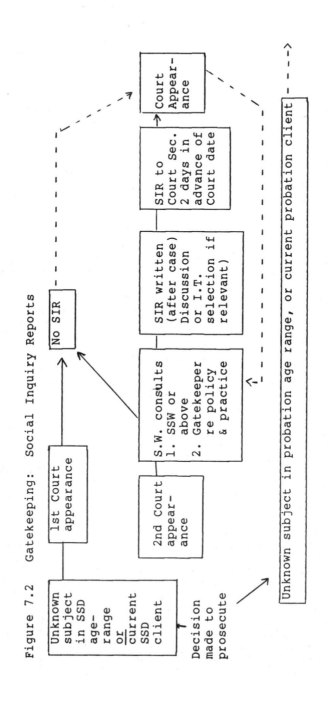

Figure 7.2   Gatekeeping: Social Inquiry Reports

departmental guidelines. The report, if agreed, is then sent on to the court section of the department for submission to the juvenile court. The department also holds <u>post mortems</u> on those cases in which the recommendation in the report was not accepted by the bench to see what modifications to content and form might be needed in such cases in the future.

Whatever the precise arrangements within any one agency, the purpose of ´gatekeeping` is common: to ´tutor` the discretion of practitioners in writing reports and to heighten their awareness of the impact of their judgments on the operation of the local juvenile justice system. (5)

The Systems´ Context within which Reports are Received

Social inquiry reports are influential documents. However, revised report writing strategies by individuals and changes in the organisational arrangements for their production will have little effect if the reasons for such changes are not understood by other agents or organisations working in the system. Magistrates have to be made aware of the need to revise practice but, so, too, do other report writing agencies, for example, the probation service, observation and assessment staff and schools. They also have to be aware of the need for a consistent approach to the use and presentation of information. In an unintegrated system, information produced by one agency can undermine the policy and practice intentions of others.

This is well illustrated with reference to the production and use of school reports in juvenile court criminal proceedings, an issue which, until recently, remained largely unexplored. Ball´s (1981) work into the influence of school reports on magistrates showed quite clearly that the ´decision to impose care orders appeared to be influenced more by the contents of the school report and by reference to educational factors in the social inquiry report than by other social work factors` (1981, 480). This influence was primarily based upon the belief that the teacher who saw the juvenile every day had a more accurate picture than the social worker who compiled the social inquiry report on the basis of one or two home visits. However, Ball went on to show that much of the material contained in school reports consisted of allegations relating to the character and conduct of the juvenile and his or her family which frequently could not be substantiated by the author and which were rarely put to the subjects of the report for rebuttal. (See also Parker et al., 1981, 200; Covington, 1984.) Subsequent surveys of school reports by a NACRO working group confirmed Ball's findings. According to Pask, a member of the working group:

> Evidence collected nationally suggests that teachers frequently yield to the understandable temptation to use the school report to the court as a forum for the expression of frustration about, or even irritation/anger towards a child, especially a child who is a nuisance in school. Teachers sometimes claim that they have foreseen for a long time that certain pupils will end up in court. In other cases a school may see the pending court appearance of a pupil as an opportunity to get rid of a troublemaker (1984, 24).

In such circumstances, it could be argued that juveniles are being punished as much for their failure to attend or work at school as for the offences which ostensibly brought them into the juvenile court.

The work of Giller and Morris (1981a) on care orders also highlighted the importance of information on the juvenile's school performance. As Emerson (1969) notes, truancy and unco-operativeness at school often provides evidence to those who judge delinquents that the juvenile is moving towards 'serious' delinquency:

> Truancy not only suggests that the youth is a "low achiever" and a behaviour problem at school but also indicates that a great deal of his time is spent without control and supervision by adults (1969, 127). (6)

Parker et al.'s (1981, 71) findings suggest that such evidence is interpreted more readily in the case of girls as a signifier of 'problematic' behaviour. This leads to more incursive intervention than would be merited either on the basis of the offence or in comparison with their male counterparts (Webb, 1984).

In the light of such evidence, attempts have been made to revise the format, content and dissemination of school reports (NACRO, 1984c). These aim to limit the information provided by the school to factually verifiable data which relate to the reason for the juvenile's appearance in court, to present positive as well as the more customary negative aspects of the juvenile and to make available for discussion the content of the report with the juvenile, his or her parents and other report writing agencies. In this way, the reports provided by schools would be consistent with the orientation adopted by the local social services department or probation service and would then form part of an integrated package of information for the court.

So far we have presented the issues of report content, their organisational setting and their systems' context as separate and distinct elements in the report writing process. In practice, they are (or should be) inter-related. However, such an inter-relationship does not imply a 'closed loop' system of influence between report writers and the bench (Davies 1974); rather by appreciating the dynamics of the social inquiry process, one can specify desired goals or targets for the system (for example, that no care orders or custodial sentences should be imposed) and evaluate the different strategies used in reports and by agencies to achieve that end.

The developments described here have been taking place over the past six years. But the form and detail of such changes are not uniform throughout England and Wales. In some parts of the country, well integrated and well understood revised policies and practices which are shared by the social services department, the probation services, schools and the juvenile courts are operating: in other areas, changes have only succeeded in altering the practice of one or two elements in the local system.

However, these practices appear to be desired professional practice as far as central government is concerned. (See, for example, draft Home Office circular and the D.H.S.S. booklet 'Reports for Courts' (1986).) While the Home Office circular is primarily directed towards providing advice for report writers in adult courts, both documents share certain principles which embody recent practice changes. They stress that reports have a limited purpose in assisting the court to assess the offence in the offender's social context and should, therefore, centre on the offence and proposals to eliminate or curtail future offending. They should also assess all of the disposals available and likely to be considered by the court and, where a recommendation is included, it should be as specific as possible with respect to how it will influence the defendant´s conduct or environment. They propose further that reports should not be routinely produced in cases where a low tariff option is likely and should not be prepared in ´not guilty` pleas as they cannot consider the context of the offence and the defendant´s culpability. These documents go on to discuss a range of issues concerning the format of reports, the use of language in them, demands placed on report writers with respect to statutory criteria, inter-agency consistency and monitoring. The clear message is that the changes which have been taking place in certain localities should become nationwide and are the preferred professional practice.

Constraints on Decision-Making

We referred earlier to the existence of criteria in the 1982 Criminal Justice Act which are aimed at restricting the use of custodial sentences. The Act envisages a three stage process being applied in deciding on a custodial sentence. First (and with the aid of a social inquiry report), the sentencers must consider whether any other disposition is appropriate. Secondly, non-custodial dispositions can only be rejected on the basis of the statutory criteria. Thirdly, the magistrates must specify which of the criteria applies in the particular case. In practice, however, research suggests that the criteria have had a limited impact in restraining the use of custody (Burney, 1985a and b; Reynolds, 1985a; Whitehead and MacMillan, 1985.)

Because of concern about the ineffectiveness of these criteria, social workers and probation officers in some areas have developed practices which assist clients (and their legal representatives) to lodge appeals to test magistrates´ interpretations of the statutory criteria. For example, Johnson et al., (1984) documented appeal practice in Wakefield and have shown that, in over 70 per cent of the cases in which the juvenile appealed, a lesser sentence was subsequently imposed. The most successful strategy adopted in these cases was demonstrating through a detailed social inquiry report that an alternative was available and had not been properly considered by the magistrates.

Moreover, since the 1982 Act allows a supplementary social inquiry report to be put to the Crown Court on appeal this is a strategy which could be widely used as it is difficult for the juvenile to contest the magistrates´ interpretation of the words ´seriousness` and ´protection of the public`. However, recent cases from the Court of Appeal suggest some principles from which this might be done.

First, the Court of Appeal held that despite the optional requirement on the court to obtain a social inquiry report this should be rarely exercised when sentencing those under the age of 21 (R v Massheder (1985, CLR 185)). Secondly, various cases indicate that the juvenile courts should not make a presumption in favour of custody merely because of the type of charge laid against the juvenile. In R v Bates (1985, CLR 601), for example, a first offender was caught with others committing a burglary in a friend´s house. The social inquiry report rejected a community service order on the basis that the offence was insufficiently serious. The magistrates, however, imposed a one month detention centre order. The Court of Appeal felt that a community service order was the most appropriate sentence and it questioned the often-held belief that cases of domestic burglary are automatically so serious that a non-custodial sentence cannot be justified. The precise context of the offence, not merely its legal category, had to be investigated and only after full consideration of the facts and circumstances should consideration of the appropriateness of custody as a penalty take place. (See also R v Grimes (1985, CLR 609).)

In R v Moffett (1984, CLR 636), the Court of Appeal considered the validity of a custodial sentence imposed on an offender (aged 20) with previous custodial experience and charged with multiple petty offences. In substituting a probation order, the Court demonstrated that where the offences themselves are not serious the lower court must consider the offender´s response to a non-custodial option for each offence and that it should not conclude on the basis of previous court appearances that the offender has reached a stage where, custody having been imposed previously, there is no further possibility of a non-custodial sentence.

In R v Bradbourn (1985, CLR 682), the Lord Chief Justice substituted a conditional discharge for a three month youth custody sentence in the case of a female sales assistant (aged 20) found guilty of the theft of £2. He suggested that the word

´seriousness` in the statute meant:

> The kind of offence which when committed by a young person would make right thinking members of the public having all the facts feel that justice had not been done by the passing of any other sentence but a custodial one (1985, CLR 683).

Whether ´seriousness` has a different meaning depending upon whether it is a care order or a custodial sentence being considered was raised, by implication, in R v Gray (1983, CLR 754). A sixteen year old girl with one previous conditional discharge was sentenced to youth custody for shoplifting goods valued at £23. While the custodial sentence was quashed on appeal, a care order was substituted, even though a qualifying criterion for the imposition of a care order is ´seriousness of the offence`.

Conclusion

This chapter has provided an overview of the context of dispositional decision-making in the English juvenile courts. The precise context varies, depending on the personnel and their practice ideologies, the prevailing ethos of the bench, the types of juveniles referred to the court and their offences, the availability of resources and the bench´s faith in them. We have stressed, therefore, the need to appreciate the localised nature of decision-making within discrete juvenile justice systems. In the 1980s, and especially since the implementation of the Criminal Justice Act 1982, the context of decision-making has begun to change and to move from the confusions in policy and practice which characterised decision-making under the partially implemented 1969 Children and Young Persons Act. In essence, juveniles´ offences are now a central and legitimate focus for decision-making.

The English position in the 1980s, therefore, is somewhat different from the schema posited by Matza (1964). Rather than the juvenile´s offence being utilized by decision-makers sub rosa as the primary criterion of judgment, as Matza suggests (and as may have been the case in the 1970s), an assessment of the offence is now explicitly viewed as a legitimate and fundamental concern in the sentencing process. We are not arguing that the offence is the exclusive criterion of judgment, but rather that it is openly the principal criterion.

Matza went on to suggest that, where the real basis of such decisions was obfuscated by the language of treatment and help, there was created in the mind of the juvenile a sense of injustice and, with this, alienation from the legitimacy of the juvenile court's processes. Indeed, he suggested that this could actually exacerbate the drift into further delinquency. Matza defined the components of justice as follows:

> It is only fair that some steps be taken to ascertain whether I was really the wrongdoer (cognisance); it is only fair that you who pass judgment on me sustain the right to do so (competence); it is only fair that some relationship obtain between the magnitude of what I have done and what you propose to do with me (commensurability); it is only fair that differences between the treatment of my status and others be reasonable and tenable (comparison) (1964, 106).

Clients' views of the decision-making process in English juvenile courts confirm the importance of these principles (Parker, 1978; Morris and Giller, 1977). They perceived the role of the juvenile court to be that of administering 'justice' in the traditional sense of the term: intervention justified on proof of the commission of an offence and the commensurability of the sentence to the offence. They expected a tariff of disposals founded in retributive ideals and it was on this basis that the efficacy of the juvenile court was measured. When deviation from these principles was observed (for example, when an individualised disposition was made or the offence was embellished by the police thereby securing a higher tariff sentence than believed to be justified), a sense of injustice and alienation arose. As Parker et al.'s (1981) work shows, however, in daily practice, deviations from the principles of justice are a frequent and routine part of the operation of the system. Such departures may be experienced not only in the juvenile court but also in the juveniles' encounters with the police, teachers, social workers, probation officers, lawyers and a range of other professionals. Parker et al., found that five out of six 'City' families and nine out of ten 'Countryside' families expressed dissatisfaction. They write that:

> Whilst working-class juveniles do voice a
> broad agreement in ranking the juvenile
> court´s range of disposals, their accumu-
> lated and experiential knowledge challen-
> ges the appropriateness or efficacy of
> these available means. In particular,
> they felt that the charges as put to them
> tended to be ´bumped up´ thus invalidating
> the fairness of the broadly ´agreed´ sen-
> tencing tariff. Half the overall sample
> also noted that a juvenile court record
> became a public badge. Hence ´You´re
> branded once you´ve been in trouble´.
> Being ´branded´ will lead to being picked
> out in particular, in future, for another
> push up the tariff ladder (1981, 118).

This realignment of the decision-making basis
in the juvenile court which has given centrality to
the offence may turn out to be a major factor in
promoting feelings of justice and fairness among
juveniles and their parents. But the juvenile
court´s decision alone, coming as it does at the end
of a process of discretionary and often ´hidden´
decisions, will not necessarily promote substantive
justice.

NOTES

1. Variations in courts´ sentencing of similar
cases is not limited to the juvenile court (Tarling,
1979).
2. There is a longer tradition of legal representation in the United States. In 1967 the
Supreme Court in <u>in re Gault</u> (387, US, 1967) held
that some of the procedural protections accorded to
adults accused of crime should be afforded to juveniles. The right to legal representation was said to
be paramount amongst these protections; the Supreme
Court stated that ´the child requires the guiding
hand of counsel at every stage in the proceedings
against him´. The Supreme Court, however, limited
this due process protection to the adjudication
stage of the proceedings and excluded it from applying to issues of pre-trial detention, intake or disposition (<u>McKeiver v Pennsylvania</u> (403, US 528,
1971); <u>Schall v Martin</u> (1984, 4681)). Challenge to

juvenile court decisions by way of <u>habeas corpus</u> proceedings as used in <u>in re Gault</u> is not possible in England and Wales; <u>R v D</u> (1976) Times 20 October, <u>R v K</u> (1978) 1 All ER 180 <u>cf. R v P</u> (1979) 143 J.P.N. 730.

3. The duration and inter-relationship of interventions also have to be considered, especially since the minimum custodial sentence under the 1982 Criminal Justice Act (in practice, two weeks in a detention centre) could be viewed as disproportionate to a three year supervision order with a ninety day intermediate treatment requirement (Rutherford, 1986).

4. While section 2(2) of the 1982 Act requires the court to obtain a social inquiry report prior to passing a custodial sentence, section 2(3) makes this optional if the court is of the opinion that it is unnecessary to do so. However in <u>R v Massheder</u> (1984, CLR 185) the Court of Appeal stated that this option should be rarely exercised when sentencing those under the age of 21.

5. Such changes mirror the proposals for legislative reform made by the Parliamentary All-Party Penal Affairs Group (1981, para. 298).

6. Comparable reasons are given by magistrates for the imposition of supervision and care orders in truancy proceedings (Grimshaw and Pratt, 1985).

Chapter 8

FUTURE DIRECTIONS

The Changing Nature of the Juvenile Court

In spite of evidence to the contrary the public perception of juvenile crime is that it is increasing at a rate faster than adult crime. The media attention given to crime in general and to juvenile crime in particular and the political significance given to the 'law and order' debate has meant that this evidence is often ignored in public pronouncements on the issue. Such a situation is not new (Pearson, 1983; Taylor, 1981). However, current changes in juvenile justice practice have fundamentally dislocated the reality of the situation from the rhetoric. (1) Two factors in particular are likely to alter radically the framework of debates on juvenile justice and provide the opportunity to question existing arrangements for dealing with juvenile offenders.

The first is the decline in the juvenile population. Between the late 1970s and the 1990s the proportion of juveniles in the population will decline by 25 per cent (Pratt, 1985a; Riley, 1986a). Whether such a decline will directly lead to a reduction in juvenile offending is, of course, debateable given that the prevalence of offending within a particular cohort can only be guessed at or investigated over time through repeated self-report instruments (see, for example, Gold and Reimer, 1975). Police practices also affect the juvenile crime rate. As Riley notes:

> The relatively low clear-up rates for recorded crime mean that the characteristics of all offenders involved in crime are much less well known than for the subset caught and processed by the criminal

> justice system. And no groups of offences
> are dominated by offenders (or victims)
> with specific age characteristics in ways
> which would allow such an approximate
> assessment of the likely impact of
> population change on the number of crimes
> committed or reported (1986a, 31).

Even more problematic, however, is whether the reduction in the proportion of juveniles eligible for
processing into the juvenile court will lead to an
actual decline in juvenile court rolls. (2) Two
factors suggest that a decline might occur.

First, as we noted in Chapter 5, the police
have recently been encouraged by the Home Office to
revise their force orders so that juvenile offenders
are more likely to be diverted from the juvenile
court. Research (for example, Crook, 1986) suggests
that police forces will respond to such pressure.
Secondly, the introduction of the Crown Prosecution
Service creates an additional sift or filter between
the police and the courts. While views on the
likely impact of the new prosecution system vary,
the existence of such a filter and these demographic
changes may well act together to reduce the juvenile
court population. Certainly, research suggests that
a juvenile court appearance for those under the age
of fourteen is becoming rare. In 1985, in England
and Wales, for example, only 10,000 children (some
16 per cent of the total dealt with in juvenile
court) were sentenced by the juvenile court compared
with some 53,100 young persons. In some local juvenile justice systems, the proportion of those under
the age of fourteen dealt with by the juvenile court
is even smaller. In Newcastle upon Tyne, for
example, during the first half of 1985, only 12 per
cent of those sentenced were under fourteen and in
the county of Surrey it was only 7 per cent (Giller,
1986).

The second factor, integrally linked to the
first, is the changing nature of the juvenile court.
The 1982 Criminal Justice Act has re-introduced
three fundamental principles which mark a return
from the welfare ethos of the 1960s to a more classical model of the administration of criminal justice. These three principles are: the appropriateness of adversarial proceedings, determinate sentences and proportionate sentences. These issues
have been discussed in earlier chapters and are
presented here in summary form only.

Twenty years ago proposals were advanced which,

if implemented, would have abolished the juvenile court in favour of a family council or service (Morris and Giller, 1978; Clarke, 1980). However, the process remained judicial rather than administrative. Moreover, juveniles´ rights to legal representation (for example, when faced with the possibility of removal from the community into care or custody) have been enhanced and ¹ the discretionary powers of local authorities to place children in secure accommodation have been considerably curtailed. Only the juvenile court is empowered to sanction the continued use of such facilities. In the 1960s, elements of indeterminacy in the sentencing structure were considered integral to the aims of reform and rehabilitation. Reformation was viewed as a continuing process and so assessment of the duration of intervention was thought appropriately determined, not in advance by the sentencing tribunal, but at the time of the maximum effect of the programme and by those administering the programme. Increasing criticism of the inequity of indeterminacy (especially in relation to the use of the indeterminate care order for offending) and a decline in belief in the rehabilitative ideal led to changes. The new sentences introduced in the 1982 Act, therefore, were all determinate in nature and this principle was applied not only to the new penalties available to the court but also to welfare measures.

There are also a number of indications in the 1982 Act that the sentences imposed by the juvenile court should be proportionate to the offence which brought the juvenile into the court. Though the criteria introduced seem not to have restricted the use of custody, they were clearly intended to reinforce a gradation of intervention related to offence-oriented factors. Moreover, again, the concept of proportionality is not restricted to traditional penalties. Similar safeguards were introduced with respect to welfare measures.

These principles which underpin current juvenile justice policy also underpin policy towards both the young adult and the adult offender. As McCabe and Treitel note:

> In the construction of a system of tariff sentencing with many stages from discharge to penal custody, the legislation has given to juvenile courts a shape and direction that does not differ materially from those for adults (1984, 28).

But it is not just the principles of sentencing which are becoming generic; many of the sentencing options are too. Custodial sentences (for example, detention centre and youth custody) have long stretched across a wide age range (from fourteen and fifteen to 21) and the 1982 Act extends the community service order, previously only available to those offenders over the age of seventeen, to sixteen year olds. Conversely, penalties which began their life in the juvenile courts have been transposed into the adult system. Schedule 11 day centre orders which were introduced in the 1982 Act for young adult and adult offenders, for example, are much like the intermediate treatment or supervised activity orders available for juveniles.

Is There a Need For a Juvenile Court?

Given this assimilation of principles and practice, the question arises whether or not there remains a need for a distinctive criminal juvenile court at all. Certainly the philosophy underpinning the civil and criminal jurisdictions of the juvenile court seem to be moving apart.

The recent publication of the DHSS's Review of Child Care Law (1985), for example, proposes a number of measures which move the juvenile court away from traditional adversarial proceedings in civil cases and a range of new powers which seek to promote consensus between the parties involved. Among the procedural changes recommended are proposals to ensure maximum disclosure of allegations and evidence before a hearing and giving all those interested in the case an opportunity to participate. Likewise, in terms of powers, the report proposes a range of orders which share responsibility for the juvenile between the local authority and his or her parents. Moreover, the report recommends that what it calls the 'free-standing' conditions of moral danger, being beyond parental control, not receiving a proper education and the commission of an offence should no longer, in their own right, be grounds for initiating care proceedings (DHSS, 1985, 102-7). While examination of the juvenile court's criminal jurisdiction was specifically excluded from the review group's brief, it is quite clear that the non-adversarial civil proceedings proposed in the report would sit uneasily alongside existing policy and practice as applied to delinquents. Also there is no indication that any government department would be willing to incorporate wholesale the

237

criminal jurisdiction of the juvenile court into a revised family court structure (Du Sautoy, 1986) and many would strenuously argue against doing so (Freeman, 1984; Adler, 1985). However, if the family court and new powers become a reality, (3) the reasons for retaining a distinctive criminal court for juveniles would need to be examined.

In the United States in the mid-1970s, perceived failure of the traditional welfare orientation of the juvenile court both to adequately deal with juvenile crime and to respect the rights of juvenile offenders led to proposals to restrict the juvenile court´s broad discretionary decision-making powers and to introduce greater legality into that setting (Morris, 1978b). While the operational basis of the English juvenile court in its criminal jurisdiction has never been as overtly welfare oriented as its American counterpart, the arguments for the abolition of the juvenile court which emerged in the United States at that time (Rubin, 1979) are pertinent to debates here.

The first argument was that juvenile courts failed to apply relevant statutory criteria and hence acted lawlessly. This is well supported in England from research into the ways in which the statutory safeguards contained in the 1982 Criminal Justice Act have been largely ignored by magistrates (Burney, 1985a and b; Reynolds, 1985a). Secondly, it was argued that the adult criminal courts would provide greater protection to juveniles´ rights than the juvenile courts, and this also seems supported. For example, while some Court of Appeal judges have resisted elaborating the statutory safeguards in the 1982 Act (R v Bradbourn, 1985, CLR 682), others have been willing to do so and have acted in a way which is restrictive of the use of custody (R v Massheder, 1984, CLR 184; R v Moffett, 1984, CLR 636; R v Bates, 1985, CLR 601; R v Grimes, 1985, CLR 609). Similarly, both published (Johnson et al., 1984) and unpublished accounts suggest that, where appeals are made against magistrates´ decisions to impose custody, many are successful in having a community-based alternative substituted.

The third argument was that as the rationale for sentencing in the American juvenile court moved from treatment to proportionality, sentences closely paralleled practice in the criminal courts. Evidence of a move towards proportionate sentences has already been mentioned in this chapter. Also relevant in this respect is the research referred to in Chapter 7 on changes in the construction and use of social inquiry reports (Tutt and Giller, 1984b). Since the implementation of the Criminal Justice Act 1982, many social service and probation departments have reviewed the form and content of their reports to juvenile courts (Raynor, 1985; Tutt and Giller, 1984b; Morris and Giller, 1983) and have withdrawn routine reports for those appearing for the first time (Baldwin, 1982). This is similar to traditional practice in the adult courts. Moreover, as professional groups (social workers and probation officers) press on the juvenile court the desirability of offence-focused procedures, the appropriateness of a juvenile court which departs from this becomes questionable.

Fourthly it was argued that diversion practices, once uniquely associated with the juvenile justice system, were established across the whole of the criminal justice process. Recent developments here show a similar trend. As we noted, the Home Office circular on cautioning (14/1985) applies to all offenders irrespective of age. The independent prosecution service also acts in both juvenile and adult courts. The final argument advanced was that if juvenile court proceedings became fully adversarial legal representatives would be able to adopt their more traditional role. Research in England does suggest a high degree of role confusion among legal representatives working in the juvenile court (Parker et al., 1981; Morris, 1983; Giller and Maidment, 1984). As we discussed in Chapter 7, the effectiveness of lawyers very much depends upon the orientation - welfare or due process - of the particular juvenile court before which they appear. An unequivocal statement that the juvenile court was a criminal court based upon adversarial principles would undoubtedly assist legal representatives in the performance of their role.

The research and information referred to in testing the strength of these arguments for the abolition of the juvenile court is derived from current policy and practice. If our interpretation and understanding of the evidence is valid, then it raises the fundamental question of what the role of the juvenile court should be? The original juvenile courts were not, of course, so distinct from the magistrates' ordinary jurisdiction. Apart from separate sittings and a modified penalty structure, they were criminal courts. Only later were special procedures and distinctive processes to determine dispositions developed. At their inception, two features of the criminal justice system were used to present the case for a tribunal which was separate from the courts which dealt with adults: the need to avoid contamination of the juvenile by the adult offender and the stigma of conviction. In addition, it was later assumed that better decisions would result if they were reached in an informal setting which facilitated communication between the bench, defendant and parents and if those with a particular experience or knowledge of juveniles made the decisions about them. Has the juvenile court achieved these objectives?

With respect to stigma, three important issues should be noted. First, despite the intention to the contrary, convictions from juvenile courts can lead to an increase or an intensification of delinquent behaviour (Rutter and Giller, 1983). For example, Farrington (1977), as part of the Cambridge Study of Delinquent Development, compared juveniles with similar self-reported delinquency scores at the age of fourteen and eighteen according to whether or not they had been convicted. The average score of the juveniles with a conviction increased over the four years whereas the average score of those who had not appeared in court fell. However, Walker (1980) argues that these findings are capable of a quite different interpretation, namely that the penalties applied on a first court appearance are so trivial that they inadequately deter those convicted. Nevertheless, other studies have produced results similar to those of Farrington (Rutter and Giller, 1983). Secondly, while the reduction of stigma is said to be a principal motive for separate juvenile court proceedings, recent research documents that despite attempts to separate such cases, in prac- tice, the mixing of juvenile and adult offenders is common (McCabe and Treitel, 1984; Parker et al., 1981). Moreover, it is naive to assume that defendants in the juvenile justice system do not see their experience as anything other than stigmatising (Parker et al., 1981). Finally, with respect to stigma, Walker has recently argued that 'the statutes which represent an attempt to control the stigma of criminal proceedings and convictions are in a confused state' (1985, 425). For example, although juveniles appearing in the juvenile court are automatically protected from identification and publicity, juveniles appearing in other courts can receive publicity unless there is a direction by the court not to. As Walker comments:

If the aim of the provisions is to protect children and young persons from stigma, it is hard to see why they should receive automatic protection when dealt with for everyday offences in juvenile courts, but not when tried for the most stigmatising offences - such as homicide or rape - in the Crown Court (1985, 293).

With respect to the participation of defendants and parents in the juvenile court process, research suggests that, rather than enhancing communication between the parties the juvenile court is frequently seen as a confusing and alien environment which transforms the subjects of the proceedings into the objects (Priestley et al., 1977; Parker et al., 1981; Badham et al., 1984). Nor does the selection of magistrates with particular experience or knowledge of juveniles guarantee particular skills in communication (Fears, 1977). Moreover, 'bench ethos' may determine how that experience or knowledge is mediated into 'acceptable' court practice. Also, if juvenile courts operate a tariff system (Moxon et al., 1985), then the need for special experience or knowledge is in doubt. More pertinently, there is no consensus about what makes particular experience or knowledge relevant and how it is to be applied.

The weight of evidence points to the juvenile court meeting neither its original objectives nor the new demands made of it. Clearly, if the juvenile court is to survive there needs to be a radical re-appraisal of the role it can play. This becomes all the more important as strategies are expanded which circumvent its jurisdiction.

Circumventing the Juvenile Court

Most jurisdictions have arrangements to transfer juveniles from or waive the jurisdiction of the juvenile court when dealing with certain 'serious' offences. In England and Wales, section 53 of the Children and Young Persons Act 1933 is the relevant legislation. Juveniles made the subject of section 53 sentences are detained in a place and under conditions which the Home Secretary directs. The Home Secretary's powers include directing the detention to be undertaken in a community home controlled by a local authority. For those under sixteen years of age at the time of the conviction, the case is usually referred to the D.H.S.S. for placement (for example, to one of the two Youth Treatment Centres or to a community home with secure accommodation (Cawson and Martell 1979; Millham et al., 1978)). During 1984, 45 juveniles were placed in child care establishments under section 53 orders and on December 31st 1984, 73 children were so accommodated (House of Commons 1985, 34-5).

In recent years, the number of juveniles detained under this section in all forms of accommodation has increased (Dunlop and Frankenburg, 1982): from eleven in 1970 to 85 in 1980 and to 104 in 1984. This increase is largely due to an extension of the crimes which make such orders possible. In its original form, section 53 was limited to offences of murder, manslaughter and wounding with intent to cause grievous bodily harm. In the words of Godsland and Fielding the order was:

> intended as a measure of social defence against a small number of dangerous juveniles rather than as a part of a range of punishments available to the courts (1985, 286).

In 1961, however, the Criminal Justice Act extended the range of offences to include all those for which an adult convicted on indictment could be sentenced to imprisonment for fourteen years or more. This brought within the ambit of the section offences of robbery, arson, certain sexual offences and burglary. The majority of those currently detained under section 53 have been convicted of property offences. In 1984, 36 juveniles convicted of robbery and ten convicted of burglary were so detained. Moreover, recently the Court of Appeal (R v Butler J., 1985, CLR 56) and senior judges (Barker, 1985) have argued for more frequent use of these sentencing powers.

Whether or not Parliament envisaged that increases in the courts' power to imprison adults would have a direct impact on the sentencing of juveniles is unclear. What is clear, however, is that section 53 'is now being used as part of the tariff system of punishment extending quite considerably beyond the function of social defence' (Godsland and Fielding, 1985, 287). While the overall number of juveniles involved in section 53 proceedings remains small, the significance of the section and its potential for marginalising the role of the juvenile court should not be underestimated. If the juvenile court is ultimately left to deal only with petty offenders, the need for a distinctive court becomes questionable.

A variety of alternative models of juvenile justice have been produced in recent years and experience of their operation in other jurisdictions is available. The models discussed here are ideal types and, as such, may not be operating in any jurisdiction in pure form. Moreover, these models are not exhaustive of the typologies which commentators have constructed (see, for example, the supplementary report to the Task Force, 1980; 350-354). While there are undoubtedly real (and often concealed) dangers associated with such modelling exercises (Martin et al., 1981), the intention here is to illustrate the nature and breadth of the debate and to highlight critical operational features. As we shall see, most systems operate with a mixture of models and it is the balance between the various elements that frequently produces operational problems. It is to these alternatives that we now turn.

Welfare and its Critics

The ´welfare model` for dealing with offenders assumes that delinquent behaviour has antecedent causes which explain it; that these causes can be (and have been) discovered; that their discovery has made possible the treatment and control of such behaviour; that delinquents share pathological conditions which make them fundamentally different from the law-abiding, though similar to others in difficulties; that delinquency gets ´worse` without ´treatment`; that ´treatment` is possible and that involuntary ´treatment` is not punishment. In essence, delinquent behaviour is seen in many ways as being similar to medical illness - it represents a kind of social illness.

In recent years, the ´welfare model` has attracted a considerable body of critical scrutiny (Morris et al., 1980; Taylor et al., 1980; May, 1971). Critics have argued that the approach oversimplifies our understanding of the causes of juvenile crime. For example, research contradicts the assumption that delinquency has a pathological base akin to a medical condition (President´s Commission, 1967). The search for unique aetiological factors, be it personality, family, peer group or environment, hasproduced inconclusive results (Rutter and Giller, 1983), even though such causes continue to be believed and relied upon by some of those operating juvenile justice systems. Given our weak

243

theoretical understanding of the causes of crime, the assumption that we have a range of treatments or interventions which we can successfully use to affect delinquency is equally flawed (Rutter and Giller, 1983). Also such interventions are seen by their recipients as punishment for crimes they have committed, despite the rhetoric to the contrary. In practice, the application of these interventions has led to stigmatising the juveniles involved and can have the effect that they remain in the criminal justice system. The discretionary powers given to those who operate welfare interventions, moreover, have frequently been used to 'widen the net' of the service. This brings into the system those 'at risk' as well as those adjudicated delinquent.

A commonly cited example of this approach is the Scottish children's hearing system introduced in 1968. We outlined this in Chapter 3 though it is important to note that the juvenile justice system there also contains elements of crime control. In 1982, 667 juveniles were sentenced in the Sheriff's Court in addition to the 10,000 offence referrals made to the children's hearings.

There is now a considerable amount of research on the day-to-day operation of the children's hearing system (Morris and McIsaac, 1978; Martin et al., 1981). This has questioned the adequacy of their observance of procedural requirements. The findings suggest that panel members often depart from the statutory procedures which were designed to assist juveniles and their parents to participate in the proceedings and to protect their civil liberties. Also, while some commentators have referred to participation by the families in the hearing and communication between the parties as a positive feature of the system (Martin et al., 1981; Asquith, 1983b; Bottoms, 1985), the research findings do not lead to such clear conclusions. Juveniles and their parents do appear to participate more in the children's hearings than in the juvenile courts. For example, in Asquith's (1983b) research, only 16 per cent of contributions to magistrates in the juvenile court were made by juveniles or their parents in contrast with 90 per cent to panel members in children's hearings. However, Asquith goes on to note that on only eleven occasions did members of the hearings disagree with the recommendations made in the social inquiry reports submitted to them compared with thirty such occasions amongst the magistrates. He provides no information on the extent to which the juveniles or their parents agreed with these recommendations and so it is possible to, at least, raise the issue that, despite their contributions, they had a limited impact on the final decision of the hearing.

Research also questions the nature of the communication taking place within the hearing. Martin et al. (1981) present a series of exchanges between panel members and parties to the hearing. These provide examples of sarcasm, denial of parents´ and their children´s accounts of or reasons for the offence, moralising and threats. Moreover, Martin et al. document that key issues believed to be the reasons for the child´s behaviour were avoided. Exchanges with parents, according to them, were:

> characterised by the evasion of sensitive
> problems and a concentration on topics
> deemed ´safe` and ´manageable` but often
> of limited relevance to the needs of the
> child in the case (1981, 136).

Despite these critical comments it is important to note that parents and children alike have expressed satisfaction with _their_ perception of the degree of participation in the proceedings and their informal nature (Martin _et al._, 1981, 191-234).

Many commentators have advocated adoption of aspects of the Scottish system in England (McCabe and Treitel, 1984; Association of County Councils, 1984; Association of Directors of Social Services, 1985). However, it seems unlikely that any such radical change will occur. Moreover, the positives commonly associated with the Scottish system - diversion, participation and better communication between the parties - are not a consequence only of a welfare approach to juvenile offenders. They can be part of systems based on quite different principles.

A frequent criticism of welfare systems has been their over-reach into the lives of juveniles for they enable greater intervention than would be justified on the basis of the presenting offence alone (Austin and Krisberg, 1981). Concerns like these led to the rejection and demise of a welfare approach in other jurisdictions (for example, in the United States).

Justice and its Critics

Influential in recent years in leading to a reconsideration of a welfare approach has been the emergence of an alternative set of principles frequently termed the 'justice model'. In brief, these involve the removal from the juvenile justice system of non-criminal behaviour by juveniles (for example, truancy) and victimless crimes (for example, drug abuse), diversion of juveniles from juvenile courts wherever possible, procedures to make visible and reviewable the discretionary practices of those working in the system and limiting sanctions available to juvenile courts by reference to principles of proportionality, determinacy, and the least restrictive alternative. We have documented the emergence of these principles and practical proposals for their implementation elsewhere (Morris, 1978b; Morris et al., 1980; Morris and Giller, 1983). The 'critical edge' of such proposals was that, in promoting the concept of just deserts, the inequalities of existing practices, including class-biases and discrimatory decision-making, would be exposed and a redistribution of the power of the state would take place (Greenberg and Humphries, 1980).

Critics of the justice model have concentrated upon five main areas of attack. First, they argue that it is overly concerned with procedural formality and due process aspects of the law. Such a focus is said not to accord with the reailty that, in the majority of juvenile cases, the facts are not in dispute (or, at least, disputes are not revealed by the court procedures). Hence, they argue that the judicial process is largely redundant (Bottoms, 1985; Asquith, 1983b; Parker et al., 1981). Secondly, there is a linked argument that, if a pro-diversion policy is coupled with a justice oriented juvenile court, this leads to a stark bifurcation in our response to juvenile offenders. The minority referred to the juvenile court would inevitably be punished severely (Harris, 1982; Bottoms, 1985). Thirdly, the justice model is said to ignore the fact that juveniles brought into the formal system do exhibit a range of social disadvantages over which they have no control. As such, the model is said to exhibit the worst form of 'eighteenth century liberalism' (Reynolds, 1981) and leaves the disadvantaged to their fate. Critics, therefore, posit the notion of a 'just' criminal justice system within an unjust society as a contradiction in terms (Bottoms, 1985, 110). As Asquith argues:

> Policies which ignore the social and econ-
> omic realities in which children find

themselves, while promoting greater equality and justice within formal systems of control, may not only ignore, but may compound the structural and material inequalities which have been historically associated with criminal behaviour (1983b, 17).

Fourthly, proponents of a justice model are said to have played into the hands of the right who are then able to co-opt the language of justice to institute tougher laws and penalties (Greenberg and Humphries, 1980; Reiman and Headlee, 1981). Finally, alternative forms of accountability for those who operate the juvenile justice system, such as popular or local justice (Brown and Bloomfield, 1979), are said to have been ignored. If juvenile justice practitioners were subject to political rather than legal accountability this, it is said, would advance two important goals. In Clarke's words:

Scrutiny of the whole array of agencies (police, magistracy, social work) seems preferable to a dependence on legal checks and balances on some (primarily social work). Secondly, representative accountability provides the ground on which arguments about juvenile strategies can be fought out. Where the justice model confines debate within the state, political accountability offers the possibility of opening up the state (1985, 420).

The extent to which the justice model has been successfully co-opted by the right in practice should not lead to the erroneous conclusion, which some commentators have reached (Rutherford, 1986, 15; Farrington, 1984, 71; Harris, 1985, 38) that it is a crude retributive or punitive model. The main philosophical justification behind the liberal version of the approach is as an expressive or denunciatory theory. In Walker's words:

The essence of expressive theories is that punishment signifies non-toleration of the offence for which it is inflicted (1983, 21).

Within the justice model, 'what is not to be tolerated' and 'how society is to signify its disapproval' become matters for open debate. The

justice model, therefore, carries within it a
critical potential to change, not only the juvenile
justice system, but also the social institutions it
wishes to regulate. It can highlight the
discrepancies between the power of the local state
and its application (Morris and Giller, 1983).
Moreover, those who argue that the justice model has
been `already colonised by the New Right` (Clarke,
1985, 418) run the risk of failing to acknowledge
the relevance of rights and justice in any
alternative social order. As Hunt (1985) has argued,
greater public representation in policy-making is a
desirable goal. But as Hunt acknowledges:

> This argument does not deal with the dis-
> tinction between participation in policy
> and its implementation. A massive increase
> in public participation in democratic
> policy-making would require an expanded
> rather than diminished role for public
> administration. And if bureaucracy re-
> mains, then the necessity of both proced-
> ural rights and rights against abuse of
> power will remain (1985, 323).

Justice and Welfare Combined

The most common response to disillusionment
with a welfare or justice approach is the development of a juvenile justice system which uses dual or
mixed philosophies and practices. Such proposals
commonly aim to divert juveniles from the formal
system where possible, but where formal action is
justified, then elements of due process, justice and
welfare are combined.

The proposals contained in the Black Committee
Report on Children and Young Persons in Northern
Ireland (1979) are a good example of this. It recommended that given the ubiquity and transient
nature of most juvenile crime, first and second
minor offenders who admitted their guilt should be
diverted from the juvenile court by police cautioning (coupled, where necessary, with voluntary social
work help). `Serious` and `persistent` offenders
and those who disputed their guilt were to be
referred to a criminal juvenile court whose main
function would be:

> to try offences in a manner which is fair
> to the defendant and easily understood by
> him and to use its power for the

protection of the public and the prevention of crime (1979, para. 6.14).

This court would have the power to sanction the
offender by discharge, fine, attendance centre
order, supervision order or a determinate custodial
sentence of between one month and two years. It
would also have the power to defer sentences and to
pass cases over to a welfare-based care court in
cases where ´care considerations are so evident that
immediate action is necessary to secure the welfare
of the child` (1979, para. 6.17). Care proceedings,
however, would not be possible solely on the basis
of the commission of an offence; the juvenile court
would subsequently determine a penalty for the
offence in the light of the outcome of the care
proceedings if it so wished. Similar proposals
which separate the two jurisdictions of the juvenile
court - care and crime - and enable a cross-over at
various points have also been made in New Zealand
(Department of Social Welfare, 1984). What is
problematic with proposals of this kind is not the
separation of the tribunals to deal with different
types of cases, but the means for identifying cases
which should be transferred from the criminal to the
care jurisdiction and the criteria on which this
discretion should be exercised. (4)
    A similar difficulty emerges in recent propo-
sals to reform the juvenile justice system by
writers who wish to retain some welfare considerations in criminal proceedings. For example, Adler
(1985), a former panel member in the Scottish
system, has proposed a re-assessment of the
children´s hearing in the light of the arguments of
those propounding a justice model. Adler argues that
a number of elements of due process could be
usefully incorporated into the Scottish system in
the light of acknowledged deficiencies in practice -
written reasons for decisions, the availability of
representation (but not necessarily legal representation) and the enforcement of procedural
requirements. More fundamentally, however, Adler
recommends:

> The Scottish experience suggests that des-
> pite the theoretical possibility of a
> single tribunal or court making decisions
> both on the basis of needs and of deeds,
> in practice it would seem that such a dual
> role is open to abuse and can be a source
> of legitimate confusion to those subject

to the different disposals. It therefore
seems that wherever possible, the roles
should be institutionally separated.
Wherever an offence is both the ground
and basis of legal intervention rather
than an indicator of a possible need for
intervention there should be separate
proceedings (1985, 137).

This recommendation is somewhat paradoxical as
over 70 per cent of the children currently entering
the children's hearing system are delinquent. Moreover, when the system was designed it was presented
as a radical new way of dealing with delinquents and
it is this aspect which devotees in England wish to
see imported (McCabe and Treitel, 1984). More problematic, however, are the criteria to be used to
determine those cases in which the offence is 'both
the ground and the basis of legal intervention' and
those in which it is 'an indicator of a possible
need for intervention'. Punishment is said to be
appropriate for the former, care for the latter.
But Adler provides no objective means whereby one
can determine which kind of offender deserves which
kind of response, other than a reference to the
'small minority of young offenders whose actions
pose a genuine threat to the public interest' (1985,
144). This is a category which, as we saw in
Chapter 4, provides no sound basis for action.
Similar logic lies behind Harris's concept of
"just welfare" (1985). After reviewing the principles and the practice of the 1969 Children and
Young Persons Act and the justice model, Harris
argues that justice and welfare can be compatibly
integrated into a single operational framework. By
distinguishing between negative welfare, that is
'doing as little as possible' and positive welfare,
that is 'doing as much as possible', Harris
proposes:

> that it is a professional social work task
> to clarify with the client which of these
> two broad approaches best meets his needs;
> and that positive welfare, where that is
> chosen, should be subject to the test of
> proportionality (1985, 40).

Apart from misunderstanding the role of welfare as
espoused by those arguing for a justice approach -
they endorse, for example, the provision of voluntary social work assistance - such proposals

pose a fundamental and insoluable equation: the
determination of the amount of welfare intervention which is proportionate to the offence charged.
There is a fundamental schism between those who
argue for a justice approach per se and those who
seek to combine with it a welfare orientation in
some (albeit residual) form. That schism relates to
assumptions about the appropriate role of the juvenile justice system. Harris articulates this clearly
when he writes:

> Let it be posited, then, that welfare as
> an ideal - that is to say meeting the
> needs of the offender - is a legitimate,
> but not the only legitimate, objective of
> the juvenile justice system (1985, 39).

For those who accept this assumption, retaining
welfare services for particular (undefined) categories of juveniles as an integral part of the criminal justice system is logical and consistent. For
those who posit a justice model, however, this
assumption is unacceptable because it is flawed:
the juvenile justice system has been consistently
demonstrated to be an ineffective mechanism for
defining welfare needs and for delivering welfare
services. Welfare considerations obfuscate the
basis of the decision-making and confuse the juveniles and families which the juvenile court seeks to
serve. By restricting and simplifying the basis of
the operation of the juvenile justice system to the
juvenile's offence, those who promote a justice
model do not deny that many juveniles in the system
have problems and difficulties which could be
assisted by social work help. They insist, however,
that the role of the juvenile justice system is to
respond to offending in ways in which social work
services can remain available to the offender (for
example, by providing services desired by the juvenile) and not to sentence juveniles to social work.

Recent Developments in the United States

In the United States, a number of models for
reforming the juvenile justice system on justice
lines emerged in the late 1970s (Institute of
Judicial Administration and the American Bar Association, 1977; Task Force on Child Care Services,
1977). In practice, none of these models have been
adopted completely by State legislatures, but
elements have been incorporated into statute and

practice. For example, a federal initiative in the form of the Juvenile Justice and Delinquency Prevention Act of 1974 attempted to achieve diversion by encouraging States through financial incentives to decriminalise status offenders, to develop community-based programmes as alternatives to institutions and to discourage States from incarcerating and detaining juveniles. The impact of the 1974 Act was mixed.

Initially it was successful in getting States to remove many status offenders from both juvenile courts and institutions. Between 1975 and 1980, the proportion of status offenders dealt with by juvenile courts declined by 25 per cent and the number of status offenders detained in custody decreased by nearly 70 per cent. (5) With the withdrawal of Federal funding for these programmes in 1982 a reversal occurred and now more status offenders are being detained (Krisberg, 1985; Krisberg et al., 1986). Moreover, it was never clear whether status offenders were truly diverted from all forms of social control (Logan and Rausch, 1985). Research suggests that a proportion of those who previously would have been dealt with by the juvenile justice system are now in the private health and education systems, which may be equally, if not more, controlling (Krisberg and Schwartz, 1983, Lerman 1980; Rutherford, 1986).

With respect to the incarceration of juveniles who commit offences the pattern was similar. Initially, the use of detention facilities and training schools declined during the 1970s, but by the early 1980s numbers were the same as when the federal initiative began. Also, the duration of detention had increased (Krisberg, 1985; Krisberg et al., 1986).

A redirection of federal effort under the Juvenile Justice and Delinquency Prevention Act has taken place since 1984 under the Reagan administration. The new policy questions whether deinstitutionalisation and decarceration should be a federal rather than a State initiative, and emphasises (among other areas) the more effective prosecution of serious and violent juvenile offenders and the promotion of accountability and just deserts (Regenery, 1986). Such a redirection mirrors the changes which have taken place in State legislatures since 1978 which, while pursuing diversion and deinstitutionalisation (especially for status offenders) have revised their legislation in such ways that tougher policies can now be pursued for some juvenile offenders.

Several States have revised their juvenile justice legislation to introduce aspects of due process and to alter their penalty structures to contain elements of determinacy and proportionality. In some, this has been accompanied by the intro- duction of the presumptive or mandatory sentence. The original intention of this was to reduce sentencing disparities which were a characteristic of welfare-oriented decision-making. Fox illustrates the constraints that this can impose on sentencers by reference to the sentencing process in Washington State:

> The Washington system...requires commit- ment for those whose offending is high on a scale of seriousness and conversely for- bids commitment of those whose offending is not serious. ´Seriousness` for these purposes is numerically computed on the basis of the child´s age, prior history of offending and the scaling of offence ser- iousness already established in the state penal code. For example, a fifteen year old who has been found guilty of the offence of rape is first given 250 points on the basis of a grid with the offence on one axis and the age of the child on the other. If it has been, let us say, 6 to 12 months since his last offence, the 250 is multiplied by a factor of 1.8, a figure also derived from a grid with offence and criminal history axis. The resulting figure of 450 is then entered into another table which then produces for the juvenile court judge the decision that the child must be confined for a period of from 40 to 50 months, followed by a maximum parole period of an additional 18 months. This is the mandated result in the ordinary case (Martin et al., 1981, 294).

Frequently, however, such changes had the effect of increasing the level and extent of intervention in the lives of juveniles. Both Washington and New York States, for example, explicitly used the justice model to toughen up penalties. In these circumstances, sentencing disparities have been reduced but at the cost of higher rates of incarcer- ation. (6)

An alternative way to introduce due process and

increase penalties is the use of waiver or direct file procedures (either at the discretion of the prosecutor or the juvenile court judge or by statutory provision). Under these arrangements ´serious` or ´violent` or ´persistent` juvenile offenders or those deemed ´not suitable for treatment` can be transferred to the adult court for disposition where more severe penalties can be applied (Feld, 1981b). Since the late 1970s, it has become easier to transfer juveniles into adult courts in most States. (7)

Definition of the terms ´serious`, ´persistence`, ´amenability to treatment` vary considerably between the States and decision-makers have wide discretion to interpret the words. The inconsistencies and criticism that this has produced (Feld, 1981a) has led some jurisdictions to draft statutory criteria more tightly. In Minnesota, for example, a matrix based on the current offence charged and previous offending history is used to establish whether or not a prima facie case is made out for certification of a juvenile to the adult court on the basis of the offender´s lack of amenability to treatment and his or her dangerousness (Feld, 1981).

Reviews of the operation of waiver procedures in the United States have also noted that their use varies considerably across States. Hamparian et al., (1982), for example, cite a range in the rate of the use of transfer of between one per 10,000 juveniles to thirteen per 10,000. Similarly, variation was noted in the type of offences which enabled waiver. While such provisions are usually justified on the basis that they will apply to violent offenders, some 40 per cent of referrals related to property offences (Bortner, 1986). Rudman et al., (1986) have shown that nearly half of the juveniles considered for transfer to the adult court were, in fact, eventually transferred. Not surprisingly, they found that transfer doubled the usual waiting time between apprehension and sentence and that the adult court usually passed a custodial sentence of longer duration than would have been available in the juvenile court.

These developments, through which aspects of due process have been incorporated with harsher sentences, are not what those who originally proposed the justice model envisaged (Greenberg and Humphries, 1980). Such co-option, however, is not inevitable. Indeed, those States, most notably Massachusetts, which pursued a strategy of deinstitutionalisation across the board in the 1970s and which did not merely concentrate on status offenders, have managed to retain this policy despite a subsequent shift to the political right in State government (Rutherford, 1986). Co-option has been most likely where liberal policy proposals have concentrated on those offenders who cause the least public concern. As Krisberg et al., note:

> The inability of reformers to provide meaningful programmes and policies aimed at serious juvenile offenders resulted in the wave of 'get tough' legislation that swept the nation during the late 1970s (1986, 30).

Conclusion

Reconsideration of juvenile justice policy and the development of alternative models have occurred in a variety of jurisdictions as a result of the perceived failure of the juvenile justice system to combat crime. In England, this was demonstrated in the debates surrounding the 1969 Children and Young Persons Act. Those seeking to reconstitute the central role of the juvenile court promoted the notion of its powerlessness to deal with juvenile crime and the provisions of the 1982 Criminal Justice Act were a direct response to this.

The supposed relationship between the format of the juvenile justice system and the control of juvenile crime is, however, problematic. A particular model or combination of models is unlikely to have more than a marginal impact on juvenile crime (Rutter and Giller, 1983). Proposals that a particular change in juvenile justice policy will have this effect - for example, proposals for more powers or more resources - are, in reality, proposals to increase the overall power of the state or to increase the power of one part of the system. The increased powers of the magistrates since the 1982 Criminal Justice Act are an example of this. Juvenile crime is unlikely to decrease as a result of these powers.

This does not mean that we should be unconcerned about the particular model of juvenile justice which prevails because all models are equally inefficient in and irrelevant to dealing with juveniles who offend. They are not. First, the research we have reviewed in this book has exposed practices which must be addressed and questions which must be answered when determining a preferred juvenile justice ideology. For example, are the procedures and practices employed by the agents of the system operated fairly? Do they discriminate against categories of juveniles on grounds which are objectionable (for example sex, race or class)? Are the rights of the juveniles respected? Are juveniles and their families given the opportunity to participate in and contribute to the decision-making process? Do they understand the basis for intervention? Is the system giving value for money? Are public resources being spent on bad practices? Is the system humane in its application? Is the least restrictive alternative used? Does the system extend the net of social control?

Questions like these take us away from the more traditional and sterile areas of evaluation such as ´does the juvenile justice system reduce crime`? But by focusing on the work of agencies and organisations in the system and their inter-face with those over whom they exercise authority, the legitimacy of policy and practice can be reviewed. If we ask such questions currently of the juvenile justice system generally and of the juvenile court in particular, there is cause for some dissatisfaction. At most, it leads to the consideration of alternative approaches, at least, it leads to the need to improve present arrangements so that the case for a distinctive juvenile court can be substantiated.

The second reason for being concerned about which model of juvenile justice is used is that the choice has implications for a critical evaluation of current ´law and order` debates. Pearson (1983) noted in his analysis of the history of youthful disorder in England that, traditionally, the language and methodology of ´law and order` and crime control - whether reformative or reactionary - blind us to dealing with those issues which lie behind the disorder. In the introduction, we referred to allied networks of social control for juveniles - families, schools and employment - each of which have a part to play. Dysfunction in any of these can have repercussions on juvenile crime and, therefore, for its control. Rather than addressing these underlying dysfunctions, currently juvenile crime is seen as the problem which must be responded to.

An example of this is the government´s response to the inner-city riots in the 1980s (Cowell et al., 1982). Factors such as limited employment opportunities, racial discrimination and poverty were acknowledged to be present, but were subsumed within rhetoric which viewed the riots as a fundamental breakdown of law and order. Lord Scarman in his Report, for example, put it this way:

> The social conditions in Brixton - many of which are to be found in other inner-city areas - do not provide an excuse for disorder. They cannot justify attacks on the police in the streets, arson, or riot. All those who in the course of the disorders in Brixton and elsewhere engaged in violence against the police were guilty of grave offences, which society, if it is to survive, cannot condone. Sympathy for, and understanding of, the plight of young black people...are a good reason for political, social and economic aid, and for a co-ordinated effort by government to provide it, but they are no reason for releasing young black people from the responsibility for public order which they share with the rest of us - and with the police (1981, 2.31).

Systems of juvenile justice cannot resolve such difficulties. Remedies lie within other social policy arenas and demand a political will (and financial commitment) to change the life opportunities of the young. But certain forms of juvenile justice systems expose rather than conceal these pressures on the young. A different kind of political exercise from the rhetoric of 'law and order' is now necessary: an evaluation of the role of juveniles in society. Juvenile justice policy and practice in England has yet to address this.

NOTES

1.   Other important social issues which are intimately associated with youth and which also cause public concern may be more resilient to public attention. Among these are schooling, drug abuse and youth unemployment.
2.   Recent evidence suggests that this has not happened in the United States, see Krisberg et al., (1986).
3.   The development of a family court is also currently being considered by the Lord Chancellor's Department (1986).

4. A connected problem is the issue of the nature and extent of intervention available to the care court which might be more incursive than that available to the criminal court.

5. In both instances the proportion of female status offenders diverted was far greater than that of males (Krisberg and Schwartz, 1983).

6. Similar outcomes can be seen recently in certain provinces in Canada where legislation - the Young Offenders Act 1984 - has been implemented (Corrado and Bala, 1985).

7. Since the Supreme Court decision in <u>Kent v United States</u> (383 US 514 (1966)), juveniles must be given the right to a hearing to determine whether or not the juvenile court can waive its jurisdiction and the assistance of counsel. The material used to make this decision is also subject to review by a higher court. Moreover, in <u>Breed v Jones</u> (421 US 519 (1975)), the Supreme Court held that the decision to treat the offender as a juvenile or as an adult must be made before beginning the adjudication process; otherwise there would be a breach of the juvenile's constitutional rights.

REFERENCES

Adler, R.M. (1985) Taking Juvenile Justice Serious-
   ly, Scottish Academic Press, Edinburgh
Adler, C. and Polk,K. (1982) 'Diversion and Hidden
   Sexism', Australian and New Zealand Journal of
   Criminology, 15, pp. 100-8
Advisory Council on the Penal System (1974) Report
   on Young Adult Offenders, H.M.S.O., London
Anderson, R. (1978) Representation in Juvenile
   Court, Routledge and Kegan Paul, London
Aries, P. (1962) Centuries of Childhood, Penguin,
   Harmondsworth
Ashworth, A. (1983) Sentencing and Penal Policy,
   Weidenfeld and Nicolson, London
Asquith, S. (1983a) Children and Justice: Decision-
   Making in Children's Hearings and Juvenile
   Courts, University Press, Edinburgh
Asquith, S. (1983b) 'Justice, retribution and child-
   ren' in Morris, A. and Giller, H. (eds.), Pro-
   viding Criminal Justice for Children, Edward
   Arnold, London, pp. 7-18
Association of County Councils (1984) Juvenile
   Courts, A.C.C., London
Association of Directors of Social Services (1985)
   Children Still in Trouble, Report of an
   A.D.S.S. Study Group, A.D.S.S., Taunton
Austin, J. and Krisberg, B. (1981) 'Wider, stronger,
   and different nets: the dialectics of criminal
   justice reform', Journal of Research in Crime
   and Delinquency, 18(1), pp. 165-96
Badham, B. et al., (1984) 'Chronicle of Confusion,
   Community Care, November 29, pp. 18-21
Baldwin, J. (1976) 'The social composition of the
   magistracy', British Journal of Criminology,
   16(2), pp. 171-4
Baldwin, J. (1982) 'Scaling the tariff barrier',
   Social Work Today, 13(34), p.1

Ball, C. (1981) 'The Use and Significance of School Reports in Juvenile Court Criminal Proceedings: a Research Note', British Journal of Social Work, 11(4), pp. 479-83

Ball, C. (1983) 'Secret Justice: the use made of school reports in juvenile courts', British Journal of Social Work, 13(2), pp. 197-206

Ball, C. (1984) 'Form and Content' in NACRO (ed.), School Reports in the Juvenile Court, NACRO, London

Barker, J.M.A. (1985) 'Some Problems in Sentencing Juveniles', Criminal Law Review, December, pp. 759-63

Barker, P. and Little, A. (1964) 'The Margate Offenders - a survey', New Society, 30th July, pp. 6-10

Beccaria, C. (1963) On Crimes and Punishment, Trans. by Paolucci, H. Bobbs-Merrill, Indianapolis (original 1764)

Belson, W. (1968) 'The extent of stealing by London boys', Advancement of Science, 25, pp. 171-84

Belson, W. (1975) Juvenile Theft: The Causal Factors, Harper Row, London

Bennett, H. (1818) 'A Letter to the Common Council and Livery of the City of London on abuses existing in Newgate', The Pamphleteer, II, pp. 277-318

Bennett, T. (1979) 'The Social Distribution of Criminal Labels', British Journal of Criminology, 19(2), pp. 134-45

Berlins, M. and Wansell, G. (1974) Caught in the Act, Penguin, Harmondsworth

Bersoff, D. (1976) 'Representation of Children in Custody Decisions: All That Glitters is not Gault', Journal of Family Law, 15, pp. 27-49

Binder, A. and Geis, G. (1984) 'Ad Populum Argumentation in Criminology: Juvenile Diversion as Rhetoric', Crime and Delinquency, 30(2), pp. 309-33

Black Committee, (1979) Report of the Children and Young Persons Review Group, H.M.S.O., Belfast

Black, D. and Reiss, A. (1970) 'Police Control of Juveniles', American Sociological Review, 35, pp. 63-77

Blanch, M. (1979) 'Imperialism, nationalism and organised youth' in Clarke, J. (ed.), Working Class Culture, Hutchinson, London, pp. 103-20

Bortner, M.A. (1986) 'Traditional Rhetoric, Organisational Realities: Remand of Juveniles to Adult Court', Crime and Delinquency, 32(1), pp. 53-74

REFERENCES

Boss, P. (1967) Social Policy and the Young Delinquent, Routledge and Kegan Paul, London

Bottoms, A.E. (1974) 'On the decriminalisation of the English Juvenile Courts' in Hood, R. (ed.), Crime, Criminology and Public Policy, Heinemann, London, pp. 319-46

Bottoms, A.E. (1977) 'Reflections on the Renaissance of Dangerousness', Howard Journal 16, pp. 70-96

Bottoms, A.E. (1985) 'Justice for Juveniles 75 Years On' in Hoath, D. (ed.), 75 Years of Law at Sheffield 1909-1984, University Printing Unit, Sheffield, pp. 95-111

Bottoms, A.E. and McWilliams, W. (1979) 'A non-treatment paradigm for probation practice', British Journal of Social Work, 9(2), pp. 159-202

Bottoms, A.E. and Pratt, J. (1985) 'Intermediate Treatment for Girls in England and Wales', Unpublished Paper

Bottoms, A.E. and Sheffield, C. (1980) Report on Feasibility of Research into Intermediate Treatment, Report to the D.H.S.S., London

Bow Group (1964) Crime and the Labour Party, Bow Publications, London

Box, S. (1971) Deviance, Reality and Society, Holt, Rinehart and Winston, London

Brown, P. D. and Bloomfield, T. (eds.) (1979) Legality and Community, People's Press, Aberdeen

Bullington, B. et al., (1978) 'A Critique of Diversionary Juvenile Justice', Crime and Delinquency 24(1), pp. 59-71

Burney, E. (1985a) 'All things to all men: Justifying custody under the 1982 Act', Criminal Law Review, May, pp. 284-93

Burney, E. (1985b) Sentencing Young People, Gower, Aldershot

Burrows, J. (1982) 'How Crime Comes to Police Notice', Home Office Research Bulletin No. 13, pp.16-19

Burrows, J. et al., (1979) Crime Prevention and the Police, Home Office Research Study No. 55, H.M.S.O., London

Cadogan Committee (1938) Report of the Departmental Committee on Corporal Punishment, H.M.S.O., London

Cain, M. (1968) 'Role Conflict among Police Juvenile Liaison Officers', British Journal of Criminology, 8(4), pp. 366-82

Campbell, A. (1981) Girl Delinquents, Basil Blackwell, Oxford

Carey, K. (1979) 'Police Policy and the Prosecution

of Women`, Unpublished paper to a British Sociological Association conference

Carlebach, J. (1970) Caring for Children in Trouble, Routledge and Kegan Paul, London

Carpenter, M. (1851) Reformatory Schools for the Children of the Perishing and Dangerous Classes and for Juvenile Offenders, Gilpin, London

Carpenter, M. (1853) Juvenile Delinquents: Social Evils, Their Causes and Their Cure, Cash, London

Carter, R.M. (1984) `The United States` in Klein, M. (ed.), Western Systems of Juvenile Justice, Sage, Beverley Hills, pp. 17-38

Catton, T. and Erickson, P. (1975) The Juvenile's Perception of the Role of Defence Counsel in the Juvenile Court, University of Toronto, Toronto

Cavanagh, W. (1966) `What kind of Court or Committee?` British Journal of Criminology, 6(2), pp. 123-38

Cawson, P. (1981) Young Offenders in Care, D.H.S.S. London

Cawson, P. and Martell, M. (1979) Children Referred to Closed Units, D.H.S.S. Research Report No. 5, H.M.S.O., London

Central Statistical Office (1982) Social Trends, No. 13, H.M.S.O., London

Cernkovich, S. and Giordano, P. (1979) `A comparative analysis of male and female delinquency`, Sociological Quarterly, 20, pp. 131-45

Cicourel, A. (1968) The Social Organisation of Juvenile Justice, Wiley, London

Clarke, A. and Taylor, I. (1980) `Vandals, Pickets and Muggers: television coverage of law and order in the 1979 general election`, Screen Education, pp. 99-111

Clarke, J. (1980) `Social Democratic Delinquent and Fabian Families` in National Deviancy Conference (eds.), Permissiveness and Control, Macmillan, London, pp. 72-95

Clarke, J. (1985) `Whose Justice? The Politics of Juvenile Control`, International Journal of the Sociology of Law, 13, pp. 407-21

Clarke, R. (ed.), (1978) Tackling Vandalism, Home Office Research Study No. 47, H.M.S.O. London

Clarke, R. and Hough, M. (1984) Crime and Police Effectiveness, Home Office Research Study No. 79, H.M.S.O., London

Clarke, S. and Koch, G. (1980) `Juvenile court: therapy or crime control: Do lawyers make a difference?` Law and Society Review, 14, pp. 263-308

REFERENCES

Clarke Hall, W. (1926) Children's Courts, George Allen and Unwin, London

Cohen S. (1973) Folk devils and moral panics: the creation of mods and rockers, Paladin, St. Albans

Cooper, B. and Nicholas, G. (1963) Crime in the Sixties, Conservative Political Centre, London

Cornish, D. and Clarke, R. (1976) Residential Treatment and its Effect on Delinquency, Home Office Research Study No. 32, H.M.S.O., London

Corrado, R.R. and Bala, N. (1985) 'Child Welfare and Juvenile Justice in Canada's Emerging Issues and Trends', Unpublished Paper

Covington, C. (1984) 'Current Practice' in NACRO (ed.), School Reports in the Juvenile Court, NACRO, London, pp. 3-12

Cowell, D. et al., (eds.), (1982) Policing the Riots, Junction Books, London

Cressey, D. and McDermott, R. (1974) Diversion from the Juvenile Justice System, Washington D.C., National Institute of Law Enforcement and Criminal Justice

Crook, J. (1986) The Limits of Diversion, Northampton Juvenile Liaison Bureau, Northampton

Crosland, R. (1963) The Future of Socialism, Cape, London

Curtis Committee (1946) Report of Committee on the Care of Children, H.M.S.O., London

Davies, M. (1974) 'Social Inquiry for the Courts', British Journal of Criminology, 14(1), pp. 17-33

Denman, G. (1982) Intensive Intermediate Treatment with Juvenile Offenders, Lancaster University, Lancaster

Department of Health and Social Security (1972) 'Children and Young Persons Act - Memorandum of a survey by the Social Work Service', Unpublished Mimeo., D.H.S.S., London

Department of Health and Social Security (1973) 'Children and Young Persons Act 1969 - Memorandum on a Further Survey by the Social Work Service', Unpublished Mimeo., D.H.S.S., London

Department of Health and Social Security (1981a) Offending by Young People: A Survey of Recent Trends, D.H.S.S., London

Department of Health and Social Security (1981b) Legal and professional aspects of the use of secure accommodation for children in care, Report of a D.H.S.S. internal working party, D.H.S.S., London

REFERENCES

Department of Health and Social Security (1982) 'Secure Unit Records', Unpublished paper, D.H.S.S. London

Department of Health and Social Security (1985) Review of Child Care Law, H.M.S.O., London

Department of Health and Social Security (1986) Reports for the Courts in Children's Cases, Forthcoming

Department of Social Welfare (1984) Review of Children and Young Persons Legislation, Department of Social Welfare, Wellington, New Zealand

Dingwall, R. et al., (1983) The Protection of Children: State Intervention in Family Life, Basil Blackwell, Oxford

Ditchfield, J. (1976) Police Cautioning in England and Wales, Home Office Research Study No. 37, H.M.S.O., London

Dixon, D. and Fishwick, E. (1984) 'The Law and Order Debate in Historical Perspective', in Norton, P. (ed.), Law and Order and British Politics, Gower, Aldershot, pp. 21-37

Donajgrodzki, A. (1977) Social Control in Nineteenth Century Britain, Croom Helm, London

Donnison, D. and Stewart, M. (1958) The Child and the Social Services, Fabian Research Series 196, Fabian Society, London

Donnison, D. et al., (1962) The Ingleby Report: Three Critical Essays, Fabian Research Series 231, Fabian Society, London

Donzelot, J. (1979) The Policing of Families, Hutchinson, London

Downes, D. (1966) The Delinquent Solution: A Study of Subcultural Theory, Routledge and Kegan Paul, London

Downes, D. (1983) Law and Order: Theft of an Issue, Fabian tract 490, Fabian Society, London

Downey, B. (1966) 'White Paper: The Child, the Family and the Young Offender', Modern Law Review, 29, pp. 409-13

Duffee, D. and Siegal, L. (1971) 'The organisation man: legal counsel in the juvenile court', Criminal Law Bulletin, 7, p. 544

Duncan, I.D. (1985) 'Social Work and Probation Court Reports: A Junior Detention Centre Perspective', Unpublished Paper

Dunlop, A. (1980) Junior Attendance Centres, Home Office Research Study No. 60, H.M.S.O., London

Dunlop, A. and Frankenberg, C. (1982) 'The Detention of Juveniles for Grave Crimes', Home Office Research and Planning Unit Research Bulletin, No. 14, pp. 41-4

REFERENCES

Dunlop, A. and McCabe, S. (1965) <u>Young Men in Deten-
tion Centres</u>, Routledge and Kegan Paul, London
Durand Committee, (1960) <u>Report of Inquiry into the
Disturbances at the Carlton Approved School</u>,
H.M.S.O., London
Du Sautoy, T. (1986) ´Family Courts - facing the
political realism`, <u>Social Services Insight</u>,
1(9), pp. 6-7
Ekblom, P. (1979) ´Police Truancy Patrols` in
Burrows, J. et al., (eds.), <u>Crime Prevention
and the Police</u>, Home Office Research Study No.
55, H.M.S.O., London, pp 17-33
Elliott, D. and Ageton, S. (1980) ´Reconciling race
and class differences in self-reported and
official estimates of delinquency`, <u>American
Sociological Review</u>, 45, pp. 95-110
Emerson, R. (1969) <u>Judging Delinquents</u>, Aldine
Press, Chicago
Empey, L. (1978) <u>American Delinquency: its meaning
and construction</u>, The Dorsey Press, Homewood,
Illinois
Ennis, P. (1967) <u>Criminal Victimisation in the
United States: a report of a National Survey</u>,
Government Printing Office, Washington D.C.
Ericson, R. (1975) <u>Young Offenders and their Social
Work</u>, Saxon House, Farnborough
Evans, R. (1982) <u>The Fabrication of Virtue: English
Prison Architecture 1750-1840</u>, Cambridge Univ-
ersity Press, Cambridge
Farrington, D. (1977) The Effects of Public Label-
ling, <u>British Journal of Criminology</u>, 17(2),
pp. 112-25
Farrington, D. (1984) ´England and Wales` in Klein
M. (ed.), <u>Western Systems of Juvenile Justice</u>,
Sage, Beverley Hills, pp. 71-95
Farrington, D. (1986) ´Age and Crime` in Tonry, M.
and Morris, N. (eds.), <u>Crime and Justice</u>, Vol.
7, University Press, Chicago
Farrington, D. and Bennett, T. (1981) ´Police
Cautioning of Juveniles in London`, <u>British
Journal of Criminology</u>, 21(2), pp. 123-35
Farrington, D. and Dowds, E. (1984) ´Why does Crime
Decrease`, <u>Justice of the Peace</u>, August 11, pp.
506-9
Fears, D. (1977) ´Communication in English Courts`,
<u>Sociological Review</u>, XXV, pp. 131-45
Feeley, M. (1979) <u>The Process of Punishment</u>, Russell
Sage Foundation, New York
Feeney, F. (1985) ´Interdependence as a working
concept` in Moxon, D. (ed.), <u>Managing Criminal
Justice</u>, H.M.S.O., London, pp. 8-17

REFERENCES

Feld, B.C. (1981a) ´Juvenile Court Legislative Reform and the Serious Young Offender: Dismantling the "Rehabilitative Ideal"`, Minnesota Law Review, 65(2), pp. 167-242

Feld, B.C. (1981b) ´Legislative Policies toward the Serious Juvenile Offender`, Crime and Delinquency, 27(4), pp. 497-521

Finnestone, H. (1976) Victims of Change, Greenwood Press, Westport, Conn.

Fisher, C. and Mawby, R. (1982) ´Juvenile delinquency and police discretion in an inner city area, British Journal of Criminology, 22, pp. 63-75

Fitzgerald, P. (1966) ´The Child, the White Paper and the Criminal Law: Some Reflections` Criminal Law Review, November, pp. 607-12

Flinn, M. (1967) ´Social Theory and the Industrial Revolution` in Burns, T. and Saul, S. (eds.), Social Theory and Economic Change, Tavistock, London

Foucault, M. (1977) Discipline and Punish: the birth of the prison, Allen Lane, London

Fox, S. (1970) ´Juvenile Justice Reform: An Historical Perspective`, Stanford Law Review, 22, pp. 1187-239

Franklin Committee (1951) Report on punishment in Borstal Institutions, Approved Schools and Remand Homes, H.M.S.O., London

Freeman, M.D.A. (1983) The Rights and Wrongs of Children, Frances Pinter, London

Freeman, M.D.A. (1984) ´Questioning the Delegalisation Movement in Family Law: Do We Really Want a Family Court?` in Eekelaar, J.M. and Katz, S.N. (eds.), The Resolution of Family Conflict, Butterworths, Toronto, pp. 7-25

Friedenberg, E. (1966) ´Adolescence as a Social Problem` in Becker H. (ed.), Social Problems: A Modern Approach, John Wiley, New York, pp. 35-75

Friedman, M. (1962) Capitalism and Freedom, University Press, Chicago

Galvin, J. and Polk, K. (1983) ´Juvenile Justice: Time for New Direction?`, Crime and Delinquency, 29, pp. 325-32

Garland, D. (1985) Punishment and welfare: a history of penal strategies, Gower, Aldershot

Gelsthorpe, L. (1984) ´Girls and Juvenile Justice`, Youth and Policy, II, pp. 1-5

Gelsthorpe, L. and Morris, A. (1983) ´Attendance Centres: Policy and Practice`, Howard Journal, 22(2), pp. 101-18

REFERENCES

Gelsthorpe, L. and Tutt, N. (1986) 'The Attendance Centre Order', Criminal Law Review, March, pp. 146-53

George, V. and Wilding, P. (1976) Ideology and Social Welfare, Routledge and Kegan Paul, London

Giller, H. (1983) 'The Cheshire Juvenile Volunteer Scheme', Journal of Social Welfare Law, September, pp. 283-95

Giller, H. (1985a) 'Proceeding with Caution', Community Care, April 11, pp. 18-20

Giller, H. (1985b) 'Social Welfare Professionals in the Context of the Juvenile Court', Paper for a ESTC/CNRS Workshop, Warwick University

Giller, H. (1986) 'Is there a Role for a Juvenile Court?'. Howard Journal, 25(3), pp 161-71

Giller, H. and Maidment, S. (1984) 'Representation of Children: Does More Mean Better?' in Eekelaar, J.M., and Katz, S.N. (eds.), The Resolution of Family Conflict, Butterworths, Toronto, pp. 405-20

Giller, H. and Morris, A. (1978) 'Supervision Orders: the routinisation of treatment', Howard Journal, 17(3), pp. 149-59

Giller, H. and Morris, A. (1981a) Care and Discretion: Social Work Decisions with Delinquents, Burnett Books, London

Giller, H. and Morris, A. (1981b) 'Law, order and the child care system', Howard Journal, 20(2), pp. 81-9

Giller, H. and Morris, A. (1982) 'Independent Social Workers and the Courts: Advise, Resist and Defend', Journal of Social Welfare Law, January, pp. 29-41

Giller, H. and Tutt, N. (1985) 'Gatekeeping in the Juvenile Justice System', in YHITA (ed.), Training Anthology, YHITA, Bradford

Gillis, J. (1974) Youth and History, Academic Press, London

Gladstone, F. (1978) 'Vandalism among adolescent schoolboys', in Clarke, R. (ed.), Tackling Vandalism, Home Office Research Study No. 47, H.M.S.O., London, pp. 19-39

Godsland, J.H. and Fielding, N.G. (1985) 'Young Persons Convicted of Grave Crimes: the 1933 Children and Young Person's Act (s.53) and its Effect upon Children's Rights', Howard Journal, 24(4), pp. 282-97

Gold, M. and Reimer, D.J. (1975) 'Changing Patterns of Delinquent Behaviour Among Americans 13 Through 16 years Old', Crime and Delinquency Literature, 7, pp. 483-517

267

REFERENCES

Greenberg, D.F. and Humphries, D. (1980) 'The Co-optation of Fixed Sentencing Reform', Crime and Delinquency, 26(2), pp. 206-25

Greenwood, V. and Young, J. (1980) 'Ghettos of Freedom' in National Deviancy Conference (ed.), Permissiveness and Control, Macmillan, London, pp. 149-85

Grimshaw, R. and Pratt, J. (1985) 'Responses to Truancy among the Juvenile Panel of a Magistrates' Court', British Journal of Criminology, 25(4), pp. 321-43

Hagan, J. and Leon, J., (1977) 'Rediscovering Delinquency: Social History, Political Ideology and the Sociology of Law', American Sociological Review, 42, pp. 587-98

Hale, M. (1971) Historia Placitorum Corona. The History of the Pleas of the Crown, Vol. 1, Provisional Books, London. Originally printed 1736

Hall, S. et al., (1978) Policing the Crisis, Macmillan, London

Hamparian, D.M. et al., (1982) Youth in Adult Courts: Between Two Worlds, U.S.Department of Justice, Washington D.C.

Hardiker, P. (1977) 'Social Work Ideologies in the Probation Service', British Journal of Social Work, 7(2), pp. 131-54

Harper, B. and Thomas, J. (1984) 'Numbers of Young People with Intermediate Treatment Requirements or Engaged in Intermediate Treatment in England and Wales' Information Street, National Youth Bureau, Leicester

Harris, R.J. (1982) 'Institutional Ambivalence: Social Work and the Children and Young Persons Act 1969', British Journal of Social Work, 12 (3), pp. 247-63

Harris, R.J. (1985) 'Towards Just Welfare', British Journal of Criminology, 25(1), pp. 31-45

Harris, R. and Webb, D. (1983) 'Social work and the supervision order', Home Office Research Bulletin, 16, pp. 35-7

Hauger, D. et al., (1983) 'Summary: Public Attitudes towards Youth Crime', cited in Galvin J. and Polk, K. 'Juvenile Justice: time for new direction?', Crime and Delinquency, 29, pp. 325-32

Hay, D. (1977) 'Property, Authority and Criminal Law' in Hay, D. et al., Albion's Fatal Tree, Penguin, Harmondsworth

Hellum, F. (1979) 'Juvenile Justice: The Second Revolution', Crime and Delinquency, 25(3), pp. 299-317

REFERENCES

Hibbert, C. (1963) The Roots of Evil: A Social History of Crime and Punishment, Weidenfeld and Nicolson, London

Hilgendorf, L. (1981) Social Workers and Solicitors in Child Care Cases, H.M.S.O., London

Hinde, R. (1951) The British Penal System (1773 - 1950), Duckworth, London

Hindelang, M. (1971) 'Age, sex and the versatility of delinquent involvement', Social Problems, 18, pp. 522-35

Hindelang, M. (1978) 'Race and involvement in common law personal crimes', American Sociological Review, 43, pp. 93-109

Hoghughi, M. (1983) The Delinquent: directions for social control, Burnett Books, London

Home Office (1965) The Child, the Family and the Young Offender, Cmnd. 2742, H.M.S.O., London

Home Office (1968) Children in Trouble, Cmnd. 3601, H.M.S.O., London

Home Office (1971) Criminal Statistics 1970, H.M.S.O., London

Home Office (1978) Youth Custody and Supervision: a new sentence, H.M.S.O., London

Home Office (1980) Criminal Statistics 1979, H.M.S.O. London

Home Office (1983) Criminal Statistics 1982, H.M.S.O., London

Home Office (1984a) Tougher Regimes in Detention Centres, Report of an evaluation by the Young Offender Psychology Unit, H.M.S.O., London

Home Office (1984b) Cautioning by the Police: A Consultative Document, Home Office, London

Home Office (1984c) Statement of National Objectives and Priorities for the Probation Service, Home Office, London

Home Office (1985a) Criminal Statistics 1984, H.M.S.O., London

Home Office (1985b) Young Offenders in Prison Department Establishments Under the Criminal Justice Act 1982: July 1983-June 1984, Home Office Statistical Bulletin Issue 2/85, Statistical Branch, Tolworth Tower, Surbiton

Home Office (1985c) Prison Statistics 1984, H.M.S.O. London

Home Office (1986a) Criminal Justice: Plans for Legislation, Cmnd. 9658, H.M.S.O., London

Home Office (1986b) The Sentence of the Court, 4th edition, H.M.S.O., London

Home Office (1986c) Custodial Sentences for Young Offenders: A discussion paper, Home Office, London

Home Office (1986d) <u>Criminal Statistics 1985</u>, H.M.S.O., London

Home Office <u>et al.</u>, (1976) <u>Children and Young Persons Act 1969: Observations on the Eleventh Report from the Expenditure Committee</u>, Cmnd. 6494, H.M.S.O., London

Home Office <u>et al.</u>, (1980) <u>Young Offenders</u>, Cmnd. 8045, H.M.S.O., London

Hough, M. and Heal, K. (1982) ´Police Strategies of Crime Control` in Feldman, P. (ed.), <u>Developments in the Study of Criminal Behaviour</u>, John Wiley, London

Hough, M. and Mayhew, P. (1983) <u>The British Crime Survey</u>, Home Office Research Study No. 76, H.M.S.O., London

Hough, M. and Mayhew, P. (1985) <u>Taking Account of Crime: Key findings from the 1984 British Crime Survey</u>, Home Office Research Study No. 85, H.M.S.O., London

House of Commons (1985) <u>Social Services for Children in England and Wales 1982-84</u>, H.M.S.O., London

House of Commons Expenditure Committee (1975) <u>Eleventh Report: The Children and Young Persons Act 1969</u>, H.M.S.O., London

Howard Association (1896) <u>Annual Report</u>, Howard Association, London

Humphries, S. (1981) <u>Hooligans or Rebels?</u>, Basil Blackwell, Oxford

Hunt, A. (1985) ´The Future of Rights and Justice`, <u>Contemporary Crises, 9</u>, pp. 309-26

Ignatieff, M. (1978) <u>A Just Measure of Pain: the Penitentiary in the Industrial Revolution 1750-1850</u>, Macmillan, London

Ignatieff, M. (1981) ´State, Civil Society and Total Institutions: a critique of recent social histories of punishment`, in Tonry, M. and Morris, N. (eds.), <u>Crime and Justice</u>, Chicago University Press, Chicago, pp. 153-92

Ingleby Committee (1960) <u>Report of the Committee on Children and Young Persons</u>, Cmnd. 1191, H.M.S.O., London

Inspector of Prisons of Great Britain (1836) <u>Report of the Inspectors Appointed to visit the Different Prisons of Great Britain</u>, H.M.S.O., London

Inspector of Reformatory and Industrial Schools (1871) <u>Fourteenth Report</u>, H.M.S.O., London

Inspector of Reformatory and Industrial Schools (1915) <u>Fifty-Eighth Report</u>, H.M.S.O., London

Institute for Judicial Administration and the American Bar Association (1977) <u>Juvenile Justice</u>

REFERENCES

Standards Project, Ballinger, Cambridge, Mass.

Jensen, G. and Eve, R. (1976) ´Sex differences in delinquency` _Criminology_, 13(4), pp. 427-48

Jensen, G. and Rojek, D. (1980) _Delinquency: A Sociological View_, D.C. Heath, Lexington, Mass.

John, E. (1986) _Development of Work with Young People at Risk and in Trouble_, National Youth Bureau, Leicester

Johnson, R. (1970) ´Educational Policy and Social Control in Early Victorian England`, _Past and Present, 49_, pp. 96-119

Johnson, R. (1975) ´Notes on the Schooling of the English Working Class 1780-1850` in Dale, R. _et al_, (eds.), _Schooling and Capitalism_, Open University Press, Milton Keynes, pp. 44-53

Johnson, T. _et al._, (1984) ´A second opinion`, _Community Care_, April 19, pp. 17-20

Jones, D. (1982) _Crime, Protest, Community and Police in 19th Century Britain_, Routledge and Kegan Paul, London

Jones, R. (1983) ´Justice, Social Work and Statutory Supervision`, in Morris, A. and Giller, H. (eds.), _Providing Criminal Justice for children_, Edward Arnold, London, pp. 89-108

Kahan, B. (1966) ´The Child, the Family and the Young Offender: Revolutionary or Evolutionary?`, _British Journal of Criminology, 6_, pp. 159-69

Kilbrandon Committee (1964) _Report of Committee on Children and Young Persons (Scotland)_, Cmnd. 2306, H.M.S.O., Edinburgh

Kilbrandon, The Hon. Lord (1968) ´The Scottish Reforms: The Impact on the Public`, _British Journal of Criminology, 8(3)_, pp. 235-41

King, P. (1984) ´Decision makers and Decision making in the English Criminal Law, 1750-1800`, _The Historical Journal, 27(1)_, pp. 25-58

Klein, M. (1979) ´Deinstitutionalisation and Diversion of Juvenile Offenders: A Litany of Impediments` in Morris, N. and Tonry, M. (eds.), _Crime and Justice: an annual review of research, Vol. 1._, Chicago University Press, Chicago, pp. 145-201

Klein, M. (1985) _Western Systems of Juvenile Justice_ Sage, Beverley Hills

Krisberg, B. (1985) ´Juvenile Justice: The Vision and the Constant Star`, Unpublished paper

Krisberg, B. and Schwartz, I. (1983) ´Rethinking Juvenile Justice`, _Crime and Delinquency, 28 (3)_, pp.333-64

Krisberg, B. _et al._, (1986) ´The Watershed of

Juvenile Justice Reform`, Crime and Delinquency 32(1), pp. 5-38

Land, H. (1975) `Detention centres: the experiment which could not fail` in Hall, P. et al., (eds.), Change, Choice and Conflict in Social Policy, Heinemann, London, pp. 311-70

Landau, S.F. (1981) `Juveniles and the Police`, British Journal of Criminology, 21(1), pp. 27-46

Landau, S.F. and Nathan, G. (1983) `Selecting Delinquents for Cautioning in the London Metropolitan Area`, British Journal of Criminology, 23(2), pp. 128-49

Langbein, J. (1983) `Albion's Fatal Flaws`, Past and Present, 98, pp. 96-120

Laycock, G. and Tarling, R. (1984) `Police Force Cautioning: Policy and Practice` in Home Office Cautioning by the Police: A Consultative Document, Home Office, London, pp. 36-47

Lerman, P. (1980) `Trends and Issues in the Deinstitutionalisation of Youths in Trouble`, Crime and Delinquency, 26(3), pp. 281-98

Lemert, E. (1970) Social Action and Legal Change, Aldine Publishing, Chicago

Lemert, E. (1971) Instead of Court: diversion in juvenile justice, National Institute of Mental Health, Chevy Chase, Maryland

Lemert, E. (1981) `Diversion in Juvenile Justice: What Hath Been Wrought`, Journal of Research in Crime and Delinquency, 18(1), pp. 34-46

Logan, C.H. and Rausch, S.P. (1985) `Why Deinstitutionalising Status Offenders is Pointless`, Crime and Delinquency, 31(4), pp. 501-18

Lombroso, C. (1911) Crime: Its Causes and Remedies Heinemann, London

Longford Committee (1964) Crime - a challenge to us all, Report of a Labour Party Study Group, Labour Party, London

Lord Chancellor's Department (1986) Interdepartmental Review of Family and Domestic Jurisdiction: Consultation Paper, Lord Chancellor's Department, London

Lou, H. (1927) Juvenile Courts in the United States, University Press, Chapel Hill, North Carolina

Low, D. (1982) Thieves' Kitchen: The Regency Underworld, J.M. Dent, London

Mack, J. (1909) `The Juvenile Court`, Harvard Law Review, 23, pp. 104-22

Mack, J.A. (1963) `Police Juvenile Liaison Schemes`, British Journal of Criminology, 3(4), pp. 361-75

REFERENCES

MacLeod, I. (1958) ´The Political Divide` in Goldman, P. (ed.) The Future of the Welfare State, Conservative Political Centre, London

Magistrates Association et al., (1978) The Children and Young Persons Act 1969, Report of a Joint Working Party, Magistrates Association, London

Marshall, T.F. (1985) Alternatives to Criminal Courts, Gower, Aldershot

Martin, F. et al., (1981) Children Out of Court, Scottish Academic Press, Edinburgh

Matza, D. (1964) Delinquency and Drift, Wiley, New York

Matza, D. (1969) Becoming Deviant, Englewood Cliffs, New Jersey

Mawby, R. (1980) ´Sex and crime: the results of a self-report study` British Journal of Sociology, 31(4), pp. 525-43

Mawby, R. and Fisher, C. (1982) ´Social Work Influence on the Cautioning of Juvenile Offenders`, British Journal of Social Work, 12(5), pp. 471-86

May, D. (1971) ´Delinquency Control and the Treatment Model: Some Implications of Recent Legislation`, British Journal of Criminology, 11 (4), pp. 359-70

May, D. (1975) ´Juvenile Offenders and the Organisation of Juvenile Justice: an examination of juvenile delinquency in Aberdeen, 1959-67`, Unpublished Ph.D. thesis, University of Aberdeen

May, D. (1977) ´Delinquent Girls before the Courts`, Medicine, Science and the Law, 17, pp. 203-12

May, M. (1973) ´Innocence and experience: the evolution of the concept of juvenile delinquency in the mid-nineteenth century`, Victorian Studies, 18(1), pp. 7-29

Mayhew, P. and Smith, L. (1985) ´Crime in England and Wales and Scotland: a British Crime Survey Comparison`, British Journal of Criminology, 25(2), pp. 148-59

Mays, J. (1954) Growing up in the City, University Press, Liverpool

McCabe, S. and Treitel, P. (1984) Juvenile Justice in the United Kingdom: Comparisons and Suggestions for Change, New Approaches to Juvenile Crime, London

McClintock, F. (1961) Attendance Centres, MacMillan, London

McClintock, F. (1963) Crimes of Violence, MacMillan, London

McConville, S. (1981) ´Editorial Note`, British Journal of Criminology, 21(3), pp. 205-9

REFERENCES

McDonanald L. (1969) <u>Social Class and Delinquency</u>, Faber and Faber, London
McHugh, P. (1970) ´A common-sense conception of deviance` in Douglas, J. (ed.) <u>Deviance and Respectablity</u>, Basic Books, New York, pp. 61-88
McKittrick, N. and Eysenck, S. (1984) ´Diversion: A Big Fix?, <u>Justice of the Peace, 148</u>, pp. 377-9 and 393-4
Melossi, D. and Pavarini, M. (1981) <u>The Prison and the Factory</u>, MacMillan Press, Basingstoke
Millham, S. et al., (1978 <u>Locking up Children: Secure Provision within the Child-Care System</u>, Saxon House, Farnborough
Millichamp, D. et al., (1985) ´A Matter of Natural Justice`, <u>Community Care</u>, June 13, pp. 25-7
Molony Committee (1927) <u>Report of the Departmental Committee on the Treatment of Young Offenders</u>, Cmnd. 2831, H.M.S.O., London
Moore, T.G. and Wilkinson, T.P. (1984) <u>The Juvenile Court</u>, Barry Rose, Chichester
Morris, A. (1978a) ´Diversion of Juvenile Offenders from the Criminal Justice System´, in Tutt, N. (ed.), <u>Alternative Strategies for Coping with Crime</u>, Basil Blackwell, Oxford, pp. 45-63
Morris, A. (1978b) ´Revolution in the Juvenile Court`, <u>Criminal Law Review</u>, September, pp. 529-39
Morris, A. (1983) ´Legal Representation and Justice` in Morris, A. and Giller, H. (eds.), <u>Providing Criminal Justice for Children</u>, Edward Arnold, London, pp. 125-40
Morris, A. and Giller, H. (1977) ´The juvenile court - the client´s perspective´, <u>Criminal Law Review</u>, April, pp. 198-205
Morris, A. and Giller, H. (1978) ´Juvenile Justice and Social Work in Great Britain`, in Parker, H. (ed.), <u>Social Work and the Courts</u>, Edward Arnold, London, pp. 8-33
Morris, A. and Giller, H. (1981) ´Young Offenders: 1. Law and order and the Child-Care System`, <u>Howard Journal, 20(2)</u>, pp. 81-9
Morris, A. and Giller, H. (eds.), (1983) <u>Providing Criminal Justice for Children</u>, Edward Arnold, London
Morris, A. and McIsaac, M. (1978) <u>Juvenile Justice?</u>, Heinemann, London
Morris, A. and Wilkinson, C. (1983) ´Just an Easy Answer?`, <u>Community Care</u>, December 8, pp. 22-3
Morris, A. et al., (1980) <u>Justice for Children</u>, MacMillan, London
Morris, R. (1965) ´Attitudes towards delinquency by

delinquents, non-delinquents and their friends`
British Journal of Criminology, 5(3), pp.249-65

Morton Committee (1928) Report of the Departmental
Committee on Protection and Training (Scotland), H.M.S.O., London

Mott, J. (1983) `Police Decisions for dealing with
Juvenile Offenders`, British Journal of Crimin-
ology, 23(3), pp. 249-62

Moxon, D. et al., (1985) Juvenile Sentencing: Is
there a Tariff?, Research and Planning Unit
Paper 32, Home Office, London

Murch, M. (1984) Separate Representation for Parents
and Children, University of Bristol Family Law
Research Unit, Bristol

NACRO (1984a) Youth Custody Sentences, NACRO, London

NACRO (1984b) The First Twelve Months: results of a
local authority survey on the sentencing of
juvenile offenders since the Criminal Justice
Act 1982, NACRO, London

NACRO (ed.), (1984c) School Reports in the Juvenile
Court, NACRO, London

NACRO (1986) J.O.T. Newsletter, Autumn, NACRO,
London

National Association of Probation Officers (1965)
`Observations on "The Child the Family and the
Young Offender"`, Probation Journal, 11, p.83

National Association of Probation Officers (1981)
Responses to the Government`s White paper
`Young Offenders N.A.P.O., London

New Society (1980) `The Law `n` Order Vote`, June
12, p. 220

Northamptonshire County Council (1984) Diversion:
Corporate Action with Juveniles, Northamptonshire County Council, Northampton

Oliver, I. (1978) The Metropolitan Police Approach
to the Prosecution of Juvenile Offenders,, Peel
Press, London

Osbourne, S. (1984) `Social Inquiry Reports in One
Juvenile Court: An Examination`, British Jour-
nal of Social Work, 14(4), pp. 361-78

Osborne, S. and West, D. (1980) `Do young delin-
quents really reform?`, Journal of Adoles-
cence, 3, pp. 99-114

Packman, J. et al., (1985) Who Needs Care?: Social
Work decisions about children, Basil Blackwell,
Oxford

Parker, H. (1974) View From the Boys, David and
Charles, Newton Abbot

Parker, H. (1978) `Client-Defendant Perceptions of
Juvenile and Criminal Justice`, in Parker, H.
(ed.), Social Work and the Courts, Edward

Arnold, London pp. 135-52

Parker, H. et al., (1981) Receiving Juvenile Justice, Basil Blackwell, Oxford

Parliamentary All-Party Penal Affairs Group (1981) Young Offenders: A Strategy for the Future, Barry Rose, Chichester

Pask, R. (1984) 'Production of Court Reports' in NACRO (ed.), School Reports in the Juvenile Court, NACRO, London, pp. 22-34

Parsloe, P. (1978) Juvenile Justice in Britain and the United States, Routledge and Kegan Paul, London

Pearsall, R. (1975) Nights' Black Angels. The Forms and Faces of Victorian Cruelty, Hodder and Stoughton, London

Pearson, G. (1975) The Deviant Imagination, MacMillan, London

Pearson, G. (1983) Hooligan: a History of Respectable Fears, MacMillan Press, London

Perry, F.G. (1975) A Guide to the Preparation of Social Inquiry Reports, Barry Rose, Chichester

Piliavin, I. and Briar, S. (1964) 'Police Encounters with Juveniles', American Sociological Review, 70, pp. 206-14

Pinchbeck, I. and Hewitt, M. (1973) Children in English Society, Routledge and Kegan Paul, London

Pitts, J. (1986) 'Black young people and juvenile Crimes: some unanswered questions' in Matthews, R. and Young, J. (eds.), Confronting Crime, Sage, London

Platt, A. (1969) The Child Savers, University Press, Chicago

Platt, A. (1978) The Child Savers, Second Edition, University Press, Chicago

Platt, A. et al., (1968) 'In defense of youth: a case study of the public defender in juvenile court', Indiana Law Review, 43, pp. 619-47

Plint, T. (1851) Crime in England its regulation, character and extent as developed from 1801-1848, Charles Gilpin, London

Pollock, L. (1983) Forgotten Children: Parent-Child Relations from 1500 to 1900, Cambridge University Press, Cambridge

Porteous, M. and Colston, N. (1980) 'How adolescents are reported in the British Press', Journal of Adolescence, pp. 197-215

Pratt, J. (1985a) 'Delinquency as a Scarce Resource', Howard Journal, 24(2), pp. 93-107

Pratt, J. (1985b) 'Juvenile Justice, Social Work and Social Control. The Need for Positive

REFERENCES

Thinking`, <u>British Journal of Social Work</u>, <u>151</u>, pp. 1-24

Pratt, J. and Grimshaw, R. (1985) `A juvenile justice pre-court tribunal at work`, <u>Howard Journal, 24(3)</u>, pp. 213-28

President´s Commission on Law Enforcement and the Administration of Justice (1967) <u>Task Force Report: Juvenile Delinquency and Youth Crime</u>, U.S. Government Printing Office, Washington D.C.

Priestley, P. et al., (1977) <u>Justice for Juveniles</u>, Routledge and Kegan Paul, London

Prochaska, E. (1980) <u>Women and Philanthropy in 19th Century England</u>, Clarendon Press, Oxford

Pullinger, H. (1985) `The criminal justice system viewed as a system`, in Moxon, D. (ed.), <u>Managing the Criminal Justice System</u>, H.M.S.O., London pp. 18-28

Radzinowicz, L. and Hood, R. (1986) <u>A History of English Criminal Law and its Administration</u>, Vol. 5, Stevens, London

Radzinowicz, L. and King J. (1977) <u>The Growth of Crime</u>, Hamish Hamilton, London

Ramsay, M. (1982) `Mugging: fears and facts`, <u>New Society</u>, March 25, pp. 467-8

Raynor, P. (1980) `Is there any Sense in Social Inquiry Reports?`, <u>Probation Journal, 27(3)</u>, pp. 78-84

Raynor, P. (1985) <u>Social Work, Justice and Control</u>, Basil Blackwell, Oxford

Reeve, C. (1792) <u>Plans of Education with Remarks on the System of other Writers</u>, Quoted in Johnson, R. (1975)(op.cit.)

Regnery, A.S. (1986) `A Federal Perspective on Juvenile Justice Reform`, <u>Crime and Delinquency, 32(1)</u>, pp. 39-53

Reiman, J. and Headlee, S. (1981) `Marxism and Criminal Justice Policy´, `Crime and Delinquency, 27(1)</u>, pp. 24-47

Reynolds, F. (1981) `In Defence of the 1969 Act´, <u>Howard Journal, 20(1)</u>, pp. 6-14

Reynolds, F. (1982) `Social Work Influence on Juvenile Court Disposals´, <u>British Journal of Social Work, 12(1)</u>, pp. 65-76

Reynolds, F. (1985a) `Magistrates´ Justifications for Making Custodial Orders on Juvenile Offenders`, <u>Criminal Law Review</u>, May, pp. 244-98

Reynolds, F. (1985b) <u>A Lack of Principles</u>, Oxford University Department of Social and Administrative Studies, Oxford

Riley, D. (1986a) `Demographic Changes and the

Criminal Justice System', Home Office Research and Planning Unit Research Bulletin, No. 20, pp. 30-3

Riley, D. (1986b) 'Sex Differences in Teenage Crime: The Role of Lifestyle', Home Office Research and Planning Unit Research Bulletin, No. 20, pp. 34-8

Riley, D. and Shaw, M. (1985) Parental Supervision and Juvenile Delinquency, Home Office Research Study No. 83, H.M.S.O., London

Romilly, S. (1810) Observations on the Criminal Law of England as it relates to capital punishments and on the mode in which it is administered, Cadell and Davies, London

Rothman, D. (1971) The Discovery of the Asylum: Social order and disorder in the New Republic, Little Brown & Co., Boston

Royal Commission on Criminal Procedure (1981) Report, Cmnd. 8092, H.M.S.O., London

Rubin, H.T. (1979) 'Retain the Juvenile Court?', Crime and Delinquency, 24(3), pp. 281-98

Rubin, H.T. (1980) 'The Emergence of Prosecutor Dominance of the Juvenile Court Intake Process', Crime and Delinquency, 26(3), pp. 299-318

Rudman, C. et al., (1986) 'Violent Youth in Adult Courts: Process and Punishment', Crime and Delinquency, 32(1), pp. 75-96

Rutherford, A. (1981) 'Young Offenders: Comments on the White Paper on Young Adult and Juvenile Offenders', British Journal of Criminology, 21(1), pp. 74-8

Rutherford, A. (1986) Growing Out of Crime, Penguin, Harmondsworth

Rutter, M. (1979) Changing Youth in a Changing Society, Nuffield, London

Rutter, M. and Giller, H. (1983) Juvenile delinquency: Trends and Perspectives, Penguin, Harmondsworth

Sanders, A. (1985) 'The Prosecution Process' in Moxon, D. (ed.), Managing Criminal Justice, H.M.S.O., London, pp. 65-86

Sanders, W. (1970) Juvenile Offenders for a Thousand Years, The University of North Carolina Press, Chapel Hill

Sarri, R. (1983a) 'Gender Issues in Juvenile Justice', Crime and Delinquency 23(3), pp. 381-97

Sarri, R. (1983b) 'Paradigms and Pitfalls in Juvenile Justice Diversion' in Morris, A, and Giller, H. (eds.), Providing Criminal Justice for Children, Edward Arnold, London, pp. 52-73

REFERENCES

Scarman Report (1981) <u>The Brixton Disorders 10-12 April 1981</u>, Cmnd. 8427, H.M.S.O., London

Schlossman, D. (1977) <u>Love and the American Delinquent: Theory and the Practice of 'Progressive' Juvenile Justice 1825-1920</u>, Chicago University Press, Chicago

Schur, E. (1973) <u>Radical Non-intervention</u>, Prentice Hall, Englewood Cliffs

Scott, P. (1959) 'Juvenile Courts: The Juvenile's Point of View', <u>British Journal of Delinquency</u>, 9, pp. 200-10

Scottish Education Department et al., (1966) <u>Social Work and the Community</u>, Cmnd. 3065, H.M.S.O., Edinburgh

Scraton, P. (1982) 'Policing and Institutionalised Racism', in Cowell, D. et al., (eds.), <u>Policing the Riots</u>, Junction Books, London, pp. 21-38

Scull, A. (1977) <u>Decarceration, Community Treatment and the Deviant: a radical view</u>, (2nd ed. 1983) Prentice Hall, Englewood Cliffs

Seebohm Committee (1968) <u>Report of the Committee on Local Authority and Allied Personal Social Services</u>, Cmnd. 3703, H.M.S.O., London

Select Committee on Criminal Commitments and Convictions (1827) <u>Report</u>, Parliamentary Papers, Vol. 6

Select Committee on Criminal and Destitute Children (1852-3) <u>Report</u>, Parliamentary Papers, Vol. 23

Select Committee on Criminal and Destitute Juveniles (1852) <u>Report</u>, Parliamentary Papers, Vol. 7

Select Committee on Factory Children's Labour (1832) <u>Report</u>, H.M.S.O., London

Select Committee on the Police of the Metropolis (1828) <u>Report</u>, Parliamentary Paper, Vol. 6

Shaw, M. (1986) 'Are parents prepared to be responsible?', <u>Home Office Research and Planning Unit Research Bulletin</u>, No. 20, pp. 43-7

Siegal, L. and Senna, J. (1981) <u>Juvenile Delinquency: Theory, Practice and the Law</u>, West Publishing , St. Paul, Minnesota

Simon, R.J. (1975) <u>Women and Crime</u>, D.C. Heath, Lexington

Smith, D. et al., (1983) <u>The Police and People in London</u>, Policy Studies Institute, London

Smith, D. and Gray, J. (1983) <u>Police and People in London: The Police in Action</u>, Volume 4, Policy Studies Institute, London

Smith, S. (1982) <u>Race and Crime Statistics</u>, Church of England Board for Social Responsibility, London

Social Information Systems (1986) <u>Custody Controlled</u>,

REFERENCES

Social Information Systems, Manchester
Society of Conservative Lawyers (1974) <u>Apprentices in Crime: the Failure of the Children and Young Persons Act</u>, Conservative Central Office, London

Society for the Improvement of Prison Discipline and for the Reformation of Juvenile Offenders (1818) <u>First Report</u>, The Society for the Improvement of Prison Discipline and for the Reformation of Juvenile Offenders, London

Sparks, R. et al., (1977) <u>Surveying Victims</u>, John Wiley, Chichester

Stang Dahl, T. (1974) 'The emergence of the Norwegian Child Welfare' in Christie, N. (ed.), <u>Scandinavian Studies in Criminology</u>, Vol. 5, Martin Robertson, London, pp. 83-98

Stapleton, W. and Teitlebaum, L. (1972) <u>In Defense of Youth</u>, Russell Sage, New York

Stedman Jones, G. (1984) <u>Outcast London: a study in the relationship between the classes in Victorian Society</u>, Penguin, Harmondsworth

Steffensmeier, D. and Terry, R. (1973) 'Deviance and Respectability: an observational study of reaction to shoplifting', <u>Social Forces</u>, 51, pp. 417-26

Stevens, P. and Willis, C. (1979) <u>Race, Crime and Arrest</u>, Home Office Research Study No. 58, H.M.S.O., London

Streatfield Committee (1961) <u>Report of the Interdepartmental Committee on the Business of the Criminal Courts</u>, Cmnd. 1289, H.M.S.O., London

Sutton, A. (1981) 'Science in Court' in King, M. (ed.), <u>Childhood Welfare and Justice</u>, Batsford, London, pp. 45-104

Sutton, A. (1983) 'Social Inquiry Reports to the Juvenile Courts: a Role for Lore in the Rule of Law?', in Geach, H. and Szwed, E. (eds.), <u>Providing Civil Justice for Children</u>, Edward Arnold, London, pp. 123-64

Tarling, R. (1979) <u>Sentencing Practice in Magistrates' Courts</u>, Home Office Research Study No. 56, H.M.S.O., London

Task Force on Child Care Services (1980) <u>Final Report</u>, Stationery Office, Dublin

Taylor, I. (1981) <u>Law and Order: Arguments for Socialism</u>, MacMillan, London

Taylor, L. et al., (1980) <u>In Whose Best Interests?</u>, Cobden Trust/MIND, London

Taylor, M. (1971), <u>Study of the Juvenile Liaison Scheme in West Ham 1961-65</u>, Home Office Research Studies, No. 8, H.M.S.O., London

REFERENCES

Terry, R. (1965) 'Discrimination in the Handling of Juvenile Offenders by Social Control Agencies', in Garabedian, P. and Gibbons, D. (eds.), Becoming Delinquent, Aldine Press, New York, pp. 78-92

Thomas, H. (1982) 'The road to custody is paved with good intentions', Probation Journal,, 29, pp. 92-7

Thorpe, D. (1983) 'Deinstitutionalisation and Justice' in Morris, A. and Giller, H. (eds.), Providing Criminal Justice for Children, Edward Arnold, London, pp. 74-88

Thorpe, D. et al., (1980) Out of Care, George Allen and Unwin, London

Thorpe, J. (1979) Social Inquiry Reports - A Survey, Home Office Research Study No. 48, H.M.S.O., London

Tildesley, W. and Bullock, W. (1983) 'Curfew Orders: The Arguments For', Probation Journal, 10, pp. 10-11

Tobias, J. (1972) Crime and Industrial Society in the Nineteenth Century, Penguin, Harmondsworth

Tutt, N. (1981) 'A Decade of Policy', British Journal of Criminology, 21(4), pp. 246-56

Tutt, N. (1982) 'An Overview of Interventions with Young Offenders: The Political and Legal Contexts' in Feldman, M. (ed.), Developments in the Study of Criminal Behaviour, Vol. 1, John Wiley, Chichester, pp. 1-26

Tutt, N. (1984) 'Report to the ESRC', Unpublished

Tutt, N. (1985) 'Attendance Centres - Should the Police Role be Extended?', in Shaw, R. and Hutchinson, R. (eds.), Periodic Restriction of Liberty, Copwood Conference Series No. 17, University of Cambridge Institute of Criminology, Cambridge, pp. 64-78

Tutt, N. and Giller, H. (1983a) The Criminal Justice Act 1982, Information Systems, Lancaster

Tutt, N. and Giller, H. (1983b) Police Cautioning of Juveniles: The Practice of Diversity, Criminal Law Review, September, pp. 587-95

Tutt, N. and Giller, H. (1984a) Diversion, Information Systems, Lancaster

Tutt, N. and Giller, H. (1984b) Social Inquiry Reports, Information Systems, Lancaster

Tutt, N. and Giller, H. (1985a) 'Doing Justice to Great Expectations', Community Care, January 17, pp. 20-5

Tutt, N. and Giller, H. (1985b) 'Directors Still in Trouble', Community Care, June 6, pp. 26-8

Tutt, N. and Stewart, G. (1986) Children in

Conditions of Security: Report of the Carnegie Study Group into Children Detained in England, Scotland, Northern Ireland and Eire, Forthcoming

U.S. Department of Justice (1981) *Criminal Justice Sourcebook*, Washington D.C., U.S. Government Printing Office

U.S. Department of Justice, Bureau of Statistics, (1982) *Sourcebook Criminal Justice Statistics 1981*, Criminal Justice Research Center, Albany

Voelcker, P. (1960) 'Juvenile Courts: The Parent's Point of View', *British Journal of Criminology, 10*, pp. 154-66

Wadsworth, M. (1979) *Roots of Delinquency: infancy, adolescence and crime*, Martin Robertson, Oxford

Walker, M. (1985) 'Statistical Anomalies in Comparing the Sentencing of Males and Females', *Sociology, 9(3)*, pp. 446-51

Walker, N. (1980) *Punishment, Danger and Stigma. The morality of criminal justice*, Basil Blackwell, Oxford

Walker, N. (1983) 'Childhood and Madness: history and theory', in Morris, A. and Giller, H. (eds.), *Providing Criminal Justice for Children*, Edward Arnold, London, pp. 19-35

Walker, N. (1985) *Sentencing: Theory, Law and Practice*, Butterworths, London

Wallerstein, J. and Wyle, C. (1947) 'Our law-abiding law breakers', *National Probation*, March/April, pp. 107-12

Walsh, D. (1978) *Shoplifting: controlling a major crime*, MacMillan, London

Watson, J. and Austin, P. (1975) *The Modern Juvenile court: for magistrates, social workers, police and others*, Shaw, London

Webb, D. (1984) 'More on Gender and Justice: Girl Offenders and Supervision', *Sociology, 13(3)*, pp. 367-81

Webb, D. and Harris, R. (1984) 'Social Workers and the Supervision Order: A Case of Occupational Uncertainty', *British Journal of Social Work, 14*, pp. 579-59

West, D. (1982) *Delinquency: Its Roots, Causes and Prospects*, Heinemann, London

West, D. and Farrington, D. (1973) *Who Becomes Delinquent?*, Heinemann, London

West, D. and Farrington, D. (1977) *The Delinquent Way of Life*, Heinemann, London

White, S. (1973) 'The Effect of Social Inquiry Reports on Sentencing Decisions', *British Journal of Criminology, 12(3)*, pp. 230-49

REFERENCES

Whitehead, P. and MacMillan, J. (1985) ´Checks or Blank Cheque?´, <u>Probation Journal</u>, 32, pp. 87-9

Williams, R. (1965) <u>The Long Revolution</u>, Pelican Books, Harmondsworth

Willmott, P. (1966) <u>Adolescent Boys of East London</u>, Routledge and Kegan Paul, London

Wilson, H. (1982) ´Parental responsibility and delinquency: reflections on a White Paper proposal´, <u>Howard Journal, 21(1)</u>, pp. 23-34

Wilson, S. (1978) ´Vandalism and "defensible space" on London housing estates´, in Clarke, R. (ed.), <u>Tackling Vandalism</u>, Home Office Research Study No. 47, H.M.S.O., London, pp. 41-65

Wines, E. (1880) <u>The State of Prisons and of Child-Saving Institutions Throughout the World</u>, University Press, Cambridge

Wolfgang, M. et al., (1972) <u>Delinquency in a Birth Cohort</u>, University of Chicago Press, Chicago

Worsley, H. (1849) <u>Juvenile Depravity</u>, Gilpin, London

Wright, M. (1983) ´Should Parents or Children Pay?´, <u>Probational Journal, 30</u>, pp. 299-317

Wyse, T. (1836) ´Education Reform or the Necessity of a National System of Education´ quoted in Johnson, R. (1975) (op. cit.)

Young, J. (1973) ´The myth of the drug taker in the mass media´, in Young, J. and Cohen, S. (eds.), <u>The Manufacture of News</u>, Constable, London, pp. 314-32

Zander, M. (1975) ´What Happens to Young Offenders in Care´, <u>New Society</u>, July 24, pp. 185-7